The Improbable Life of
the *Arkansas Democrat*

The Improbable Life of the *Arkansas Democrat*

AN.ORAL HISTORY

Edited by JERRY McCONNELL

The University of Arkansas Press
Fayetteville
2016

20   19   18   17   16   5   4   3   2   1

Designed by Liz Lester

☉ The paper used in this publication meets the minimum
requirements of the American National Standard for
Permanence of Paper for Printed Library Materials Z39.48–1984.

Library of Congress Control Number: 2015948195

Dedicated to the people who worked
for the Arkansas Democrat
because they loved to report the news.

CONTENTS

ACKNOWLEDGMENTS

This book is based on the oral histories of the *Arkansas Democrat* and *Democrat-Gazette* that were conducted under the auspices of the David and Barbara Pryor Center for Oral and Visual History at the University of Arkansas. It is also the result of the efforts of a lot of people who love Arkansas and history and newspapers, and all those big and small stories that have been investigated and written and edited and printed in the pages of two vibrant newspapers over a period of almost two hundred years. We can't name all those people in this brief space, but a lot of them will be named in the pages of this book, as they were named in the pages of the oral history of the *Arkansas Gazette*. We can't thank all those people here either, but we can thank several of them, including Walter Hussman Jr., who made this oral history project possible by paying for a lot of it.

My part as director of this particular project was inspired by Dr. Jeannie Whayne, who was then head of the History Department at the University of Arkansas and still teaches history there. She became the first director of the oral history program. She was the one who encouraged Hussman to support and fund the *Democrat* project; he suggested me for the job, and she encouraged me to take it and explained how it would operate.

This book is based on a series of taped interviews, which had to be transcribed, read, and approved by the interviewer, the interviewee, and me (all three of us might and usually did make corrections) and then posted on the Internet. Keeping track of all the interviews, and the corrections, was not an easy task, and for that I must thank Lindley Shedd, James Defibaugh, Jason Pierce, and Susan Kendrick Perry. Transcribing the interviews was perhaps the hardest job, because not all of the tapes were of pristine quality, and not all the people on them always spoke clearly. In my view, easily the best transcriber was Cheri Pearce Riggs, who quickly learned all the important names and knew how to spell them. She was also the fastest at posting them on the Internet.

The overall program started out in the History Department, but it quickly became too big for the department to handle, so it was moved in alongside Special Collections in the basement of the Mullins Library. Tom Dillard was head of Special Collections, and he may have never been technically the head of the oral history program, but he was the one whose office I sometimes used and whom I went to see when I had a problem, and he was unfailingly helpful. For a long time Cheri was his secretary. She did the transcriptions on her own time at night, and she is still doing them, although she married an archaeologist in 2008, and they moved to Austin, Arkansas, for his job.

Of course I must thank all those people who conducted interviews, read them, made corrections, and took care of the correspondence with the oral history center. They also provided their own tape decks and tapes, although we did pay them a small stipend. Their names are listed elsewhere in this book. And of course I must thank all those people who agreed to be interviewed and sat there for one, two, or three hours and answered questions and didn't get paid. Not all of the people who still worked at the *Democrat-Gazette* agreed to be interviewed, but most of them did, and I thank them for their cooperation.

As one of our interviewees said, putting together a daily newspaper filled with news, ads, comics, and features was a daily miracle, especially at the old *Democrat.* Here's to all those people who helped bring it off. I hope you readers never have to exist without such miracles to keep you better informed.

The Cast

Following are brief biographies of the people who are quoted in this book. They constitute only a relatively small segment of the *Democrat* staffers who were still alive when this project began in 2004. However, they were chosen so we could paint a broad picture of what was happening at the *Democrat* and what kind of paper it was in the era when they worked there. For that reason we chose to interview more than just reporters and editors. Thus, included below are people who worked in the composing room before computers took over and after. Also included are a number of people who worked on the business side of the newspaper because they played such a key role in the *Democrat*'s war with the *Gazette* and understood the strategy that helped topple a giant. At the end is a list of the people who conducted the interviews. Some conducted several interviews each, which you can discover by checking the *Democrat* Web site at the Pryor Center. The format of the book is fairly straightforward. When someone is quoted directly, their full name appears in boldface the first time they are quoted in each chapter. Thereafter their last name appears in boldface. When I introduce a chapter or explain some development, my comments appear in italics.

Charles Allbright began his career as a sportswriter at the *Arkansas Democrat*, later joined the *Arkansas Gazette* as a reporter and then a columnist, and wrote editorials for two years before eventually going to work for Governor Winthrop Rockefeller. After Rockefeller died, Allbright returned to the *Gazette* as a columnist. He then joined the *Democrat-Gazette*, which inherited his contract.

Amanda Allen started at the *Paragould Daily Press* as a reporter and left after two years for the *Arkansas Democrat*, where she quickly moved to the copy desk. There she held most of the top positions over the next ten years and eventually wound up as the travel editor at the *Atlanta Journal-Constitution.*

Jim Allen grew up working for the *Democrat,* as a paper boy, mail-room staffer, circulation aide, and newsroom clerk, and became a reporter when he graduated from the University of Arkansas, Little Rock (UALR). After three years he joined the Associated Press, first in Little Rock and then in San Francisco. He ended up as public relations manager for two big corporations, first CNF, the old Consolidated Freightways, and then Hess (Oil) Corporation.

Philip Anderson was the lead attorney for the *Democrat* in the antitrust suit filed against it by the *Arkansas Gazette,* in which the *Democrat* won a unanimous verdict. He had represented the *Democrat* since the Hussmans bought it in 1974. An Arkansas native, he has been president of the American Bar Association and chairman of the Arkansas Bar Association.

George Arnold graduated from the University of Kansas, got a journalism degree from the University of Missouri, and eventually went to the *Democrat* as night editor on the copy desk. He was named state editor by John R. Starr, worked briefly at the *Gazette,* was managing editor at El Dorado for fifteen years, and wound up working on the *Democrat-Gazette*'s Northwest Edition.

Jim Bailey started to work in the *Gazette* sports department in late May 1956 and was still there as the newspaper's star sportswriter when it closed on October 18, 1991. He went to work for the *Arkansas Times,* switched to the *Democrat-Gazette* as a freelance columnist in 1994, and soon became a regular staff member. He retired in 1998 but continued to write a column.

Julie Baldridge Speed went to work as a copy editor for the *Gazette* in 1970, moved to the *Democrat* in 1974 to write the "Answer Please" column, and left in 1976 to work for Bill Clinton in the attorney general's office. She became Clinton's press secretary when he was elected governor, left to have a child, and later worked for Ray Thornton in Congress and then at the UALR Law School.

Allen Berry graduated from the University of Arkansas with an MBA in 1968, worked for five years for one of the "Big Eight" accounting firms, and then went to work for the Hussmans in 1972. He became the controller and then the treasurer for WEHCO Media and was the go-to guy to find the necessary money from WEHCO when the *Democrat* fought its war with the *Gazette*.

Arminta Berry graduated from Lindenwood College and then went to work for the *Democrat* in display advertising in 1948. There she met Stanley Berry, the nephew of owner K. A. Engel, who became co-owner of the paper when Engel died in 1968. Arminta, a violinist in the symphony, left the paper when she and Berry married in 1950. Stanley died in 2005.

Cary Bradburn, who obtained history degrees from Hendrix College and the University of Arizona, started working for newspapers for Cone Magie at Cabot. Three years later, in 1981, he went to work for the *Democrat*, where he covered the infamous Mary "Lee" Orsini murder trial. He eventually switched to the *Gazette* in late 1985 and stayed there until it closed.

Phyllis Brandon received a journalism degree from the University of Arkansas in 1957 and joined the *Democrat* but quickly left. She served two stints at the *Gazette*, around pregnancies, and then retired for sixteen years to raise her two boys. After a few years in other jobs she was rehired by the *Democrat* to edit the "High Profile" section, which was highly popular and a boost to the paper in its war with the *Gazette*.

Fred Campbell, who had been a paper boy for the *Democrat* as a kid, went to work as an apprentice in the *Democrat* composing room in 1942, in the "hot metal" days, when type was set by linotype machines. He worked his way up to foreman, managing sixty-eight workers, and retired after fifty years, when computers took over and he was down to five employees, soon to be none.

Ralph Casey worked for several years delivering the *Democrat*, starting in 1927. He moved into the circulation department in 1934 and worked his way up to city circulation manager, with time out to work as a railway mail clerk during World War II, then handled "Audit Bureau of Circulation" reports in later years, retiring at age seventy-five in 1989. He died in 2012 at age ninety-seven.

Wayne Cranford got a journalism degree from the Arkansas State Teachers College (now the University of Central Arkansas), taught school for three years, and eventually joined the *Democrat* as a reporter. He was recruited by Bob McCord to work on the Sunday magazine; left for the Chamber of Commerce; and soon formed the public relations-advertising firm Cranford & Johnson, which quickly became one of the most successful in several states.

Sheila Daniel grew up in a newspaper family, received a journalism degree from the University of Arkansas, and went to work for the *Gazette*. She left during a union hassle and switched to the *Democrat* as a copy editor, then was offered a job by the *Chicago Tribune*, where she worked for three years. She later switched to the *Los Angeles Times*, left after three years, and became a foreign correspondent.

David Davies took a broadcast degree in journalism from the University of Arkansas, worked in radio for a year and a half, worked in newspapers and radio around a semester sojourn in Europe, and joined the *Democrat* in 1983 in the middle of the newspaper war. He switched to the *Gazette* in 1985, left in 1989 to earn a doctorate, and is now head of the Honors College at the University of Southern Mississippi.

Barbara Day, after getting an advertising degree, first went to work for stores in Tulsa and then in Lincoln, Nebraska. She became ad manager at Pfeifer's in Little Rock; worked for Dillard's after it bought Pfeifer's; and then switched to the *Gazette* ad department in 1980. She was fired and won a discrimination suit against the *Gazette* and then went to work for the *Democrat*, retiring in 2001.

Jerry Dean worked at the *Democrat* three different times, as well as serving a long stint at the *Gazette*. He worked at the *Democrat* from 1965 to 1967, went into the air force for five and a half years, returned to the *Democrat* and stayed until 1979, and then switched to the *Gazette*, staying until it closed in 1991. He returned to the *Democrat-Gazette* in May 1992 and stayed for three years.

Sam Dickinson studied mostly archaeology in college and became an editorial writer for the *Gazette* and then the *Democrat* after graduation. He started at the *Gazette* in 1944 but didn't like either owner-editor J. N. Heiskell or editor Harry Ashmore, who arrived in 1947. Dickinson left a year later, taught college for one year, and then worked at the *Democrat* for thirteen years. He was opposed to integration. He died at age ninety-five in 2007.

Gerald Doty was circulation manager for the *Dallas Times-*

Herald when Walter Hussman Jr. offered him a similar job the month he bought the *Democrat* because his circulation department was in such bad shape. Doty took the job and made progress, but he was undercut, according to sources, by someone who wanted his job. He was fired by Hussman, then took the same job at the *Houston Post*.

Michael Dougan, a retired history professor at Arkansas State University, wrote *Community Diaries: Arkansas Newspapering 1819–2002*, a history of the Arkansas Press Association. His master's thesis focused on the Little Rock press during the Civil War, and he wrote his doctoral dissertation on Confederate Arkansas. He was also author of *Arkansas Odyssey*, a history of the state.

Frank Fellone started at the *Democrat* as a Friday-night sportswriter, working part-time, then took a full-time job at the *Jacksonville Daily News*. He left to work at the *Batesville Guard* for three years and was hired as a reporter at the *Democrat* early in the newspaper war by John R. Starr, who named him state editor. He later became the paper's political editor and is now its deputy editor.

Arlin Fields started working in sports at the *Democrat* while he was still a junior in high school. He was soon recruited to switch over to the city side as a general assignment reporter, covering police and politics for a time, and then became the paper's entertainment editor. He was at the *Democrat* when the new regime under Gene Foreman and Bob McCord took over. After five years, he left to go to the *Gazette*.

Gene Foreman started at the *Gazette*, was promoted to state editor, and was then hired by the *New York Times*, which was soon hit by a strike. At that point he became managing editor at the *Pine Bluff Commercial*. He was hired to try to resurrect the *Democrat* after owner K. A. Engel died in 1968. After three years he became executive news editor of the newspaper *Newsday* on Long Island.

Marguerite Gamble, a reluctant debutante, worked in society news at the *Gazette* while attending Vanderbilt and later became the paper's assistant society editor. She left when she thought her job had hit a dead end and switched to the *Democrat* to work in society with Dorothy Dungan Carroll, also covering fashion shows for two and a half years.

Chester Garrett worked in circulation at the Fort Smith papers for seven years, served as a medic throughout World War II, and joined the

Democrat in 1946. He became the paper's circulation manager and then replaced Stanley Berry as its business manager when Berry became publisher. In 1981 he became its purchasing agent, a job he held until he retired at age eighty-seven in 2002. He died in 2005 at age ninety.

Marcus George served as a navigator on a B-24 bomber during World War II, finished a journalism degree at the University of Texas in 1947, and then joined the *Democrat,* owned by his uncle K. A. Engel. He started as a cub reporter, covering North Little Rock and the state capitol, and subsequently became assistant and then city editor. When Engel died in 1968, George became the paper's co-owner and editor, selling it to the Hussmans in 1974. He died in 2010 at age eighty-six.

Larry Graham, hired in circulation by Knight Newspapers, became circulation director at Tallahassee, Florida, and then city director for the *Kansas City Star.* He was hired as city circulation manager by the *Democrat* in 1980 and quickly became interim manager when Tony Biggs left. He led the *Democrat's* circulation planning throughout the paper's war with the *Gazette* and is now vice president in charge of circulation.

Omar Greene attended Subiaco Academy, where he became a standout boxer. He eventually graduated from Hendrix but kept job-hopping and place-hopping: he studied in England; worked for papers in Hobbs, New Mexico, Berkshire, Massachusetts, and Fort Smith, Arkansas; spent two years in the Peace Corps; joined the *Democrat* staff; and got married in Bob Starr's office. Greene and his wife left after a flap with Starr, and Greene became a lawyer.

Ramon Greenwood worked for an army newspaper in Greenland (the country, not the city) and for a weekly in Warren, got a journalism degree from the University of Arkansas, and took a job at the *Democrat.* He was quickly assigned to help cover the state capitol beat and later went to work in public relations, working for some of the top companies in the nation. He died in 2014.

Tim Hackler, who had been editor of his college paper at Hendrix, was recruited by Bob McCord and then Gene Foreman to join the new regime at the *Democrat.* He started in 1968 and worked as a reporter and copy editor. In 1970 he went to graduate school at Columbia. He returned to the *Democrat* for a short while and eventually wound up as press secretary for Senator Dale Bumpers.

Wally Hall worked briefly for Orville Henry at the *Gazette*, joined the air force for three years, and then worked for the *Democrat* sports department and at United Press International (UPI) in New York. He returned to the *Democrat*, staying there until he was fired, and then worked for Houston Nutt Sr. at the Arkansas School for the Deaf. Bob Starr later hired him as an investigative reporter, then named him a gallivanting sports columnist and sports editor.

Lynn Hamilton, a Fresno, California, native, was hired by his older brother, living in Conway, Arkansas, to work at a small data processing firm that later became Systematics. He spent three years in the navy, was hired by Walter Hussman Jr. for WEHCO Media in 1974, and was named business manager of the *Democrat* in 1979. Promoted to vice president for operations (production) in 1982, he was named president and general manager of the *Democrat* in 2013.

Eric Harrison, who went to college at Haverford, "on the mainline in Philadelphia," wound up at the *Democrat* as a copy editor but soon began to review restaurants, movies, and music. He became the paper's entertainment editor during the newspaper war and still holds that position twenty-eight years later (in 2015), partly because he is also active in theater (amateur and professional), choral groups, and standup comedy.

Steele Hays graduated from Yale and joined the *Democrat* in 1976 as a fledgling reporter, covering stories ranging from murders to a congressional race. He left in late 1977 to travel in Europe but while traveling was recruited by both the *Democrat* and the *Gazette*. He joined the *Gazette* and stayed at the paper for over four years, covering the state capitol for three, before he left to go to graduate school at Columbia.

Gene Herrington graduated from the University of Arkansas in 1941 with a journalism degree. He worked briefly for two weeklies and then joined the *Democrat* in early 1942. He served in the air corps during World War II but soon returned to the *Democrat* as assistant city editor. He became city editor in 1954, holding that job throughout the Central High crisis, and then was managing editor for ten years.

Alyson Hoge started at the *Democrat* as a clerk in May 1979, shortly after the beginning of the newspaper war and a big expansion in space and staff. She quickly worked her way up the hierarchy, making state capitol reporter after one year and going through thirteen coworkers in three and a half years. She served as night city editor for two years and then as state desk editor for six years, when the newspaper war ended.

Walter Hussman Jr., born into a newspaper family, became publisher of the *Democrat* at age twenty-seven in 1974, when his father agreed to buy the paper. When Hugh Patterson of the *Gazette* rejected his joint operating offer in 1978, Hussman launched a blitz of innovations that provoked the *Gazette* into suing the *Democrat*. The *Gazette* lost the suit and was sold to Gannett in 1986; Gannett gave up and sold the *Gazette*'s assets to Hussman in 1991.

Bill Husted taught school for a year, worked for the Russellville paper for a year, and then switched to the *Democrat* under Gene Foreman. There he became a featured reporter and was named city editor. He befriended the incoming managing editor, John R. Starr, or vice versa, but was fired by Starr when he had the honesty to warn Starr he was interviewing for another job, which he didn't have yet.

Estell Jeffrey grew up around newspapers, throwing a paper and working in the back shop at the *Searcy Citizen*. He went to work for the Conway paper in 1966 and became its advertising manager. Paul Smith hired him in 1984 to be the promotions manager at the *Democrat*, where he ran an in-house advertising agency designed to act quickly in the newspaper war.

Ken Kaufman graduated from Westminster College after serving in the navy during World War II. He went to work for the *Rogers Daily News* in 1950, quit after four or five months, and wound up at the *Democrat*, where he covered North Little Rock and then the state capitol. He led the paper's coverage of the new state highway department and early conflict over desegregation but quit so he could make enough money to get married.

Charles Kelly got started in television in the army and later took a job with a TV station in Shreveport but was quickly hired as news director at Channel 11 in Little Rock, the station whose major owner was K. A. Engel. Kelly left Channel 11 after eleven years to join Arkansas Power & Light.

Jon Kennedy, hired by owner K. A. Engel, started at the *Democrat* in August 1941 and was probably the first professional artist hired by an Arkansas newspaper. He enlisted in the army and worked mostly as an artist for almost three years during World War II. He returned to the *Democrat* in 1946 and chose his own topics as the paper's editorial cartoonist until he retired in 1988.

Martin Kirby, who held degrees from Tulane and Johns Hopkins, had worked at papers in three large cities but was freelancing when he took a job with the *Democrat* in 1969. He quickly became a top reporter for the paper: he had scoops on the Little Rock bank flap, covered Ross Perot's trip to Vietnam, penned a long series on Arkansas prisons, and left after three years to start his own magazine, the *Arkansas Advocate.*

Gerald Koonce flunked out of two colleges but then won three degrees and almost a fourth, working for newspapers in between. He took a job at the *Democrat* as a copy editor in 1976 and then went to the *Gazette* a year later, working there as a copy editor until it closed in 1991. He later helped the *Democrat-Gazette* set up its new editing system.

Bob Lancaster attended two colleges briefly. He was fired from their newspapers for criticizing the wrong people or groups and went to the *Pine Bluff Commercial,* where he wound up writing editorials. Hired to write a front-page column at the *Democrat,* he won the prestigious Nieman Fellowship in 1971 and then moved to the *Gazette* to write the "Arkansas Traveler" column. After leaving the state briefly to live in Philadelphia, he returned to Arkansas.

Mara Leveritt graduated from UALR in 1974, applied for a job as a copy editor at the *Democrat,* and was hired. After a year she switched to reporting, covering education and then general news. She moved to the *Arkansas Times,* worked at the *Gazette* for two years, and then returned to the *Times.* She has written two crime-related books, including *Devil's Knot.*

Rod Lorenzen started to work in sports at the *Democrat* in 1966, the week he turned fifteen. He was laying out the sports section by the time he was eighteen and went to West Memphis to work as a managing editor in 1972, the year he was twenty-one. He soon returned to the *Democrat* so he could finish his degree at UALR. He helped start the *Arkansas Times* in 1973 and then opened his own bookstore in 1974. He sold that store in 1988 and started another.

Mike Masterson started at the Newport, Arkansas, paper and then worked for six years at the Hot Springs paper, ending up as its executive editor. He worked for one year at the *Los Angeles Times* and then moved to the *Chicago Sun-Times,* leaving when Rupert Murdoch bought it. He wrote for all WEHCO Media, including the *Democrat,* for four years and also wrote for the *Arizona Republic.* After a stint as a professor at Ohio State, he took at job at the *Arkansas Times;* he is now a columnist for Hussman in Northwest Arkansas.

Deborah Mathis became a clerk at the *Democrat* straight out of Central High, was promoted to reporter in a few months, and was hired by a TV station (Channel 11) in two years. She was soon grabbed by a Washington, DC, station and became a coanchor with Maury Povich. She returned to Little Rock to start a family, signed with Channel 4, and then switched to Channel 7; after she quit television news, she became a columnist at the *Gazette* until it closed.

Al May, who earned a master's degree in journalism from the University of Missouri, joined the *Democrat* in 1974 and was sent to Hot Springs to open a bureau. After about eight months he moved to Little Rock and was eventually sent to the capitol to cover politics, which was his goal. He left in early 1978 to join the *Raleigh News and Observer* in North Carolina, a job for which he had been recommended by Ernie Dumas of the *Gazette.*

Jerry McConnell graduated from high school in Greenwood, Arkansas, in 1945 and then from the University of Arkansas in 1951. Two days later he went to work for the *Democrat,* where he covered the police, city hall, the state capitol, and Orval Faubus. He then covered sports for the *Gazette* for sixteen years before returning to the *Democrat* as managing editor for seven years, four of them under Hussman. McConnell later took a job as executive sports editor of the *Oklahoma City Times* and the *Daily Oklahoman.*

Bob McCord started at the *Democrat* while he was in the tenth grade and then went to the University of Arkansas, where he became editor of the *Traveler,* had one of his pictures chosen to win a national award, and was elected national president of Sigma Delta Chi. He was later instrumental in passing Arkansas's freedom of information (FOI) law and owned a North Little Rock weekly. He returned to the *Democrat,* where he was named executive editor by Hussman, but left when Starr arrived, moving to the *Gazette* to start the op-ed page.

Fred Morrow attended the University of Missouri for three and a half years, served in combat in Vietnam, and was hired as a sportswriter at the *Pine Bluff Commercial*, also holding the job of sports editor for a year. The *Democrat* hired him in 1970 as sports director, replacing Jack Keady as head of the department. In that position he wrote columns, covered the Razorbacks, and became known as anti-Frank Broyles. He left in 1976 to work for the *Rocky Mountain News* in Denver.

Randy Moss grew up around Oaklawn Park in Hot Springs. By the time he was in the eleventh ᵉgrade, he was picking the "Morning Line" for the *Gazette* under an assumed name. Orville Henry hired him full-time from college as a reporter and handicapper, but the *Democrat* lured him away in 1984 by doubling his salary from $15,000 to $30,000. He stayed at the *Democrat* four years before going to the *Dallas Morning News*, then ESPN, and then the NFL.

Rex Nelson worked as the sports editor for two papers in Arkadelphia, one weekly and one daily, before entering college. When he finished at Ouachita in 1981, he became a sportswriter at the *Democrat*; he left for a while and then returned as assistant sports editor until Bob Starr grabbed him to go to Washington and cover politics. He left the paper in 1989 but was rehired as its political editor in 1992.

Mark Oswald, after graduating from Catholic High, attended Notre Dame for a year, studied in France for a year, and switched to study journalism at the University of Texas. He worked for the *Democrat* in 1974 as an intern before his senior year and returned as a reporter after his graduation, covering the police beat and city hall. He left in late 1978 to go to the *Gazette*, remaining there until it closed.

Ralph Patrick started working at the *Democrat* while he was still in college before returning to the Arkansas State Teachers College (now the University of Central Arkansas). He got his master's degree at Oregon, worked on the Rockefeller campaign, and was hired by Bob McCord at the *North Little Rock Times*, where he became editor. He returned to the *Democrat* as city editor in 1969 and stayed for ten years before leaving to start his own magazine. He wound up working at the *Atlanta Journal-Constitution* for twenty years.

Leslie Newell Peacock graduated from Bennington College with an art degree and went to work on the copy desk at the *Democrat* in 1976. She became assistant wire editor, left in 1979, and later worked briefly for Bill Clinton. Peacock returned to the *Democrat* as a copy editor in 1980 but was fired by John R. Starr for "disloyalty." She was eventually hired by the *Gazette*, remaining there until it closed.

Fred Petrucelli, a Connecticut native, started working at the *Democrat* in 1945. He covered North Little Rock for about a year and then switched to sports, becoming the assistant to sports editor Jack Keady and writing a Sunday column. Years later he switched to the news side and became a rewrite man and then assistant city editor.

Gary Rice began writing for a daily newspaper when he was only fourteen. After high school, at the age of sixteen, he went to work for the *Wichita Eagle,* the biggest newspaper in Kansas. He stayed there for three years before he came to the *Democrat,* where he had a series of scoops over the next two years. He then went to the *Kansas City Star,* then to Austin, Texas, where he taught college and got his bachelor's, master's, and doctoral degrees in about six years. He is now a professor at California State University, Fresno.

Ron Robinson started working in the *Gazette* sports department while he was still at Hall High School. He worked as a *Gazette* stringer for a while when he was at the University of Arkansas. After graduation he served as an air force officer for five years and then went to work for Cranford and Johnson, the large advertising agency that represented the *Gazette* for many years. There he was in charge of the *Gazette* account and was named president of the firm in 1984.

Jim Shuemake started work in street circulation for the *Democrat* in 1954, joined the army for two years in 1957, returned, and soon went to work in the paper's composing room as an apprentice union mechanic. He left the union at Hussman's urging, became the *Democrat*'s production manager, and took care of the paper's computers and other vital equipment almost single-handedly throughout much of the newspaper war.

Griffin Smith, the son and grandson of lawyers, graduated from Rice Institute, got a master's degree from Columbia, studied at Oxford University in England, and earned a law degree from the University of Texas. He helped found and edit *Texas Monthly* magazine, worked as a speechwriter for President Jimmy Carter, and began editing the travel section of the *Democrat* in 1987, before becoming the paper's executive editor in 1992.

Paul Smith started to work at the *El Dorado News-Times,* a Hussman paper, at age nineteen as an ad salesman. He left, was rehired, and started a competitive paper in Texarkana. He then was rehired as the El Dorado ad director but was soon chosen by Walter Hussman Jr. to serve as the business manager at the *Camden News.* Smith followed Hussman to the *Democrat* as its ad manager and was named the paper's general manager in 1981, devising much of its strategy during the war with the *Gazette.*

John R. Starr graduated from Pine Bluff High School in 1945 and from Southwestern College as a member of Phi Beta Kappa in 1952. He worked as a sportswriter for the *Memphis Commercial Appeal;* joined the staff of the Associated Press (AP) in Little Rock in 1957, serving as the AP's capitol correspondent; and then was named bureau chief in 1966. He resigned to teach journalism at UALR in 1976 and then enrolled as a graduate student at the University of Tennessee.

Rusty Starr, the youngest of three children born to John Robert and Norma Starr, worked at the *Jonesboro Sun* while attending Arkansas State University. After graduating, he worked at papers in Gadsden and Florence, Alabama, and then at the *Wilmington (NC) Morning-Star* before becoming the publisher of the *Palatka (FL) Daily News.*

Tucker Steinmetz, a Hendrix graduate, planned to be a Methodist minister but had second thoughts. He taught school in El Paso, Texas, went to work for Bob Fisher at the weekly Crossett paper, and was soon hired by Gene Foreman at the *Pine Bluff Commercial.* Steinmetz followed Foreman to the *Democrat* and played an active role in tense efforts to remake the paper. When Foreman left, Steinmetz switched to the *Gazette.*

Carol Stogsdill, fresh out of Arkansas State, worked briefly for the state's tourism department and the *Pine Bluff Commercial* before being hired as a copy editor at the *Democrat* in 1971. She became the paper's wire editor and then its deputy sports editor. She left in late 1975 to go to the *Rocky Mountain News,* before moving to the *Chicago Tribune* and then the *Los Angeles Times,* where she became senior editor.

Ozell Sutton became the first African American to work for a major newspaper in Arkansas, and either the first or second in the

South, when he went to work for the *Democrat* in February 1950. He was at first segregated from the other reporters, but that soon changed. He covered black activities in Little Rock and across the state until he left in March 1957 to work for Winthrop Rockefeller.

Bill Taylor started delivering the *Democrat* in 1941, just before his thirteenth birthday. He never stopped working in circulation because he liked it, working his way up to a motor route and also working in the mailroom on Saturday and in the business office in the morning. He became a district manager, then a zone manager, and then the state manager. He took over the *Democrat* credit union in 1971 but maintained his job in circulation.

David Terrell worked for his high school paper in Conway; wrote for the *Conway Log Cabin Democrat* daily paper while getting a philosophy degree from Hendrix; and started at the *Democrat* in 1974, covering general assignments, the federal building, and then politics. He switched to the *Gazette* in 1976 and followed a similar trajectory to the state capitol. He left in 1980 and wound up in government.

Teri Thompson was hired by Fred Morrow in 1975 to cover sports for the *Democrat*, one of first women sportswriters in the country. She covered all sports despite some access problems. Thompson switched to a Colorado Springs paper after two years, moved to the *Rocky Mountain News* in Denver, and earned a law degree. She later became Sunday sports editor and investigative editor of the *New York Daily News*.

John Ward was a stereotypist, a college music student, a linotype operator, a jazz musician, and a band director before joining the *Democrat* as a reporter in 1958. At the paper, he handled many big stories but left in 1968 to become director of public relations for Winthrop Rockefeller, running two of his campaigns for governor. He then became managing editor of the *Conway Log Cabin Democrat*.

Mel White was hired as a copy editor at the *Democrat* in 1974. At his request, he became a reporter, covering school news and the federal building. Also a musician, he eventually left to write jingles for a recording studio. He returned to the *Democrat* as the entertainment editor but left in 1977 to write jingles again. He later became a writer and editor at the *Arkansas Times,* then a writer for *National Geographic.*

Lynda Zimmer-Straw worked for the newspaper in Tucson while getting a journalism degree from the University of Arizona. She then worked for the AP Bureau in Phoenix. After her husband was transferred to the Little Rock air force base, she went to work for the *Democrat,* soon making a foe of North Little Rock mayor William F. "Casey" Laman with her vigorous coverage.

The interviews for this project were conducted by Amanda Allen, George Arnold, Clay Bailey, Jim Bailey, Phyllis Brandon, Elisa Crouch, Dan Farley, Frank Fellone, Arlin Fields, Jackye Finch, Denise Gamino, Tim Hackler, Steele Hays, Charles Hemingway, Collins Hemingway, Garry Hoffmann, Alyson Hoge, Bob Holt, Gerald Jordan, Sam Krebs, Mara Leveritt, Jerry McConnell, Bob McCord, David McCollum, Meredith Oakley, Gary Rice, Jeanne Rollberg, Carol Stogsdill, Celia Storey, David Terrell, Pamela Terrell, Brenda Tirey, and Mel White. Roy Reed, who conducted the *Gazette* oral history project, interviewed Walter Hussman Jr. for that project before anyone knew there would be a *Democrat* project. Hussman was prepared, and that interview, which lasted four hours, covered such detail there was no need to repeat it. I quote liberally from it in some sections of this book. I also interviewed Hussman about other areas, and I quote from those interviews too.

CHAPTER 1

A Friendly Beginning

THE ARKANSAS DEMOCRAT *came into being in the 1870s as the second major newspaper in Little Rock, and it maintained that position behind the* Arkansas Gazette *for nearly all of the next 113 years. It trailed the* Gazette *in prestige, income, and circulation but remained a viable second source, and sometimes the main source, of news throughout that time. There is evidence that the two long-time owners of the papers, J. N. Heiskell at the* Gazette *and K. August Engel at the* Democrat, *were content with that situation. Heiskell never made an effort to put the* Democrat *out of business, and Engel never made an effort to take over the number-one slot. Heiskell seemed happy to have a well-edited newspaper of record that covered most of the state. Engel seemed happy to have a newspaper that filled in the gaps and always made money.*

As long as Heiskell and Engel were alive, there was no newspaper war in Little Rock. If there had been, the winner would almost certainly have been the Arkansas Gazette, *the oldest daily newspaper west of the Mississippi River and one of the most prestigious. But both men died, times changed, other people took over the newspapers, and there was a war, with shocking results.*

This oral history is partly a story of that war, mostly from the Democrat *perspective, since that is what this oral history is designed to cover. But first it is a story of how the two papers coexisted peacefully for a hundred years, how the* Democrat *sometimes produced some exemplary work and made an impact on the state, and how a belated attempt to make the* Democrat *a better paper may have indirectly led to the showdown with the* Gazette.

It is also a story of how Heiskell and Engel competed with honor and how their deaths may have had some unexpected consequences. It is a story fraught with great ironies, none greater than that the Gazette *had two chances to own or control the* Arkansas Democrat *and thus avoid what eventually happened.*

Heiskell always denied that the Gazette *ever owned the* Democrat, *but he eventually conceded that the owners of the* Gazette *owned the* Democrat *for a few years in the early part of the twentieth century. That was first reported in a book written by Fred W. Allsopp, business manager of the* Gazette *and one of the major stockholders when he and the Heiskells bought the* Gazette *in 1902. Allsopp had joined the* Gazette *in the mid-1880s and become business manager in 1896. In 1922, he published a book called* History of the Arkansas Press for One Hundred Years and More. *In that book he wrote, "In 1909 [George] Naylor was stricken with paralysis and soon afterwards the* Arkansas Democrat *was sold to the owners of the* Arkansas Gazette. . . . In 1911 *the* Democrat *was sold to Elmer E. Clarke, who published the paper until 1926." (John M. Branham was also listed by the* Democrat *as one of the purchasers.)*

The claim arose again years later, during a ceremony dedicating a plaque on the Gazette *building to Heiskell, when a speaker said that Heiskell had at one time owned both newspapers but that he didn't think it was healthy for both newspapers in the community to be owned by the same person and didn't keep the* Democrat *for that reason.*

Margaret Smith Ross, who was the Gazette *historian for twenty-eight years, a job Heiskell created for her, said he never challenged that statement. When she asked him about it, he said that he never owned the* Democrat, *and the* Gazette *never owned the* Democrat, *but when she asked if the same people who owned the* Gazette *had owned the* Democrat, *he said, "Well, I guess you could say something like that." Ross, who died in 2002, said that after Heiskell died at the age of one hundred in 1972, she found an instrument in his personal papers that proved his ownership.*

Ross said she had become suspicious of Heiskell's denials when she found a story in the Gazette *about the sale of the* Democrat *to Elmer Clarke and John M. Branham, but it never mentioned whom they had bought it from. Similarly, the new owners' publisher's announcement about the purchase in the* Democrat *never mentioned whom they had bought it from. It did, however, include this line: "The new publisher is assuming the good will of the past publishers of the* Arkansas Democrat *along with its name and physical plant." The only explanation for the "coincidence" is that the two parties had agreed not to reveal the seller.*

That goodwill seemed to carry over for years. The two papers apparently had a tacit understanding (not entirely rare in the newspaper business) that they would not raid each other's staff. Sam Dickinson, who worked for a while as an editorial writer for Heiskell, said he decided to leave after Heiskell hired Harry Ashmore.

Sam Dickinson: I left about a year after Ashmore arrived [in 1947]. I knew I had a job at the *Democrat*, but in those days the two papers had a policy that they didn't hire from each other. You had to be gone from one paper a year before you could go to work at the other. So I went to Arkansas State Teachers College [now the University of Central Arkansas, in Conway] and taught English courses and one on Arkansas folklore. Then I left there and went to work writing editorials at the *Democrat*.

Chester Garrett: As long as the old timers, Engel and Heiskell, owned them, there was no competition, so to speak. It was competitive, but it wasn't a knock-down drag-out. It was just an honest, day-by-day, competitive situation. Both made money, for all these years, they were bound to make money. They made enough money in the newspaper to buy TV stations, good things.

Bill Taylor, who worked in circulation at the Democrat *for forty years, recalled that when there was a fire in the* Gazette *pressroom in the 1950s, Engel offered the* Gazette *the use of the* Democrat *presses if they needed them to get the paper out. He said the* Gazette *made repairs and didn't need the* Democrat *presses.*

Bill Taylor: I was told that Mr. Heiskell and Mr. Engel were at some social occasion and got into a conversation, and Mr. Engel said, "Mr. Heiskell, do you subscribe to my paper?" Mr. Heiskell said, "Well, yes, Mr. Engel, I subscribe to it, but I don't read it." So Mr. Engel said, "Well, what do you do with it?" And he said, "Well, I feed it to my goat." So Mr. Engel said to him, "Mr. Heiskell, one of these mornings you're going to wake up—your goat's going to be smarter than *you* are."

Perhaps the classic example of the apparent goodwill between the newspapers occurred after the hullabaloo over the two papers' positions on the integration of Little Rock Central in 1957. Because the Gazette *was perceived as being more favorable to integration, both advertisers and subscribers boycotted it, putting a big dent in its income. For the first time in history, the* Democrat's *circulation surpassed that of the* Gazette. *In 1956, the* Gazette *led the* Democrat *in Sunday circulation by 105,040 to 90,632 and in daily circulation by 94,033 to 80,297. By 1959 the* Democrat *had forged further ahead on Sundays by 100,796 to 93,556 and daily by 86,419 to 84,011.*

At about this time the Democrat *was approached by some wealthy landowners from East or Southeastern Arkansas, where resistance to integration was the fiercest, to offer help if the* Democrat *would go into direct competition with the* Gazette *by offering a morning paper.*

Gene Herrington, then the city editor, met with them because managing editor Ed Liske and Engel were out of the office.

Gene Herrington: There were about four or five or six who came up. I talked with them in Liske's office. This was after the situation had started burning. They said they were disgusted with the *Gazette,* but wanted a morning paper because that's when they needed it. They wanted the *Democrat* to put out a morning edition. I said I didn't have authority to do anything, but I would be glad to talk with Mr. Engel, who owned the paper. They were going to assure us a certain amount of circulation—I don't even remember what it was—to help us get started. I figured it wouldn't be much trouble. We get out six editions now. One more is not going to take too much trouble. We can just [print it] in the morning. [Herrington may have underestimated how much trouble that would be. Walter Hussman Jr. found out years later how costly it was to publish both a morning and an evening edition.] Anyway, I went down and talked with Engel the next morning, and he said, "Gene, you never treat a friend like this when he's down." That helped me to like Engel as much as anything he ever did.

It is clear that Engel made more money during the time when his circulation surged past that of the Gazette, *because he also picked up additional advertising. There is no evidence that Engel ever used any of that extra revenue to make the* Democrat *a better paper, nor did he use it to install air conditioning. The* Gazette *did put more money into its product, and by 1962 it had forged back into the lead in circulation. The gap steadily widened after that until the newspaper war began to change the fortunes of both sides in the 1980s.*

The second time the Gazette *turned down a chance to control the destinies of both papers came in the late 1970s when Walter Hussman Jr., the new publisher of the Democrat, proposed a joint operating agreement with the Gazette, having decided that it would otherwise have to fold. His proposal would have given the Gazette a major share of the profits and would have locked in the Democrat as the region's afternoon paper. Hugh Patterson, Heiskell's son-in-law, who had taken command of the Gazette after Heiskell died, turned Hussman down three times. Hussman then decided to challenge the Gazette head-on, and one of his first major moves was to make the Democrat a morning paper (more about that later on).*

But first the story of how these two papers arrived at such a startling denouement. The Democrat didn't start off too auspiciously. In fact, it isn't certain when it did start. The Arkansas Democrat used to date its beginning from October 2, 1871, when Daniel O'Sullivan arrived in Little Rock, but that's a rather cavalier use of the word "beginning." The founding date of the Democrat should probably be listed as either 1875 or 1878. Based on the Democrat's own history, when O'Sullivan arrived in Little Rock in 1871, he went to work as a reporter for the Little Rock State Journal, which suspended operations in the spring of 1873. O'Sullivan then started his own newspaper, the Weekly Chronicle, on May 24, 1873. That venture lasted about six months, and O'Sullivan then went to work as a reporter for the Republican. He again entered the publishing business with a paper called the Evening Star, which printed its first edition on May 4, 1875. On August 14, 1876, O'Sullivan sold that paper to a former Arkansas Supreme Court judge and candidate for Congress named John "Poker Jack" McClure. O'Sullivan remained on staff as a local editor. McClure sold the paper in February to his colleague Henry Cooper, who then sold out to the printing firm of Webb and Burrows on July 18, 1877. The paper suspended operations on April 9, 1878. Two days later, J. N. Smithee purchased the Star's presses and began publication of his new paper, which he called the Arkansas Democrat. There has been a paper identifiable as the Democrat ever since.

Smithee, forced to dispose of the Democrat in September 1878, sold it to General W. D. Blocher, former owner of the Arkansas Gazette, and James Mitchell, who also worked for the Gazette. Mitchell edited the Democrat for the next twenty-four years and led it into prominence.

Michael Dougan, a retired history professor at Arkansas State

University, covered this period in a book he wrote about the Arkansas Press Association called Community Diaries: Arkansas Newspapering, 1819–2002. *Dougan, who read a number of newspapers from that era, said the* Democrat *was the more progressive paper in the later decades of the nineteenth century.*

Michael Dougan: There's no question about that in my mind. That has to do a lot with the personality and character of James Mitchell. The Mitchell family was from northwest Arkansas ... and he was from the beginning a very literate and educated child. ... I seem to remember that he taught at the Arkansas Industrial University [now the University of Arkansas, Fayetteville]. He was always called Professor Mitchell.

The quality of printing is greatly superior on the part of the *Democrat* at this time. The layout is greatly superior. But, most importantly, the elevation of moral tone is greatly superior. Now, it's interesting if you take some of the critical events in that period of time and compare the two newspapers, they're not necessarily that far apart on what they're saying, but they're certainly far apart on how they're saying it. And, of course, the critical issue was the rise of the farm labor movement, which threatened the Democratic Party. The farm labor union reached out to black voters, and black voters were allowed to vote as long as they voted Republican, and Republicans couldn't win anything. But if, in fact, the white vote became divided, then the black vote became important, and the black vote had to be destroyed. And that's what happened to black civil rights in Arkansas in the late 1880s and early 1890s. And you find both of these newspapers defending that, so there's not a difference in that. But if you follow some other issues, there are some differences. One of the editorials from the *Arkansas Gazette,* during the time when the whole South—in fact, almost America generally—in the late 1890s and early 1900s—was ablaze in lynchings, said that "no respectable Negro was ever lynched." Mitchell had rather a lot to say on that. In the first place, there had been a lynching in Texarkana where they had burned a boy, and that was defended by the local editor down there. And Mitchell's comment on that was, "Shame!" And there was a second lynching in Pine Bluff, and the *Graphic,* one of Pine Bluff's newspapers at that time, defended that as well, and Mitchell quoted what the *Graphic* said: "The best of order prevailed throughout. The citizens met for a common good, and did it effectively and fearlessly." And Mitchell's take on this, and I'm quoting him here, was, "It is time to halt. The *DEMOCRAT* will always be found fighting on this line. To defend the mob is to invite ruin and utter destruction of every interest of society."

The other thing that Mitchell was most noted for was women's rights and at one point turned the *Democrat* over to women to put out a women's issue. The Gazette was opposed to women's rights.

Dougan said there were two significant events in Arkansas newspapers in 1902: Mitchell died, and the Heiskells bought the Arkansas Gazette.

The Democrat *was operated from 1902 to 1906 by George C. Naylor and William S. Mitchell, the heir to the newspaper. During that time the* Democrat *ran into a lot of problems, including trouble with the union when the* Democrat *tried to operate an open shop. Dougan said the paper no longer maintained the high moral tone it had under James Mitchell.*

The paper was sold in 1906 to Naylor and the Little Rock Publishing Company, but the Mitchell heirs retained ownership of Democrat Printing and Lithographing, a job printing business, which often made up the most lucrative part of a newspaper business during that era. The country soon was hit by the Panic of 1907; Naylor died, and the paper was apparently sold to some of the owners of the Gazette.

When the paper was later sold to Elmer Clarke and John Branham in 1911, Clarke brought in as business manager K. August Engel, who had previously worked for him at the San Antonio Light *and the* New Orleans Item. *When Clarke retired in 1926, Engel acquired a major interest in the newspaper and became president and general manager. He led the* Democrat *until his death in 1968.*

CHAPTER 2

Not Your Average Man

KUNO AUGUST ENGEL was born in 1889 in Luckenbach, near the heart of the Texas Hill Country area, which was heavily settled by Germans. His grandfather was a circuit-riding Lutheran minister who emigrated from Germany to Texas in the 1840s. His father was a farmer and ran a general store at Cranes Mill, seventeen miles northwest of New Braunfels. Cranes Mill was covered by Canyon Lake in the 1960s, but it once had its own post office, and in 1872, according to Texas history, the postmaster was a minister named August Engel, who was succeeded by his son, also named August. It seems more than likely that they were the grandfather and father of K. August Engel.

It didn't take K. August Engel long to leave the farm. At the age of seventeen, he went to work for the San Antonio Light *newspaper, in accounting. His family and friends say he was always fascinated by financial matters. He used to joke about his grandfather, posing this question: "Can you imagine someone riding around preaching when he could be looking for oil?"*

Not long after Engel went to work for the San Antonio Light, *Elmer E. Clarke joined the paper as the business manager. When Clarke left San Antonio to become associate publisher of the* New Orleans Item, *Engel went with him. And when Clarke and John M. Branham bought the* Democrat *in 1911, Engel became its business manager. When Clarke retired in 1926, Engel became the principal owner and president and general manager of the* Democrat. *Those who worked with him for the next forty-two years, until he died in 1968, could testify to his financial acumen, his devotion to the* Democrat, *and his frugality.*

The late Ralph Casey, who worked with him for thirty-four years, said Engel spent virtually all of his time at the Democrat. *He came to* work in the morning, stayed throughout the day, and in early evening would walk down Capitol Avenue for dinner at Franke's Cafeteria and then return to the office and stay until ten thirty or eleven.

A long feature story on Engel's career, published in the Arkansas Democrat-Gazette in 1998, noted that he lived for about thirty years in the Capital Hill Apartment Hotel (which was across the street from the state capitol) and then spent his remaining years at the Albert Pike Hotel, two blocks from the Democrat, on Scott Street. People who worked at the Democrat said that someone always had to deliver a copy of the Sunday paper to Engel on Saturday night, whether at the Capitol Hill or the Albert Pike.

Engel did find time to serve on the boards of the St. Louis Federal Reserve Bank; the American Exchange Trust Co., Arkansas's largest bank at the time; and the Guaranty Building and Loan Association. He was the treasurer of the Arkansas Press Association for twenty-three years and served as a director of the American Newspaper Publishers Association and president of the Southern Newspaper Publishers Association. The 1998 Democrat-Gazette story also noted that in 1954 the University of Arkansas awarded him an honorary doctor of law degree for his contribution to the community as an editor and publisher.

In a 1930 feature story about Engel in Editor and Publisher magazine, he said, "I have no nuggets of advice to pass on to others in the newspaper publishing business." To understand how he operated, you'd have to follow his actions over a period of years and listen for the occasional "nugget" he dropped here and there. And even if you could fathom how he operated, you still might not know why. He was, by most accounts, a rather secretive man.

In all those years, if Engel ever spelled out his methods and motives in any detail, it hasn't come to light. He apparently didn't even discuss his approach with his nephews (and heirs apparent) Stanley Berry and Marcus George, who took over operation of the Democrat after Engel died in 1968.

Berry, who served as the paper's publisher, died just before we started this oral history project. I did interview George, with whom I worked as a Democrat reporter for four years, but he was already fatally ill and on oxygen and could not always remember details about the paper. In a search for that information, I went to Berry's wife, Arminta, who worked at the Democrat *herself until she married Stanley. I asked her how closely Stanley kept her abreast of conditions at the* Democrat.

Arminta Berry: He didn't. He was *very* close-mouthed. He didn't talk about it. He never said anything about the way Mr. Engel ran the paper. And he didn't even tell me how much money they were losing per day until it was sold because he was just a person who kept things to himself. He was secretive [laughs]. It was not only Stanley—it was Mr. Engel. When Marcus and Stanley [took over], they didn't have a clue about a lot of things. Didn't Marcus tell you that?

Jerry McConnell: No, he didn't.

Berry: Marcus is secretive, too. It runs in the family. I think "close-mouthed" would be the word instead of "secretive."

Engel did drop one nugget in a speech to the Southern Newspaper Publishers Association in 1951, when he said, "The high cost of operation can destroy a newspaper just as quickly as a national dictator." As far as I know, he did not discuss either the likelihood of a national dictator or a likely candidate.

So these sections on Engel and his paper are an exploration of how he operated and the impact he had on journalism and the state of Arkansas and the people who worked for him. Some of them may still be mystified.

Jon Kennedy worked for Engel as his editorial cartoonist for twenty-six years, and he saw him this way: "K. A. Engel was not your average man. He never married, though he came close once. Never had a family to support, never owned a home, never went to church, never traveled, except to publishers' meetings and an occasional Razorback game. On the whole, he was a happy man with a pleasant disposition. When I got down here in 1941, he was a pillar in the community. It struck me when I first saw him that he looked like a central casting publisher, you know? He looked the part."

Most of the people who worked in various business departments under Engel always spoke of him admiringly.

Chester Garrett: Mr. Engel was not necessarily an oddball at all, as some people might think. He was a bachelor. He had a sweetheart for three or four years when he was young, and then the girl abruptly broke it off and married another man. He never dated another girl. This was before he came to Little Rock. He turned his attention toward business.

Was Engel a good manager? One of the best. You won't believe this, but I know it for a fact—because Mr. Engel told me. We were kidding about being the second paper—and he said he would rather make money and be the second paper than be number one and not make any money. I could say, and I will say, he was a mathematical genius. He had some funny ways about different things, but he never would fail to listen to you. If you wanted to talk to him about anything, he would listen. He would weigh it, and then he would tell you what's wrong with it, and then he would say—when I was circulation manager—"This is the way it will work." I would go in with an idea and he'd tell me, "This could happen and that could happen," and then he would end up telling me to weigh the two against [each other] and say, "You make the decision." When I was circulation manager he never rebuked me for anything.

Fred Campbell: The pressmen were always unionized, including those who ran the letterpress that printed the regular newspaper. But they had a [separate] small press down there that they used to print the Sunday *Democrat* comics on. A little-bitty press, just to print the comics and print the Sunday magazine. [Union rules called] for just so many people doing this because it was a small press. The pressmen kept insisting that they wanted one more man to help operate that press. Well, Mr. Engel refused to give them one more man. He just wouldn't negotiate with them, and they kept on and kept on. Finally, one day he got fed up with them keeping on about wanting a pressman. He shut it down and fired the whole bunch of them. He shut the press down, and they never started it again. He went out and bought his comics already printed. I had some dealings with him when I became a foreman at the paper. When he'd make up his mind for something, that's the way it was going to be. He was a very good businessman. We used to get our newsprint from Canada, and they were on strike at one time. We began to run low on paper and didn't have enough newsprint, so Mr. Engel cut out all advertising in the paper, except the classifieds, to save newsprint. And he ran a twelve- to fourteen-page paper every day with just news in it, plus the classified section, in order to save newsprint. He was able to maintain that the whole time the strike was going on. We never did have to shut down the newspaper.

Even the people who admired Engel had to admit he was extremely frugal.

Ralph Casey: Sometimes we'd see him come out of his office and go look in the wastebaskets for the little [worn-down] pencils people had thrown away; he'd pick them up and take them back to his office. Anytime you'd see him use a pencil, it was just a little short pencil that he had gotten out of a wastebasket. If he would write you a note, it would be on newsprint, not good paper. If you wrote him a note on good paper, he didn't get another piece of paper. He'd just answer it on that piece of paper and not waste any paper.

Garrett: He did not pay a lot of money, that's true. I was talking to him one time about the turnover we had, in district advisors and everything. He said, "What do you think is wrong?" I said, "Well, the only thing I can figure out is if all you're going to pay is peanuts, all you're going to hire are monkeys." He laughed, reared back in that chair and laughed. The people that worked there were satisfied. There wasn't any animosity between the company and Engel or anybody. They [were] hired to do a job, and they got paid [for] what they were hired to do. What we were doing was taking care of them in a time in their life when they needed money to live on, so to speak. As soon as we trained them and got them back on their feet and they straightened themselves out financially where they could find the time to get a better job, that's what happened to them. We trained a lot of people.

Garrett, whom everyone liked, apparently didn't talk much to the reporters and editors. They didn't feel so kindly about Engel's practices. Jon Kennedy, who may have been fonder of Engel than most, could cite details about his frugality on salaries.

Jon Kennedy: When I was working at the *Springfield [MO] Leader-Press*, I heard the *Democrat* was looking for an artist, and I sent them some clips [clippings]. I got an envelope full of clips—cartoons that I had done—and sent them down there to Mr. Engel. And I waited. I thought I'd hear from him in a couple of days, but I waited a week, two weeks, and three weeks. I didn't hear a word. Finally, I wrote to Mr. Engel. I said, "Would you please send me back those clips?" Those were the only copies I had. I needed them back. And I waited another week. Finally, he sent me a letter saying he would start me at forty-five dollars a week and more as years go by. I accepted immediately. After my first year there, I scored a small raise by threatening to take a job offer in Kansas City. Engel said if five dollars a week would keep me at the *Democrat,* they could handle that. Then I had to wait about three or four weeks for a raise to go through [laughs]. That was the custom at the *Democrat*—that your raise had to "go through" before you would get it. But he did what he said [he would do]. He paid fifty dollars. He was always very nice to me. One time I went to a Cotton Bowl game in Dallas in 1946—along in there. I don't remember who our opponent was. [It was Louisiana State University.] I went down with our ad manager and his wife. They stayed at the Adolphus Hotel. I got a room in a cheaper place. One night I walked into a restaurant where Mr. Engel was with Clyde Lowery. They were partners, you know, until they sold the business they had. They invited me to sit down and eat with them, so I did. We had a nice little session there while we were eating. When we got through, they got into an argument over who would pay the checks [laughs]. "I'll get it." "No, August, I'll get it." I sat there and listened to it. Finally, I said, "Well, it doesn't make any difference who gets it, you're both millionaires."

John Ward, who worked as a reporter for the Democrat *for six years and left to go to work for the less frugal Winthrop Rockefeller, said, "Mr. Engel was a fine fellow, but he was as tight as the bark on a tree, and he was not interested in paying real salaries. I don't think he ever really quite figured out that reporting was important to newspapers. You know, selling ads was, but reporting wasn't all that important."*

Casey: I've understood, right or wrong, that the *Democrat* really made more money than the *Gazette,* but they [the *Gazette*] paid their employees more.

Engel apparently had an eye for a good deal. In 1955 he and some partners started a new television station in Little Rock, KTHV, making it the third TV station in the city.

Casey: One year when I was calling on Clyde Lowry at National Old Line Insurance on another matter, he said, "You know, you told me you worked for the *Democrat,* didn't you?" I said, "Yes, sir." He said, "August Engel called me and said, 'Clyde, I'm fixing to start a TV station and just wondered if you'd be interested in it.' And I told him, 'Heck, yes!'" He said that anything August Engel put his money in had to be good or he wouldn't be getting into it.

The question remains of why Engel operated so frugally. Was it partly because he and the early owners had made some kind of a com-

mitment to the Heiskells? Was it because he thought it was too risky to try to expand the business? Or was it because he was most interested in the profit margin and believed in keeping expenses as low as possible?

Because I thought it might be informative to see how he operated a different business, I sought out two sources to see how he ran the television station. Engel apparently still devoted most of his time to the Democrat, *but he hired B. G. Robertson as general manager of the TV station, to run it as he wished.*

Charles Kelly, who was news director at the station for ten years, said that Robertson told him once, with pride, that he had filed a report with the Federal Communications Commission (FCC) about the operation of the station and that the FCC called him and told him they didn't realize it was possible to run a TV station that cheaply.

Ron Robinson, who worked for the large advertising agency Cranford and Johnson, could testify about one of the station's cost-cutting methods.

Ron Robinson: In the 1974 United States Senate race, when Dale Bumpers and Bill Fulbright competed in the Democratic primary, we [Cranford and Johnson] represented Senator Fulbright. This was during a period of time when politicians still made television programs. They would make fifteen- or thirty-minute television programs. And so the night before the election, we bought a fifteen-minute program for Senator Fulbright, and Senator Bumpers was going to add his fifteen minutes. We recorded it at Channel 11 that morning. And that night, both programs were on from six thirty to seven o'clock. Well, Mr. Engel made the people in the production studio use old videotape that sometimes they didn't erase as well as they should have. And so, the night the television program ran with Senator Fulbright—I'll never forget this for as long as I live, and it made me paranoid about television productions from then on. The senator came on and began speaking, and in the background you could hear—just faintly, but distinctly enough to know what it was—you could hear an old Lawrence Welk television show in the background. And the senator would be talking about, "This is the most important election in America," and behind him you'd hear Welk going, "And now the Champagne Lady will sing 'Tiny Bubbles in the Wine.'" I think at that moment my heart stopped. I thought my career had ended at that particular point in time. And I do remember that because of this—it was faint retribution, but they didn't charge us for the television program because of that.

McConnell: Are you aware how Channel 11 ranked in the Little Rock market?

Robinson: I would say that they were considered to be the number-three station in the market but [were] probably number one in bottom-line profitability.

Kelly, who came from a well-run station in Shreveport, jumped at the chance to become a news director in Little Rock. After a week on the job, however, he wanted to beg Shreveport to take him back but couldn't force himself to do it.

Charles Kelly: I thought we eventually built one of the finest news bureaus in the country. CBS told us we did. We were one of the few stations that they would assign stories to cover, because of the competency of the people we had. What we didn't have—and this gets into the financial aspects of it—is good anchor people. I could not keep good people. We never could put that kind of anchor people on the air and leave them there. We would get somebody good, and Channel 7 would tape them and send it off to a station somewhere [laughs], and they'd hire them. You know, we just didn't have the bells and whistles that the other stations had. I don't want to make it sound like they were brutal or anything like that. I think their concept was that our job was to make money. We'd cut a product good enough to make money, but as long as we were doing that, we were not going to worry about the quality too much.

The 1998 Democrat *feature about Engel noted that under Engel,* Democrat *editorials often focused on agriculture. The paper endorsed diversified farming, quick-freezing vegetables, creating a state fair and livestock show, reforming the state hospital, improving election laws, improving education, and expanding Little Rock Junior College into a four-year institution. There are not a lot of controversial issues there, and by all accounts, Engel wanted to keep it that way.*

Kennedy: I always respected and admired him but was disappointed when he took no stand on the Central High crisis of 1957. Here was one of the top stories of the twentieth century right in his own backyard, but he ignored it. He *did* permit his writers to go their own way, and since most of them were friendly to Orval Faubus, most readers considered the *Democrat* to be pro-Faubus. Why did Engel stay neutral? He worked very hard to build and keep circulation and didn't want to upset the apple cart. I think that was the reason.

Sam Dickinson: He didn't want to rock the boat. He didn't want to stir up trouble [or] get into any arguments. We were against integration, but we couldn't say so. It wouldn't have been a very good thing for a newspaper to advocate defying the federal government, although the Shreveport paper did. We said it was the law of the land, and it should be obeyed. It would have been stupid to defy it. We couldn't have won. He [Engel] was against integration, and so were Mr. Heiskell and some other members of the Heiskell family. Heiskell's father fought for the Confederacy and was very much in favor of it. [Harry] Ashmore and [Hugh] Patterson talked him into it [supporting integration]. I think Mr. Heiskell was getting senile, and he had always dreamed of winning a Pulitzer Prize.

Charles Allbright: I thought it [the paper] was not bad, but editorially, it didn't exist—I mean, in terms of taking positions. That really came to the forefront in the 1957 crisis.

Gene Herrington: I don't think we got involved in the editorials like [the *Gazette*]. I don't know what Engel's policy was. I think he was for law and order, and I think he was for doing right. I don't know that we ever did anything that was less than in the middle. Now, it may have appeared that way because coverage of some things will look like that.

Bob McCord: Mr. Engel didn't want the editorials to get too tough about Central High either, I'm sure. And occasionally, the paper would write an editorial about it, but it was just, "Now, everybody just be careful, and don't overdo anything." Some people said that the *Democrat* was on the side of the rioters. That never happened. That's not true. I mean, Engel said, "Now, let's don't lose our mind here, let's be calm." They were pretty quiet about it. They didn't come out with any strong positions or anything. Karr Shannon, the long-time columnist, wrote about it, and he was—I guess you'd have to say—of the whole group, he was about the only one that ever showed any sympathy to the gang of thugs. And it wasn't all that much.

McConnell: Through most of this time that you were at the *Democrat*—say, from the late 1940s—they just didn't take a very strong editorial stance on anything, did they?

McCord: No. And that's just the way Mr. Engel really wanted it.

While the Democrat's own editorials were always fairly moderate, Engel did hire a number of syndicated columnists, who for the most part ranged from conservative to radically conservative. In fact, he may have held the edge on the Gazette in using well-known and popular columnists. At that time major newspapers and other groups syndicated their own columnists and made those columns available to other newspapers around the country for a comparatively small fee. Thus smaller newspapers could afford to carry commentary by some of the best-known writers of the day. The syndicates would deal with only one newspaper in a market, so the largest and most affluent paper had the first pick. However, the Gazette seemed to prefer writers syndicated by the New York Times, most of whom were liberal. Thus Engel was able to pick up writers from the New York Herald Tribune, which included Stewart Alsop, Joseph Alsop, and Walter Lippmann, as well as George E. Sokolsky, who became a right-wing radical.

CHAPTER 3

Engel's Newsroom

THE PEOPLE WHO worked in Engel's newsroom in the middle of the twentieth century tell a story of primitive working conditions, poor pay, long hours, and intense pressure, often allayed on and off the job by alcohol. They also reveal their pride in their work and the camaraderie of working with other people they knew were also doing their best in difficult circumstances.

Many of the good ones stayed only a short time and then started shopping around for better jobs, in or out of the newspaper business. One of the good ones who put in more years at the Democrat *than most was Bob McCord, who started as a photographer when he was barely in high school and too young to drive, won a national photographer's award while still a college student, became editor of the student newspaper at the University of Arkansas, and later earned a master's degree in journalism from Columbia University. He also had more direct contact with Engel than most, for all the good it did him. McCord returned to the* Democrat *after getting his master's degree.*

Bob McCord: Well, I didn't have any other place to go. I thought all these big-shot eastern newspapers would give me a job, but nobody did, so I came back here. Mr. Engel came up to New York City while I was at Columbia. Mr. Engel was not known for his social activities, you know. He was an all-business man, but he came up for the American Newspaper Publishers Association convention at the Waldorf Hotel. The next thing I knew, he called me on the phone and said, "I wish you and your wife would come in and have dinner with me at the Waldorf." I thought, "My God." And I said, "Well, we would love to do that." Muriel [Moo] was seven months pregnant, and we went to that fine hotel and sat there with Engel, and he told me, "Well, I'm glad you're coming back," and, "We'll be looking for you," and so on, and that was a great thrill when he introduced me to all those other publishers. Well, I came back and I was doing general assignment—kind of what I was doing when I left—and I was traveling. I wasn't making enough money to really stay alive, and we were in a little apartment in North Little Rock with the baby, so I hooked up with the *Christian Science Monitor* and with *Business Week* to cover Arkansas stories for them. They were especially glad to have me when [the Little Rock school integration crisis of] 1957 came along. They paid really well, and I didn't have to do too much. With that and with what I got at the *Democrat* I was doing okay. I'd do about one piece a week for *Business Week* and maybe a couple of pieces for the *Christian Science Monitor.* They really were fine people. Later Mr. [Ed] Liske [the managing editor] called me into his office, which was kind of unusual, and he said, "How would you like to be editor of the Sunday magazine of the *Democrat*?" And I said, "Well, I don't know, Mr. Liske." "Well, I really do need somebody." I said, "Why, what's happening to the editor?" So Liske got up and went over and closed the door to his office, and he said, "You know, I knew something was going on, and almost every week there was a story or a picture in there of a barber." He said, "I just figured it out. I wrote their names down, and I called two or three of them." And he said, "That guy was trading for his haircuts—he would put their pictures and a story about them in the magazine." And Liske said, "I just can't have that." They didn't fire him, but they moved him out into the newsroom, but Gene Herrington wouldn't have him. So he finally left. Liske said, "All right, we'll give you five dollars more a week." Well, that was a lot of money then, and I said, "Well, okay." And so that's what I did.

McCord edited a much-praised Sunday magazine for about four years and then left to buy the weekly newspaper in his hometown, the North Little Rock Times. *He returned to the* Democrat *ten years later, after Engel died.*

Here are some other views of Engel's newsroom in that era from some talented writers and editors.

Ramon Greenwood: I got my journalism degree in 1950 and worked in the retail lumberyard [in Warren] for a few months so I could get married and was always thinking about the newspaper business. So I went up and interviewed with the *Democrat*. The next day I had the job, so we moved to Little Rock. I was on general assignment for about a month, and then Mr. Tilden said that he was going to give me a tryout at the state capitol. Ken Francis and Marcus George were on assignment out there, and they needed somebody else, so I took it as quite a compliment. He picked me to go out there and work with them, which was really, really interesting and sort of a plum opportunity. I covered kind of the second-level stuff—the health department, the forestry and education [departments], and that sort of thing. It was just a romantic kind of time. Martha and I hadn't been married very long. Interestingly enough, she was making more money as a secretary than I was as a reporter. She had had about six weeks of shorthand—that was her whole training. I had started at forty dollars a week, and she was making forty-five dollars a week. I thought [the *Democrat*] was an excellent newspaper. I remember more than anything that I sort of felt like, in looking back on it, we were sort of the last go-around of the traditional newspaper people, you know, like the classic newspaper I guess you grew up reading about and hearing about. So it was just—it was kind of a romantic time. We felt we were doing something, you know?

But as happened with a lot of others, the time came when romance alone was not enough.

Greenwood: When probably the worst tornado that ever hit Arkansas occurred, we were having a staff picnic out at a city park [Boyle]. Somebody had their car radio on. Gene Herrington [the assistant city editor] was there, and he kept sending people to go here and there. And it got down to where there weren't many reporters left. So Gene said, "Well, come on, let's you and I go up toward Beebe and Judsonia—and see what we can do up there." So we went in his car, and it was pretty dark. And the devastation was just *incredible*. We visited the hospitals and so forth, and he and I turned around and got back to Little Rock about daylight and went to the newsroom and wrote our stories. And I wrote about being in the hospital and seeing these parents sitting on the floor in the hallway holding a baby in their arms, and there was blood and the baby was injured, and they were sitting waiting there for the doctor. So I wrote that in my part of the story. Well, that got picked up by the AP [Associated Press], and I got calls and letters from all over the country about that segment of the story. So, anyway, we had worked around the clock and then had to get the Sunday paper out, and I told Martha—I said, "Well, it's a really an experience. Of course, we'll be paid for all those extra hours." When he came in Monday to go to work, Mr. Liske called us all together. He said, "Now, you all put in a lot of overtime, but we thought it would be better—instead of paying you for the overtime, we'll just give you time off." So, anyway, we had time off, which didn't sit very well with us.

Comp (compensatory) time was a typical newspaper way (at least at the Democrat) of avoiding shelling out extra money by giving employees time off when things weren't so busy.

Incidentally, those tornadoes hit on March 21, 1952, and killed at least 112 people. Seven people were killed at Dierks, and at least 8 were killed at England as the storms moved to the northeast, but the destruction was worse the farther they went. More than 50 were killed in two small towns only four miles apart in White county, 36 in Judsonia and 18 in Bald Knob, which is where Herrington, Greenwood, and others wound up. It wasn't long after this that Greenwood began to be tempted by offers of other employment.

Greenwood: A fellow named Fred Lang was the state forester, and I saw quite a bit of Mr. Lang [at the state capitol]. He said, "Would you be interested in talking with a friend of mine about working in a trade association?" I said, "Well, yes. I'll talk to anybody." So he got me set up with an interview with a fellow from Washington, DC, who had been previous state forester in Arkansas. When this guy was in Little Rock, he interviewed me and offered me a job. And as I said, at that time I was making forty dollars a week, and Mr. Gillette, the guy from Washington, offered me one hundred dollars a week, mileage that would let me buy a new car, and to make me district manager for his trade association. I came back, and I told Mr. Tilden what was happening. So he went in and told Mr. Liske what was happening, and Liske said he ought to talk to Mr. Engel about this. So after a little bit, Mr. Liske came back and called me into his office, and he said, "Well, we don't want you to leave. Here's what Mr. Engel says we can do for you." He said, "You've been here about a year now, or going on a year." He said, "You're making forty dollars a week. You're due to be raised to forty-five dollars a week in the normal course of events. And now that this has come up, because we want to keep you, we can raise you to fifty-five dollars a week." So I said, "Well, Mr. Liske, don't you understand? I just told you that these other people offered me one hundred dollars a week and a car—mileage and so forth." So he said, "Well, that's the best we can do. What are you going to be doing? What does this job entail?" And I said, "Well, it's public relations for the forest product industry." He said, "*Public relations!*" He said, "Ramon, do you not know that this public relations business—it's not here to *stay?*" [laughs]. So I said, "Well, Mr. Liske, I guess I don't have much choice." So I had to leave or *thought* I had to leave.

Greenwood did leave and became head of public relations for a series of major American companies, including the Crossett Co., Morton Salt, Consolidated Foods (now Sara Lee), and American Express, as well as serving as head of public affairs for eighteen months for the US Department of Transportation.

Jerry McConnell: What kind of fringe benefits did you have at the *Democrat?*

Greenwood: Gosh, I don't know that we had [laughs]—I don't remember *any.* Of course, I wasn't too interested in it then, but I don't believe we *had* any. You know, I never thought about that. Hell, no, we didn't.

Another compatriot of that era, who wound up working at both the Democrat *and the* Gazette, *leaving both then returning to both, was Charles Allbright.*

Charles Allbright: I worked on the newspaper at Little Rock High School. Rabbit Burnett, who was coach then of the football team, said, "Allbright, you're not doing anything here." We were [working out] at the practice field. He said, "We're not going to miss *you.* Take this stuff up to Miss Middlebrook in the *Tiger* office." So I did. I was relieved not to get beat up another day by Fred Williams [a future Razorback and NFL player]. At the *Tiger* office I sat down. Dallied as long as I could so as not to go back to practice. I thought, "I can write better than this." It was so dreadful. I decided right then, "I think that's what I want to do—write sports." And that's what I did. One day a journalism teacher came to me and said, "Mr. Jack Keady, [the sports editor] at the *Arkansas Democrat,* wants to know if you will come visit with him." I went. I was seventeen, and he hired me. It was dreadful, Jerry. The writing was just what you'd write at seventeen. Every run was *scintillating*, and every fire *raged*. When my stuff was put into the archives at the University of Central Arkansas, I prayed about, "Am I going to include this crap, too?" I did, so it's there, and it's embarrassing. But that's how I started. One day when I was going to the university, the *Democrat*'s managing editor, Edwin Liske, came to me. It was a summer day. He said, "Red, on Monday, don't wear your tennis shoes." I wasn't wearing tennis shoes. I was in the sports department, but you don't tell that to the ME [managing editor]—point out your shoes. So, that was the end of sports. He moved me to the news side—on general assignment.

Later Allbright enrolled at the university, worked on the Traveler, *was the Fayetteville correspondent for the* Democrat, *and then returned to the* Democrat *in the summer. He became editor of the* Traveler *in 1951–52.*

Allbright: The year I was editor, I got so beat up—so *used* up, I decided, "I can't go back to school now. I've got to take a break." I was at the *Democrat* then, and here came Horace Heidt with his musical [big band] group. Well, I interviewed Heidt. His show had already come to Fayetteville, and I wrote a really bad review for it, being your usual excessive kid critic. Then I wrote a piece about Heidt coming to Little Rock. He called me from Jackson, Mississippi, which was his next stop, and offered me a job. I took it and did his public relations and traveled with the band for about a year....

McConnell: What was your starting pay at the *Democrat*?

Allbright: Twenty-six dollars a week, but, really, for seven days. When I left to go into the army, I think it was about fifty-six dollars.

McConnell: Did you get paid any overtime when you were working seven days a week?

Allbright: I remember that I got to go home at two thirty in the afternoon [an hour early] instead of getting any more money.

Allbright had no trouble remembering that drinking alcohol was very common at the Democrat.

Allbright: We had some pretty heavy drinkers at the paper. They were in key spots. I might have recalled that a couple of them would come to work every other Monday morning with their eyebrows singed off. They had been at home, cooking something. The oven just blew them out [laughs]. Drinking was another thing in those days. It was somehow traditional. Those of us who didn't do that weren't feeling superior, but we were probably more aware than these other guys were. I knew staffers who, right after we got through [having breakfast at] Walgreens—went on to city hall, and on the way drank beer for breakfast. It was tolerated because some of the people who had to tolerate it were also drunk.

Ken Kaufman: I started first with the *Rogers Daily News*. It was a nice little paper. I was dating the captain of the girls' basketball team. It would have continued, but I got bored with Rogers, and she did not want to leave Rogers. I could see very little career there. I quit and told them I was going someplace else. My first choice was the Fort Smith paper. They offered me forty-nine dollars a week. I felt that was an insult. That was the same as I was making at the *Rogers Daily News*. And I thought, "Well, why should I come all the way down from Rogers to work for them for the same amount of money?" Well, their theory was it was such an honor to work on the Fort Smith daily paper that I should be willing to jump into it. I drove to Little Rock. I arrived at about five o'clock on a Friday afternoon. I went into the [*Arkansas*] *Democrat*. I remember [Allen] Tilden was working late, and I went up to him and said that I was looking for a job. He quizzed me a little bit, and then he said, "Well, we'll take you on Monday morning." I said, "That would be fine. What will I get paid?" He said, "Forty-nine dollars a week." Then he said, "When can you start?" I said, "Well, I can start on Monday." Then he said, "Be here at six o'clock in the morning and we'll put you on." Then Tilden said, "I guess you need something to eat, too, don't you?" I said, "Yes." He said, "Well, I'll tell you what I'll do. I'll put you on the civic club circuit, and you can earn one meal a day covering civic clubs, and that should keep you from starving to death."

It didn't take long for Ken to demonstrate his ability, and he was soon promoted to the number-three spot at the state capitol (he may have replaced Greenwood), where he soon produced some excellent stories on developments in the new state highway department and provided top coverage of perhaps the first flare-up in Arkansas over the Supreme Court ruling ordering desegregation of the schools, this one at Sheridan. He was interviewed by phone while he was in a health-care facility in Wichita, Kansas, suffering from the Parkinson's disease that would soon kill him. He could not remember everything about his career at the Democrat, *but he could remember a lot. He stayed at the* Democrat *about three years.*

McConnell: Ken, why did you leave the *Democrat*?

Kaufman: I always said I would never marry as long as I was in newspapers because I didn't think they paid enough. I remember I'd go to somebody's house, and they'd barely have enough to eat. One of the few pastimes that I can remember us having was playing poker. We kind of had a little poker group—maybe about four or five. I applied for a job at Southwestern Bell Telephone Company. So I quit and went to work for the telephone company. Then Mary [Arnold] went to work for the state Parks and Tourism Department. We got married almost immediately.

Kaufman stayed with the telephone company for thirty-seven years, rising to head of its public relations department, and worked for four years at American Telephone and Telegraph in New York City. He also returned to college while he was still working and earned a doctorate in history from St. Louis University. His doctoral dissertation was published as a book by the University of Missouri Press. It was called Dred Scott's Advocate: A Biography of Roswell Field. *Dred Scott was a slave who sought his freedom in court; when the US Supreme Court denied his freedom, it helped inflame opinion against slavery. Roswell Field was his lawyer. The book received favorable reviews.*

Not everyone left the Democrat *after a few years. Gene Herrington stayed around for twenty-eight. Herrington graduated from the University of Arkansas in 1942 and first found employment with some little Arkansas weeklies but soon started looking around.*

Gene Herrington: I was walking down the streets in Little Rock and ran into Matilda Touhey, who I had known at the university and was now working for the *Democrat*. Tuohey suggested I call Allen Tilden, the city editor at the *Democrat*. I called the next day from McGehee. He said, "Come up, and let's talk." So I came up. He said, "I'll start you at twenty-five dollars a week." He promised a raise in three months. When Tilden hired me, he said, "Gene, I can't pay you much, but I'll give you a free lunch every day. You can cover a luncheon club every day so you won't have to bring your lunch, or you won't have to go buy one." And, you know, it sounds like a penalty—because you're poor, you're going to have to do it. But it turned out that I met more leaders in Little Rock in one year than some people ever knew in their lifetime.

This was during the war, and Tilden eventually assigned me to cover the military at Camp Robinson. Since I didn't have a car, I went to Camp Robinson every morning and came back every afternoon on the bus. The brass at the camp loaned me a bicycle so I could travel all over the camp. I ate at the staff mess hall.

Herrington eventually enlisted in the US Army Air Corps. When he was discharged, he returned to Little Rock and went back to the Democrat *to see about a job. Tilden had gone into the army as a captain and had not yet returned. His replacement offered Herrington his old job back, but at the same pay, fifty dollars a week. Herrington turned it down and took a job for fifty-five dollars a week with the state employment security division, a job he didn't like.*

Herrington: After Tilden came back, I went to see him, and he said, "Gene, why in the world aren't you here where you're supposed to be?" And I told him, "Five dollars a week?" He said, "Will you come back if I can get you the five dollars?" I said I sure would. I wasn't having any fun there. "Well, I can get it," he said, and did. Anyway, I became the assistant city editor with the job of assigning reporters, checking the *Gazette* for stories they ought to look at and see what's going on. I came in at six o'clock and worked usually until about one thirty or two o'clock. I'd get to work Saturday night, too.

McConnell: You were working a six-day shift, weren't you? Monday through Saturday.

Herrington: The Saturday was two shifts.

McConnell: Were you doing seven shifts a week?

Herrington: Yes.

McConnell: What kind of fringe benefits did you have?

Herrington: I'm looking for them. When I left after twenty-eight years there [and serving as city editor and then managing editor], they gave me a little attaché case.

McConnell: They didn't have health care, did [they], at that time?

Herrington: No health care, no sick leave, no retirement.

John Ward: I was at the *Log Cabin Democrat* as a reporter during the 1957 crisis in Little Rock and even went down there a time or two and covered some of that. But I went to work at the *Democrat* in 1958, and I was there until 1964. Marcus George was the city editor and my boss. Gene Herrington was the managing editor. Marcus, frankly, took a liking to me and encouraged me to develop my reportorial skills and also enabled me to pursue my interest in photography. I wound up doing lots of my own photography, and I wound up with the best job there, which was traveling around making my own assignments, making my own photographs. I covered all the Arkansas River development. I'd go to Tulsa and up and down the river—that was one of my assignments. I later wound up covering the big stories, whatever they were. You know, the boys' industrial school fire at Traskwood. And the air force jet crash in Little Rock. The *Democrat* was an interesting place. We didn't make very much money. We were poorly paid, and the people there were there because they were relaxed about things. They were not three-piece-suit guys and intense stuff. It was a relaxed place to work. We did a lot of decent reporting. We were not the *Arkansas Gazette*. It was secondary to that paper. It was an afternoon paper in those days. It was not a great newspaper. The *Democrat* was always secondary in the newspaper market in Little Rock. But the *Democrat* was a very profitable paper because of the way it was operated like that. It wasn't anything like the *Gazette*, but we had a good circulation. We didn't feel competitive, really, with the *Gazette* because they were morning [and] we were afternoon. We didn't think we were in their league. We all were wise enough as reporters and journalists to know that they were putting the most resources into local reporting, and the quality of their stuff was just—it was pretty high. But we didn't have an inferiority complex about it. Everybody tried to do the best they could. I think if you would go back and review those papers and look at the quality of the reporting, a lot of it was pretty good. Some of it wasn't so good, but most of it was pretty good. But it was always "Try to find the cheapest way to do things"—that was Mr. Engel's style. We had No. 5 Underwood typewriters, and Stanley Berry, one of Mr. Engel's nephews, one of his jobs was to come up and oil the typewriters and change the light bulbs. It was such a strange, kind of low-budget-type thing.

Because their pay was so slight, several journalists supplemented it with other jobs, frequently signing up as correspondents with out-of-state papers or national magazines, as did McCord. Fred Petrucelli was one of the most innovative.

Fred Petrucelli: I think the *Democrat* paid me thirty dollars a week to start [in 1945]. I had married, and thirty dollars a week was not a lot of money, even in those days. I was interested in [professional] wrestling, and I became the wrestling agent in town. I'd do the stories before the matches and after the matches and help in any other way. I think the promoter Leroy McGuirk paid me about thirty or forty dollars a week. He would send me a list of the matches. I would give them publicity. After the matches, I would write stories and send the stories to the *Gazette* and the Associated Press and then the *Arkansas Democrat*. I would help the wrestlers get organized in hotels and whatever they needed when they were visiting here in Little Rock. These guys coming in didn't know where to go, so we ran a little headquarters in the Marion Hotel. They'd just drop in and get some information about places to eat, or one thing or another. I also did work for Hazel Walker. [Walker was an All-American basketball player from Ashdown, and she put together her own team, the All-American Redheads, and toured the country playing men's teams, usually pickup teams.] I was her booking agent, and that was a pretty darn good job, although I just happened to run into it. Henry Levy was a fight promoter in Little Rock. He booked some matches in Robinson Auditorium. I got to know Henry pretty well because I was covering the matches. He was dating Hazel Walker, which was a curious match in itself. She was six feet whatever, and Henry was just a little-bitty guy. Levy put me next to her, and we talked about the job. I took it from there, and I booked games for her all through the South, you know. It was just lots of telephone work, where I got on the phone and called police departments, or fire departments, or boys' clubs, and so forth, and set up arrangements. Hazel wanted to play every blasted night, too. Oh, she was fantastic. It was a heck of a job to get her games all of the time, but she wanted to do it.

One year [1951] the *Democrat* sent me to Florida to cover the Little Rock Travelers baseball team during spring training. Ray Winder, the general manager of the Travelers, put me on his payroll and paid me just enough to cover my meals.

In addition to the tight financial arrangements, everyone who worked there in that era remembers the Democrat *building, especially the newsroom. Their memories may vary a little, but not by much, because it was pretty memorable. The* Democrat *was located then, as it is now, at Capitol (Fifth Street) and Scott. It was in an old YMCA build-ing, where Engel moved the paper in 1930. As a YMCA it had housed a swimming pool in the basement and a basketball court and showers. The newsroom then was on the second floor, and it looked as though it hadn't changed in decades. The floor was well-worn hardwood that was oiled to keep down the dust. To clean it, the janitors sprinkled sawdust on it to absorb the other dust and then swept it with big push brooms. In the hot weather, they kept the windows open and had big fans sitting around the room, which stirred up a breeze and everything else. Before noon, you could run your hand across your forehead and wipe off the grime. Some people said the fans edited more copy than the editors.*

Rodney Lorenzen: It was kind of run-down when I started there in the 1960s. They had an elevator that barely worked. I usually avoided getting on that. But, actually, the steps weren't much better; they were kind of shaky, or you'd bounce on them just a little bit going from the ground floor up to the sports department on the second floor. The place just was kind of dingy. The desks were old. The typewriters were really old and very hard to operate. You really had to pound them.

Ward: I remember Mr. Engel didn't even air-condition the news-room. When I was working the Saturday-night shift, which I fre-quently had to do to get the Sunday paper out, we would raise all those windows, and, of course, the bugs would just be in there by the millions—grasshoppers and flies and everything else. It was really, really very interesting.

As Herrington recalled, there was no sick leave policy. Marguerite Gamble, who worked in the women's department, recalled a glaring example.

Marguerite Gamble: Joe Crossley was on the desk, I believe. [He was the news editor and a graduate of Harvard.] Joe had also worked there forever. He had some sort of serious male operation. And they paid him his two-week vacation but no sick leave. After his two weeks of vacation were up, they cut off his salary till he could get back. They did take him back. I don't know if it was the same salary or the same job or whatever. But he was at an age when he could not afford to quit; he would have had no place else to go. They were just were ugly to a lot of their employees. They didn't give them raises. For Christmas, every-body got a twenty-five-dollar bonus. But they took out five dollars in income tax, so you only got twenty dollars. Of course, twenty dollars was a whole lot more in those days than it is now, but still.

Anyone who has ever worked at a large newspaper could regale you with stories about the characters (not so say oddballs) who worked there, but if you pressed them they'd admit they knew more talented, dedicated people than oddballs, even at the old Engel Democrat. In the former category you'd have to include Bob McCord, who started there when he was fourteen or fifteen and left having been the editor and partial owner. Along the way he became the national president of Sigma Delta Chi, which became the Society of Professional Journalists.

McCord: I think the thing that really started it is that I was a photographer. You know, North Little Rock was kind of a tough town back in those days, and my dad didn't want me to get involved in a lot of things I could have gotten involved in. It was a railroad town, then—really, that was all that was here. And he bought a real fine camera for me, and we set up a little darkroom in my house. I was about twelve years old, and I was a pretty good photographer. I got into about the eighth grade down at Fourth Street Junior High School—and our basketball team beat East Side in Little Rock, and we just couldn't get over it. I made a picture of the team and the coach, and it was a good picture, and one of the teachers said, "You know, I bet that the *Gazette* would print that picture." I said, "You do, you think so?" And she said, "Yes." So I got on the streetcar and went over there. Orville Henry was still in high school, but he was working down there for sports editor Ben Epstein, and Henry came out and looked at it and he said, "Oh, that's a good picture, I'd like to run that, but you know, paper's scarce"—this was during World War II, and paper for newspapers was scarce. Well, Epstein said no because it would take up about three columns, "and we just can't do that." So I took it back to the same teacher, and she said, "Well, what happened?" I told her. And she said, "Well, why don't you just put two people vertically—two here, two here, and two here, and you could get it all in one column." I said, "Well, I never thought of that." So I got them together down there, and I made the picture and took it back over there [to the *Gazette*], and Orville said, "Gosh, that's a good idea. Let me take that in to Epstein," and he put it in the next day's paper. And if you think I wasn't proud of that one-column picture of the basketball team—I think that's where my journalism career started. When I got to high school, I started to work at the *Democrat* and would go over there—I couldn't drive, because at first I wasn't old enough to have a license—but my dad would get up and take me to work at six thirty a.m., and I would work in the darkroom. I would catch the bus and come back over to high school. Sometimes I would work in the afternoons, after school. But I worked daily every summer until I went off to college. So you could say from 1945 [on], I was on a daily basis of working for an afternoon newspaper. I was making pictures, and I started to write some. Oh, yes, police reporting—that's what they make all the new ones [do]. You know, until the war was over, newspapers still had mostly women, and there were a lot of places women just could not go in those days, especially women photographers. I used to go out to all these crime [scenes], and, of course, I would try to look as old as I could. Old Joe Wirges, the well-known photographer [and police reporter] at the *Gazette,* took a liking to me. And the cops a lot of times would say, "Get away from here, kid. You don't work for a newspaper"—and Joe would say, "Ah, let him in, he's a good fellow." And I would get to go in and make a picture just like he did.

When he graduated from North Little Rock high school, McCord enrolled at the University of Arkansas in Fayetteville and immediately went to work for the Arkansas Traveler.

McCord: I mainly made pictures for one year because I just kind of liked to do it, and I had all my equipment up there, even a little darkroom in the trunk of my car, and that was something really hot in those days. My junior year, I think I was either assistant managing editor or managing editor. I must have been managing editor because Muriel [Stuck] came up to apply for a job, and [John] Troutt was the editor. I interviewed her, and we are still married. She worked for the Traveler those last two years. Then I was the editor of the *Traveler* for the last year.

McCord came back and worked at the Democrat for the first two summers after he enrolled at the university. He was working mostly as a reporter but still did some photography.

McCord: When they got into a tight [spot], I did. That was kind of what happened on that picture that won the AP [Associated Press] prize. I was in the darkroom that morning, developing O. D. Gunter's film—he had been somewhere. The city editor came running in and said, "Look, Bob, pick up a camera and run down there real quick and get a picture of the president coming down Main Street. (This was in 1949, and [Harry] Truman was attending a reunion of the Thirty-fifth Division, and they were marching down Main Street.) I looked like hell. I had on a t-shirt and what have you, but I just grabbed this four-by-five Speed Graphic [camera] and ran down there and made this picture. The first shot I made—why, just as I pressed the trigger. President Truman threw his arm over [in front of his face] to wave to somebody, so I knew I had to make another one. So I started going backwards, and, of course, they were moving real fast. Governor McMath was on this side of Truman, and then on the other was all of his Thirty-fifth Division friends. I kept backing up, and I kneeled down and made a second picture, and I thought, "Well, that was pretty good." All of a sudden, these two guys picked me up by the arms, hauled me out of the street, and plunked me down on the sidewalk, and they said, "Who in the hell do you think you are, running out there and making a picture of the president of the United States?" They were Secret Service agents. I said, "Well, I work for the *Arkansas Democrat,* just right down the street. I'm a newspaperman." "Yes, yes, you get your butt out of here and don't ever let me see you again." Now, I guess they would have shot you if you did something like that. Scared me to death.

The picture made the Democrat's *first edition and was spread over six columns, unusually wide for that era. It was selected as the* Associated Press Picture of the Year nationally.

McCord: They sent it in for the Pulitzer [Prize], and, of course, it didn't make it. There had been a murder up in New York, and a picture about it in the old *Herald Tribune* won it.

It was not the first time that one of McCord's pictures made national news. While he was still a student at Fayetteville, he and Bob Douglas were the only members of the media present when Silas Hunt entered the University of Arkansas Law School, becoming the first black to enter a law school in the South. Douglas, who also worked for the Traveler, *later became managing editor of the* Arkansas Gazette *and then head of the University of Arkansas Journalism Department. He wrote the story that was sent out with McCord's pictures, which were picked up all over the nation. Allbright, who worked with McCord at the* Democrat *and was managing editor under him on the* Traveler *and was always the master of a tongue-in-cheek statement, had this observation: "McCord could've been a great all-time photographer internationally if he hadn't gotten hung up on thought."*

Ozell Sutton remembers McCord in another context. *Sutton was hired by the* Democrat *in 1950, the first black hired as a reporter at a major newspaper in Arkansas and the first or second in the South.*

Ozell Sutton: Now, how the *Democrat* decided to hire a black is but a supposition on my part. There were great divisions between the two papers. The *Democrat* was considered by blacks to be the most conservative paper, and the *Gazette* the most liberal. The *Democrat*, in order to impact the black circulation without changing its conservative policy, decided to hire a black affairs writer. Now, that's my supposition, and I found it to be pretty well true. So I went to work for the *Democrat*. Now, in light of those days, they segregated me. The city desk was [stretched] across the room, and then the reporters were in line [in front of] the city desk. Well, they didn't put me, at first, in line, they put me on the other side of the city desk. I was behind Allen Tilden [the city editor]. When I'd come in, I would go to my desk—nobody sitting over there but me—and work. You know, for one thing, it was kind of contributing to my development. The reason was that I was not a trained journalist, and I didn't even know how to type at that time. I was unhampered and unbothered by anybody—because nobody spoke to me at that time. Bob McCord was very friendly toward me, and he was the first person that would even come back [to] where I was and say hello. And that was the way it went. I came in one day, and my desk had been moved from being behind Allen Tilden to beside Allen Tilden. I've always been a person who approached crazy situations in sort of a crazy way. So when I walked in and my desk had been moved, I walked over to Tilden. I said, "Chief, where is my desk, or have I been fired?" He said, "Here's your desk right here, Ozell." I said, "Oh, is that so? Am I an editor?" He said, "No, not quite, but here's your desk." So I sat down there by Allen Tilden. I stayed there about six months, and then I came in—my desk had been moved again. I was in line, now, with the other reporters. I was next to Karr Shannon? He was one of the editorial writers.

At first I covered whatever I could hustle up in the black community. I had no assignment. I certainly didn't have [a] city desk assignment. I had no city hall assignment or school assignment. I just was sort of a general assignment reporter, working the black community and their affairs. That happened until 1954 [when the US Supreme Court voted to desegregate the schools]. At that time, I was the vice president of the Little Rock chapter of the NAACP [National Association for the Advancement of Colored People]. And I was Daisy Bates's lieutenant. So I became a little more important at that particular time to the paper. I became sort of statewide in my coverage of the black struggle. And since I was probably the most knowledgeable person in the state about black efforts to desegregate themselves, I started covering those kinds of events—but then I was privileged to begin to cover the middle-class black activities. And as they sought to advance themselves, what might be termed the *Ebony* [magazine] kind of black movements in Arkansas.

The *Democrat* never used courtesy titles for black women. The *Gazette* did. But the *Democrat* had a problem because I absolutely refused to write a black woman's name without a courtesy title. Now, that's the atmosphere out of which I grew up. Tilden was always on my case. I'd write a story, and I'd write, "Mrs. So-and-so," and he or his staff would go through this story and scratch "Mrs." But they never could get me to write it that way. Tilden said, "Now, Ozell, you know we don't use courtesy titles for black women." I said, "Chief, we have a problem. You don't use courtesy titles for black women, and I don't write black women's names without courtesy titles." Tilden was a good man. I really didn't have any difficulty out of [him]. It's just a policy on their part. And we came to an impasse. What I started to do, I didn't write, "Mrs. Joanna Sutton," I wrote, "Mrs. Ozell Sutton." Then if you wrote it without a courtesy title, then you're identifying the wrong person. That's when old man Liske came in. He called me into his office. And that was back in the days when you called blacks "Doctor." Liske always called me Doctor. That was in lieu of calling me "Mr." He said, "This whole subject of courtesy titles—we seem to be going around the horn on that one. You win." I said, "I win? What do I win?" He said, "The *Democrat* has decided to start using courtesy titles for blacks."

I left the *Democrat* in March—I believe it was March—in 1957. I went to work for Winthrop Rockefeller up on top of Petit Jean Mountain. By then, I was totally and wholly disillusioned about my own career. I was going nowhere, the *Democrat* was not giving me any raise—well, they gave you about a five- or ten-dollar-a-week raise sometimes. So I wasn't getting promoted. They weren't about to make me an editor. They were not about to make me *anything*. I got that five-a-week raise, and that's all. I had a wife and two children at that time. I needed to do better. So I got a job working for Win Rockefeller; folks don't realize that I was Winthrop's butler for two years. He had the best butler you ever seen in your *life*. And that's what I did from 1957 until 1959, was to serve as a butler to Win Rockefeller. Mr. Rockefeller was a good man. I was able at that time to be more than just a butler. Because Win had all these big affairs up there, and I was in charge of special events. When he'd have those big cattle sales up there and those rich people coming in from all over the world, who was in charge of events? Ozell. I left there and came back down to Little Rock and went with the Little Rock Housing Authority as a relocation supervisor. I stayed there from 1959 until 1961, and then I became the associate director of the Arkansas Council on Human Relations.

Wayne Cranford: While I was assistant state editor [at the *Democrat*], Bob McCord had already started a rather new Sunday magazine and hired me as a writer for the Sunday magazine. In a very, very small room, Bob McCord, Roberta Martin, a young woman named Julia—I believe her last name was Naylor—and I had a desk and put out what we thought was the best Sunday magazine that we had ever seen or have seen since. Will Counts was the photographer. He and I had gone to college together. We were fraternity brothers. I really enjoyed working at the Sunday magazine, and I learned a *lot* from Bob McCord. Well, I learned a lot while I was working at the *Democrat* from Marcus George and others, but I really learned a lot from Bob McCord. So, suddenly, I was offered a job as director of public relations for the Little Rock Chamber of Commerce. Bob promised me that if I wanted to take that job, I could still do freelance stories for the magazine, which I did continue to do for a couple of years—three or four, maybe. Among the stories were—for example, one of our first ones was going to Piggott, Arkansas, where they were filming [the motion picture] *A Face in the Crowd* [1957]. It was Lee Remick's first movie. She was eighteen years old. The director was Elia Kazan. It was a great experience. We did a fabulous feature in Pangburn, Arkansas, on a Boy Scout who had saved another kid's life and got the Medal of Honor from the Boy Scouts of America. Things like that.

Perhaps the best-known and most controversial reporter at the Democrat *for a period of thirty years or more was George Douthit. Everyone who worked with Douthit had generally strong views about him, one way or the other. He became somewhat famous during the Central High crisis. Douthit eventually quit the* Democrat *in a huff during a new regime in 1970, but more about that later. Douthit was born in Texas and started his career as a sports reporter in San Antonio at the age of sixteen. He went to work for the Associated Press in Fort Smith in 1932, transferred to Hot Springs in 1935, and then went to work for the* Democrat *in 1936. After five years in the army, he returned in 1945.*

McCord: George Douthit, just back from World War II, was the best reporter in my early days. I mean, he could go to a tornado and find out what was destroyed and how many were killed in thirty minutes. And George would always be back to get the story in the eleven o'clock a.m. paper. It was just amazing. And he knew somebody everywhere. He knew a way to find out anything. He didn't write very well, but he was a hell of a good reporter.

Petrucelli: Douthit covered the integration crisis for us. At one point Governor Faubus went into hiding when President Eisenhower was trying to serve him with a writ. Nobody could find him—federal agents didn't know where to serve it. They couldn't find him. The only person who knew where he was was George Douthit. That's true. George would send us stories about Faubus—what Faubus was doing—never telling us his location. He considered it his beat, and he wasn't telling anybody. He didn't tell anybody what he knew. He would give us stories from Faubus's headquarters. He would scoop the *Gazette* every damned day. They would have to rewrite George Douthit every time. AP was rewriting. All over the country they were rewriting George because he was the only one who could get to Faubus. And that went on for several days. The end came when the agents finally got to Faubus when he returned to the capital building. The *Gazette* called Douthit Faubus's Boswell. George didn't mind. He was getting a story. He was getting a scoop. We didn't care either.

Ward: In fact, my first expense account—when I first got there— Douthit came over and sat down with me afterwards and said, "Now, let me give you some instruction about this." He didn't like the way I'd done it—I was real honest and straight. "No, that's not the way we do it." Douthit was so funny.

Greenwood: I remember George Douthit had great contacts—a short, stubby little guy—self-important sort of fellow. I don't recall he hardly ever left the newsroom, but he worked the phones.

Jerry Dean: One of the key reporters at the time was George Douthit. George was a bit cantankerous. He covered Orval Faubus and state capitol news for the most part. He could be very easygoing and a likeable fella, but every morning when people started arriving at the *Democrat*, we had what the interns started to call "George Douthit Hour," because George would take the newspaper that had come out the afternoon before and take it apart page by page, column by column, and would make vitriolic comment about everybody that, in his eyes, had screwed up the day before.

McCord: There were a lot of good people and good journalists—male and female—at the *Democrat* when I was first there. Dorothy Carroll, the society editor, knew everyone in Little Rock and wanted the pictures I took for her to be just right.

Dorothy Dungan Carroll was society editor of the Democrat *for twenty-nine years and may have given the* Democrat *an edge in society news for some time. She was a charter member of the Junior League of Little Rock and a board member of the historic Mount Holly Cemetery, where she was buried, as was her son John Dungan Carroll, who was killed in a military air crash at the age of twenty-two in 1943.*

Gamble: Dorothy Carroll, who was then the society editor of the *Democrat,* called and asked me to come down and talk to Mr. Liske, and he hired me. And I worked as women's editor. I went to work there in the summer of 1954, and right away I got sent to New York to cover the fashion openings for the New York Dress Institute, which made it a whole lot more palatable. We had that long office on the northwest corner of the building. And Lelia Maude Funston, who was the religious editor, was at one end, and Dorothy Carroll and her assistant and I were at the other end. And Miss Dorothy and Miss Lelia Maude did not speak [to each other]. So Miss Dorothy would say, "Marguerite, go and ask Miss Funston so and so and so forth." And I would get up—and, of course, Miss Funston could hear this. So I would go down, and I would say, "Miss Funston, Mrs. Carroll wants to know so and so forth." And she'd say, "Marguerite, you tell Mrs. Carroll so and so and so forth." So I'd go back and I'd say, "Miss Dorothy, Miss Funston says so and so forth." It was the most absurd situation I've ever been in.

Dorothy had been there for years and years. She took time off during World War II to go work for the Red Cross full-time, but she had been there, I guess, since the early 1930s and maybe before. And this was in the 1950s. And she was quite a character. I was very fond of her. And I think in her own way she was of me

But I remember one time there was a black debutante ball, and Ozell Sutton, our first black reporter, brought a picture over to Dorothy Carroll, who was not noted for being tactful to people who were not "in." And she was lovely with him; she said she really didn't think the community was ready for that yet. And she said, "These are very nice girls, and I'm proud of them, and I'll write them a letter and congratulate them. Whatever I can do, I'll do, but I can't run your picture."

CHAPTER 4

Dead Papers Don't Float

WHEN K. A. Engel died in 1968, there was a feeling in some quarters that the paper was adrift, even more than usual, and that the time had come to try to do something about it. Marcus George and Stanley Berry, Engel's nephews, inherited the management of the paper and took over as editor and publisher, respectively. They immediately contacted Bob McCord, who had left the paper ten years earlier to buy the weekly North Little Rock Times, *and invited him to return as editor of the editorial page. McCord and George then hired Gene Foreman away from the* Pine Bluff Commercial *to run the newsroom.*

Foreman had started his career at the Arkansas Gazette *but left to take a job at the* New York Times, *which promptly was hit by a long-lasting strike. To make ends meet for a growing family, Foreman had taken a job at the* Pine Bluff Commercial, *which he made into an exceptional small-town newspaper in five years. He eventually ended up as managing editor at the* Philadelphia Inquirer, *which won seventeen Pulitzer Prizes in his twenty-five and a half years at the paper. For those who don't keep up with such things, that's fifteen more than the* Gazette *won (two) in its history and seventeen more than the* Democrat *ever won. At the* Democrat *Foreman faced some immediate problems. The owners apparently never did tell Gene Herrington, the managing editor who had been with the paper since 1942, that his authority to run the paper was being turned over to Foreman.*

Gene Foreman: That was mid-1968. It was in July, as I recall. Marcus [George] was, of course, most interested in news and editorials and Stanley [Berry] in business and the production of the paper. That's kind of how they divided it: right down the middle. But Marcus had hopes that we would improve the paper, and McCord, a good friend of mine, was the editorial page editor. So in talking first with Bob and then with Marcus, we felt that we were at a point where we could work something out, and we did. So I came up in July, and my title was news editor. But the understanding I had with Marcus that was brokered by Bob McCord was that I would have broad authority to try to improve the paper across all the fronts, except for the editorial page. That's what I started doing in July of 1968. I was interested, if we could, to stay in Arkansas. JoAnn [Foreman's wife] and I both liked Little Rock particularly, and that was appealing to us. And the hope that we could put something together that would improve the paper and make it a worthy and formidable competitor to the *Gazette* was something that I found very challenging.

Jerry McConnell: You say, "broad authority." How broad an authority? Did that go as far as hiring new people and relieving old people?

Foreman: Yes, it did, and we kind of finessed it there. Gene Herrington, who was a very decent person to me, kind of understood the situation. In fact, Gene went on after a few months to AP&L [the Arkansas Power and Light Company] to a PR [public relations] job. I then became the managing editor, which essentially was what I already was charged with doing.

McConnell: Did Bob and Marcus make some kind of representation to you to what their hopes for the paper would be and what they were shooting for?

Foreman: I can recall that in only very general terms, which is to say we drastically would improve the quality of the paper, the quality of the reporting, the way the paper looked, the way it read, [and] the way it was edited, to be a strong competitor [of the *Gazette*], which I didn't think it had been. And I felt the *Gazette* had some very good people. I'm very fond of the *Gazette* and always was. The sort of newspaper war that occurred years later was not anything that we had in mind. Somebody might say it's wishful thinking that with p.m. [afternoon] papers starting to fold across the country, this could happen. But it was a hope that we could do it. What we saw was kind of a gentlemen's battle with the *Gazette*. We'd win some; they'd win some. Then, like the National Football League players, after beating up each other for two (or three) hours, we'd shake hands and say, "We'll beat you next time." It didn't turn out that way. I don't think that I could've been a part of the newspaper war as it eventually evolved. I just had too many friends over there. I knew the circulation at the *Democrat* was already starting to dwindle. Our hope was, of course, that we'd gain circulation. Put out a better paper, gain circulation. But, as we know, the next three years it continued to decline. And part of that assumption—again, wishful thinking—was that the advertising and circulation departments would be similarly rejuvenated. That they would be aggressive in battling the *Gazette* in a competitive situation that we hoped would be more evenly matched than what it had been.

McConnell: From stories that I'm hearing, I don't believe that the advertising department made those changes, or the circulation department, either.

Foreman: Definitely not the circulation. No, the advertising didn't, either. It also became evident that there were strong differences in approach and goals between Marcus and Stanley. I think the division of authority between the two was cumbersome and held the paper back. You know, I don't fault either one of them. Stanley is dead now [George died later, after this interview], but both were honorable gentlemen. But it was not a good business model, as I was to learn. I don't think he [Stanley] shared Marcus's hope that we could improve the situation. I hope I'm fair to him, but I think he was more willing to settle for a distant second place than to really be a true competitor.

McConnell: Is there anything specific that you did to try to change the paper?

Foreman: We were at day one. It was a hot morning in July. I got to work at six thirty, and Si Dunn, the veteran desk man and telegraph editor, showed me how things were done. I was listening and trying to learn that day. I said, "Si, where are the page dummies?" Si said, "Well, there aren't any." I said, "Well, how do we know how much copy to send?" And he said, "Well, I'll send a note up." So he wrote a note out and said, "How many pages today?" He put it on the conveyor belt that went from our desk there on the second floor to the composing room on the third floor. So Freddy Campbell, the composing room foreman, a few minutes later sent back a note that said, "Sixteen pages open at this time." I said, "Si, we really ought to have dummies." [Page dummies were replicas of a page on which an editor could mark where a specific story was to be placed.] That was one of the things I took up that first week with Marcus: "We have no page dummies. I don't know of any newspaper that doesn't have page dummies." I think the practice was that the printers placed the news content with some minimal supervision from the news editor, who went up there before the deadline. I think the only pages that were dummied would be the front page and some other special pages [and] maybe a sports front. But it was minimal involvement of the news department in the preparation of the paper. Marcus then got together people from the advertising department, and we met with them. I remember the ad manager saying, "Maybe we wouldn't get as many ads left out if we had page dummies." Very soon, within a week or two, we started getting page dummies. That was step one, a very fundamental thing. But it was only indicative of the sort of changes that I had to make over the coming months and years.

We had an inadequate desk staff, just in terms of numbers. And there wasn't a read-back function or anybody in charge. So, fairly soon, we moved to create a copy desk with a slot. We created a layout desk that would do all the page layouts. We had a slot who would oversee all the copy editors. Then we created a wire desk. We also added the *Los Angeles Times—Washington Post* news services, which gave us some stories with more depth than AP generally gave and also stories that the *Gazette* would not have. The *Gazette* had the *New York Times* news service in addition to AP. But this gave us more depth reporting that was exclusive to us in Little Rock. We were trying to rejuvenate the reporting. One of the things on the reporting side that I didn't think was acceptable was the fact that they rewrote the *Gazette* without verifying anything they wrote. They did this as quickly as they could in the morning. The editors would hand out stories to be rewritten, and no phone calls would be made to sources. And if the *Gazette* had made a mistake, we made it too. So we started saying, "If we're going to rewrite the *Gazette*, we've got to verify it." Well, this doubled, tripled, quadrupled the amount of reporting time. And George Douthit, the veteran capitol reporter, who was my leading critic in the newsroom and made no bones about it, told everybody in sight, "This is madness." We were both right and wrong, in hindsight. On the one hand, I was right. If we were going to report the same thing the *Gazette* did, we ought to verify it. But I think that George was right by indirection. I should have focused more on enterprise. I think we did a lot of good enterprise, more than the *Democrat* had done in the past. But I should've recognized that we had limited resources. And a lot of stories that were in the *Gazette*, we should've just kissed off and said, "We're not going to try to match them on that." It's clear to me now that we should've enterprised more than what we did.

I understand the veterans, how they probably felt about that. And maybe in retrospect, some things could have been done to try to soothe their feelings or to reach out to them. But I don't think that anything could have really resolved the main issue, which was that we wanted a paper that was not the sort of paper they had in the past. And that meant, in terms of people in a couple of key jobs, that we needed what the management guru of the time, Laurence Peter, called a "lateral arabesque," lateral somebody out of a job where they were impeding our ability to change the paper. And the city editor was one, and the sports editor was another. I've read Fred Morrow's [interview] on that. Fred knew his job was essentially to do what [sports editor] Jack Keady had been doing all this time, but we wanted somebody who had different approaches. We moved Jack out. Jack was a very harsh critic of me, but I understand how he felt. But we needed to move ahead. We kept Jack's column, but we said, "That is what we want you to do. Fred is going to run the sports department." Rod Powers was the city editor, and we tried to find a place for him. I'm sorry about that, but that's what we felt we had to do. So Rod moved on at some point. I think that we gave it a try. But it was clear that we were not in sync. And this enabled me to make what I thought was probably the most important appointment: Ralph Patrick to be city editor. Ralph rejuvenated the staff—led them every day.

The *Gazette* was a good newspaper, but I thought that they were coasting, and in terms of being a competitor that could win some battles with them, I thought that could be done. In fact, that did happen, but it didn't help circulation. I thought the better the paper got, the more circulation we lost. But the *Gazette* demonstrated to me that because of its tradition for excellence—something that we were trying to create from scratch—which they, even on cruise control, could do better day in and day out than we could. It was hard, day in and day out, to beat their solid reporting staff. The difference was experience.

It's all understandable, but it was the most hostile environment [in which] I ever worked. On the one hand, I was really thrilled by the outstanding work that the young staffers were doing—how hard they were working and how well they were doing. On the other, it was constantly battling through the tension. And the same sort of situation could have occurred in Philadelphia [later on], but it was not nearly that tense.

One of those at the heart of that battle was Tucker Steinmetz, who had worked for Foreman at Pine Bluff.

Tucker Steinmetz: I'd go anywhere Foreman asked me to go. He went up there, and he called me. He said, "Would you like to come to work up here?" And I said, "Yes." So I moved to North Little Rock, my old hometown, where I had graduated from high school. I moved there and started work for the *Democrat* for Foreman. It was really an interesting and challenging experience from the beginning because he had been told, "Change things. Remake this paper." I'm sure they had their resource limitations. I mean, the paper wasn't that well-heeled. It was a challenge. It was tense at times because the old hands were not particularly enamored of the changes Foreman was making. The old hands were a little suspicious, and I can understand that. There had been a changing of the guard. You had people who had been there for years. Some of them regarded Foreman with great suspicion because he was so direct, so knowledgeable, and he really didn't mince words. He was not unkind, but they tested him. So I came in, and at first I was covering city hall and then some other places, sort of general assignment work. And then pretty soon Gene decided that he wanted me to be assistant city editor. Rod Powers was not a real assertive city editor. And Fred Petrucelli, who's a delightful guy, was the assistant city editor. And I took that job on. And Gene told me to be very firm, because I was pretty good at rewriting and at editing. Gene was a good teacher, and I think I learned a lot. He wanted me to be very assertive in making people go out and do their work. And years later, John Robert Starr, who periodically [on three or four occasions] would just sort of gratuitously jump on me, and he wrote that I was Foreman's hatchet man. You know, that's not exactly an endearing term or something that one likes to have. I probably still wouldn't in polite company say, "Well, I was his hatchet man." But in a sense, I guess—being very honest—I was because he said, "I want you to rewrite and rewrite people. If they're not doing it right, then show them what you're doing and don't accept things that are sloppy." Well, I made some people mad. I mean, you know, I was this young firebrand, and I tried to not be overbearing about it, but, I mean, he pretty well gave me a job, and I did it—probably clumsily. But I don't regret it. I felt like the paper needed to be redone—that it could be a good paper. So I started stirring people up pretty quickly, and I guess most notable was that I stirred George Douthit. I liked George, but I disagreed with some of George's style, and I felt like George's personal biases came into his stuff a lot. But he was a hard worker. I couldn't fault him. He was already fairly old. He wrote something one day that came in late. We had an AP story on it. George sent a quickly written story that was just kind of impossible to follow. Now, you know, maybe I was overzealous. I don't know. When he came in, he said, "Did you get my story?" He kind of growled at me. I said, "Yeah, but I didn't use it. I used the AP story." And he threw a fit in the newsroom—a *horrible fit*. And I got kind of concerned because he had had a stroke one time throwing a fit, I think at the capitol. And I said, "George, calm down. You're going to have a stroke." He said, "I've already *had* one!" And it was terrible. I'm a little hazy on these details now, but I think that's when he quit. You know people would get mad at George, but he *was* an institution around there, and so I was certainly not popular with the old crew at *that* point because I had provoked George. I *liked* George. We would argue occasionally, but I liked him, and I did feel bad about that. He [left the *Democrat*] and went on and did his news service, and it was probably better for him—may have prolonged his life some because it wasn't as stressful. But I felt bad about that because I had rewritten some of his stuff already that made him very angry. That was a very cataclysmic day.

Bob Ferguson I rewrote ruthlessly. Bob was such a nice guy. Well, Bob has died in the last few years. And Bob left and went to the *Benton Courier*, and a lot of his complaint was that he was tired of my rewrites. I don't like playing that role, and I've never wanted to be in that role since because I don't like it. I was the bad guy and kind of the messenger. I was probably ruthless at times, in rewriting and in sending people back to do it themselves.

We had a fellow who came in every Saturday morning—Bud Lemke. I faulted the paper over the years for not getting him help or kind of forcing him to make a decision about what he was going to do with his life and his drinking. I guess now as a recovering alcoholic I can speak about that. On Saturday mornings, Bud sometimes was my only reporter, which meant I *had* none. So Bud would come early, do a few *Gazette* rewrites haphazardly, and vanish. A press conference was called for nine o'clock one Saturday morning. Mabel Berry got the call. She told me. I said, "Mabel, who do we have?" And I look out over this empty newsroom, and she said, "Bud's the only one on today." Bud would always park his car on a meter, and then when meter time came, he would come and say, "I've got to go move my car." And then he'd disappear. You never saw him again. And they let him do that for *years.* Bud would be gone to the Brunswick. On Saturday morning he got to leave *real* early, and apparently they always let him. But I just said, "Mabel, we've got to have him. I don't have anybody else. I can't leave. We've got to cover this press conference." She said, "I can get him." Mabel gave kind of a determined little look. But she had the number memorized, so she just dials the Brunswick Pool Hall, and Bud gets on the phone, and I heard her say, "Bud, the boss needs you." And I could tell he was arguing from her end of the conversation. And she says, "I don't know. He said you need to get here immediately. We *need* you, and do not delay. Come straight to work." Well, I was work- ing on something, waiting on him to get there, and I heard someone say, "Well, goodbye." And I looked up, and Bud's leaning over the desk, and you could smell the alcohol, and his eyes were kind of whirling. I mean, he was a *mess.* And I said, "What?" And he said, "I'm gone. I'm out of here. I quit." I said, "What?" He said, "I don't have to take this shit." And I said, "Well, I just called you over to work. I believe you're still on the clock." And he said, "I'm out of here. I'm gone. I'm going down to see Chester [Garrett] and get my money."

So then at some point I became a kind of special assignment reporter. I finally told Foreman that the city desk stuff was really get- ting to me. I didn't want to hear a phone ring. I was real jumpy. I probably had blood pressure problems that I didn't know about. But I went home in a foul mood. I stressed out. And I said, "Gene, I need relief." And he said, "Well, why don't you do special assignment?"

By this time there had been a real changing of the guard. Those who left, for whatever reason, included Herrington, the managing editor, who had been with the Democrat *since 1942; Douthit, the most experienced reporter, who had been with the paper since 1936; Lemke, who probably joined the staff in the late 1940s; Rod Powers, the city editor; Fred Petrucelli, the assistant city editor, who had been with the paper since 1945; copy editors Ted Woods and Leon Hatch, both veterans; Si Dunn, a veteran desk man; and several of the top reporters, such as Maurice Moore, Bob Ferguson, and others. Of course, Foreman had been busy hiring their replacements.*

Foreman: Paul Nielsen, who had worked for me in Pine Bluff, left the *Commercial* for Little Rock and became the slot, and he would be in charge of the copy desk. And the wire editor became Bill Terry, who scanned all of these wires and really put a lot into that. I thought we were getting a very decent wire report. The pages looked good because our page layout person did it, and that became Richard Allen, who is now at the *Herald Tribune* in Paris, France. Ralph Patrick became the city editor. Ralph rejuvenated the staff, led them every day. He's an outstanding journalist. Over a period of time, we hired quite a few reporters. I think that anybody looking at this could say, "Well, it's young versus old," and I guess that's the way it played out. It wasn't deliberate. The fact is that we didn't pay a lot of money, and we wanted to hire good people, or at least people who had the potential to be good. And if a person had ten or fifteen years of experience and had proved himself or herself to be a very good reporter, we couldn't afford them. So we were trying, as we had in Pine Bluff, to scout out talent who had not proved themselves yet. Martin Kirby was one of our hires. Martin had just gotten a degree in writing from Johns Hopkins [University], so I called down to McGehee to the family's home. Martin was not there, but I got his grandmother on the phone. I talked to her and told her who I was and that I was interested in talking to Martin. She said, "You're not going to try to hire Martin for a little bit or nothing, are you?" I said, "Yes, ma'am." But Martin came on for a little bit or nothing and made a very good reporter.

McConnell: When you brought Fred Morrow in, did you give him any particular slant that you felt he ought to pursue as far as covering the Razorbacks or anything else in his sports coverage?

Foreman: I don't know that I did give him any specific instructions. Fred became the anti-Orville [Henry] in that he was maybe more critical of the Razorbacks than he needed to be. But he gave us a fresh approach. People who were reading about the Razorbacks could certainly get some insights that they weren't going to get from the *Gazette*. But I was basically trying to just upgrade the coverage across the board. And, obviously, in Arkansas the Razorbacks are going to be the number-one beat.

Morrow quickly found himself being squeezed two ways, first by the old-timers at the Democrat *and second in trying to cover the Razorbacks against Orville Henry, who had the inside track to Frank Broyles.*

Fred Morrow: I went there in August of 1970 [as sports director]. You know, it was not a pleasant situation. It was like combat all over again. People were falling left and right. [Morrow was in combat in Vietnam in the First Air Cavalry.] They gave me a title like sports director because Jack Keady was still there. He kept the title as sports editor, and he sat at one end of that big room behind a desk, and they had me down at the other end. It was uncomfortable. I never had any problems with Jack, but he was obviously upset. He didn't have any [role in the] decision process. He just wrote a column every once in a while. He had a nice job then. He would come in and write a little column and leave.

McConnell: What do you remember about your career at the *Democrat*?

Morrow: I had kids then, and just the trouble of making a living—I remember that. It was a lot of work, but it was fun. We were young, and we were so downtrodden and beat up by the *Gazette,* you know. We just let it fly. I hired a bunch of young kids, and some of them were really good. There was Teri Thompson and John Bloom and John Brummett. Bloom and Brummett were still high school kids when they came to work for me. Teri Thompson—it just dawned on me that it would be nice to have a female in the sports department. At that time it was a revolutionary thing. There might have been one or two more in the country, in larger papers of circulation, at that time.

We were way down in experience and underfunded. We were probably not nearly as good [as the *Gazette*], just to be truthful about it. But we'd do things that they wouldn't do, you know what I mean?

We tried things whether they were right or wrong, and probably because of me we sort of became the antiestablishment paper, at least in that sports section, because I was always after [Frank] Broyles. Not as much as he perceived, I don't think. But you know Frank was like God, so with any kind of a little strike, you know, he's not going to take that very well.

When I came there, I found out real quick that anything that came out of the University of Arkansas was going to be the privilege of Orville Henry [sports editor of the *Gazette*]. I mean, how do you fight that? Even if I'd have sucked up to Arkansas, all scoops still would have gone through Orville first. What's the point of that? Don't get me wrong because I liked Orville. At that time, Gene brought in a lot of young, aggressive guys and girls that tried to do those stories that maybe the *Gazette* wouldn't do. Got after it, and it was hectic, and it was fun. But the *Gazette* had it over us in [that] mainly they had a lot of seasoned veterans. We were a bunch of kids just stumbling along—half of us were probably trying to think how we could get a job selling insurance and the other half thinking, "How can I get a job with the *Washington Post?*" We had something they didn't have. We had nothing to lose, basically. We were way below them, and we had a lot more energy.

The more I think about it, I really feel bad about a lot of the older people that were just [shunted aside]. [Society editor] Betty Wood's husband, Ted—I remember he was run off. There wasn't anything wrong with Ted. He was a bright guy, but he just happened to be the old order there—you know, had some age on him. A lot of those people—and Gene was bringing in all those young guys and girls and wanting them to do things his way. I loved Betty Woods. She was wonderful. She was raised by Owney Madden, who was a noted mobster. Madden dated her sister, I guess, when he lived in Hot Springs.

Some of the newcomers provided some excellent journalism, and nearly all of them remember Foreman with fondness and admiration.

Martin Kirby: Well, in earlier times I had liked the *Gazette* a lot better, although at McGehee we subscribed to the *Democrat,* and I read it every day. I was particularly fond of Karr Shannon's column, even though I didn't understand a lot of the issues that he wrote about. I finally met him when I worked for the *Democrat.* I had gotten more sophisticated about things as I grew up. I decided that the *Gazette* was a real good paper, and the *Democrat* wasn't much of a newspaper. I hesitated before going to work for the *Democrat*, because I thought it was so much worse than the *Gazette*. But Gene told me that they were in the process of making it better. I didn't really have any other options at the time, so I decided I would go on back to work as a reporter. I went to the *Democrat*. I thought it was a pretty good paper while I was there. It could have paid better.

Rodney Lorenzen: Well, Gene Foreman was a very demanding boss. He was probably the best and the toughest guy I ever worked for. He had very exacting standards for the way that he wanted things done. I think people really worked hard for him, and he just demanded that. Lots of times you would get something torn out of the newspaper, and it would be marked up with a red grease pencil, and it would be a note from Gene, calling your attention to some error you'd made. I think most everyone in the newsroom really wanted to avoid getting those in their boxes. But Gene was a hard worker, and he just wanted that from everybody he worked [with]. He was interested in having a good product; he was interested in good journalism standards. Unlike a lot of people I've worked for in the newspaper business, that was just a priority with him. And to illustrate the kind of guy he was, when he had a hernia operation, he spent all of his time recuperating in writing a new stylebook for the newspaper.

Ralph Patrick: Foreman edited all of the page-one copy himself, laid it out, and wrote the headlines. He was one of my two mentors. [Bob McCord was the other, for whom Patrick had worked at the weekly *North Little Rock Times*.] I learned a lot from Foreman about just how to run the desk every day. There's a lot of difference in a weekly paper and a daily, an afternoon paper with several editions that you're trying to [make the deadlines for]. And, a lot of times, not many people to do the work.

When I was the city editor, one of the best writers we had, of course, was James Scudder. The late James Scudder was a Methodist minister, actually. When he came to work for us, he had been managing that dinner theater out in southwest Little Rock. He had a dramatic flair and had written a little thin book of poetry. He was given a week's tryout, I think. And before the week was over, we knew we wanted to hire that guy, and we did. The best writer they ever had there was named Bob Lancaster. He was the best writer in town, as far as I was concerned, and still is.

Amanda Allen: You look back on those days with a great deal of fondness?

Patrick: I do now. I think there was a long period when I didn't, but I do now. And a lot of that has to do with having worked at the *Atlanta Journal-Constitution* for twenty years and six months. I *never* had as much fun there as I had at the *Democrat.*

Not long before Foreman left, many employees became unhappy with the pay and lack of fringe benefits and perhaps other issues and began to discuss what to do about it.

Arlin Fields: I remember the management called a huge staff meeting and herded everyone over to the [Lafayette] hotel. Marcus George made a little talk about how they absolutely would not tolerate a union. I guess he had read somewhere that you should start any discussion with a little humor or something to lighten the mood, so he told a little joke. He asked if anybody in the room knew how to make a dead baby float. There was kind of a silence. He said that it took two scoops of ice cream and a dead baby. There were several jaws that just dropped.

I've wondered if Marcus meant more than met the eye, or the ear, with that message; if he meant that trying to resurrect a dying newspaper was like trying to resurrect a dead baby.

About three years into that experiment, Foreman decided to leave to take a major job on one of the country's fastest-growing papers, Newsday, *which was located on Long Island, an extension of New York City that juts out into the Atlantic Ocean.*

Foreman: I left at the end of the summer in 1971. Pat Owens had been at *Newsday* as a columnist, and he engineered a job offer for me. [Owens had worked with Foreman at Pine Bluff.] *Newsday* was going to a Sunday paper. It may seem strange today, but a lot of papers were still just six-days-a-week or five-days-a-week and did not have Sunday papers. In the decades since then, publishers and editors recognize that a Sunday paper, which people have more time to read, is a very remunerative paper to have. When Colonel [Harry] Guggenheim sold the paper to the *Times Mirror*, the new owners said, "We've got to have a Sunday paper." That was happening during the summer of 1971. David Laventhol was the editor, and he was going to put Dick Estrin, who had been the daily news editor, in charge of the new Sunday paper. So he was casting about for someone to take the title of executive news editor to be in charge of producing the paper six days a week. I would be in charge during the week and oversee the news and copy desk. Patrick Owens convinced Laventhol that I was a person who would do that, so Dave made me a very good offer to come east again. One of the things I got was that if there were a strike, I would keep on getting paid. I had felt that it was time for new leadership in the *Democrat* newsroom. Both Ralph and I were wearing down. I do want to say that I appreciate all the work that these young staffers did. There was a lot of camaraderie among them, and they just knocked themselves out trying to put out a good paper.

McConnell: The *Democrat* had continued to struggle financially, though.

Foreman: Yes, it was really evident that afternoon papers were struggling against the tide. And in most cities in the country they were moving toward just the morning paper, and we've naturally seen that happen everywhere now in the decades since then. But the trend was taking shape in the late 1960s and early 1970s. And as we saw in the latter stage of that, even in towns where a publisher owned both papers, they consolidated into a single paper published in the morning. Clearly, for a lot of reasons, morning papers were the way to go. And that meant not the *Democrat*.

So Foreman left, and I came on board on August 1, 1971. I was the managing editor at the Democrat *during that seven-year period after being hired by Marcus George and Stanley Berry to replace Foreman. During those seven years the management at the* Democrat *still tried to figure out ways to compete with the* Gazette *and stop the losses at the* Democrat. *For almost three years under George and Berry they tried to forge ahead with some of the innovations made under Foreman, as well as fine-tuning some of them and changing others. Basically they were still trying to put out an attractive, readable newspaper that contained less news and features than the* Gazette. *The management had already started the move to cold type, which would eventually revolutionize the way newspapers were produced.*

The 1970s constituted a period of mammoth change in the newspaper industry, as well as at the Democrat. During that time the paper converted completely from hot type to cold type; became one of the early users of computers in preparing, editing, and processing copy; underwent a change in ownership; underwent a union election in the newsroom; and underwent a strike by the pressmen.

At some point, in either late 1973 or early 1974, the editorial employees decided to seek a union at the Democrat, declaring they wanted to affiliate with the International Typographical Union (ITU). At about the same time, Arkansas Gazette newsroom employees decided to try to form a union affiliated with the Newspaper Guild. George and Berry were still in charge of the Democrat at that time.

The ITU nationwide was also beginning to lose membership, which put more pressure on current members to pay enough dues to provide strike benefits and retirement funds. This was a time when newspapers were just beginning to switch over to computerized typesetting, which would soon make linotypes and other typesetting processes obsolete.

During this period, George and Berry sold the newspaper to the Hussmans, who owned the old Clyde Palmer chain in south Arkansas, and Walter Hussman Jr. was put in charge of the Democrat. Walter retained me as the managing editor and told me he wanted me to remain in charge of the management position in fighting the union. By this time I had become concerned with our lead attorney, Gaines Houston, who was also the lead attorney for the Gazette. I feared that he would devote more time to the Gazette case because the Gazette was a much bigger paper with more employees and more prestige. I had also become concerned with his approach.

I went to Walter and told him I wanted to change lawyers. He asked me why, I told him, and he said okay. The new attorney, Bill Toney, was from a Tulsa firm that had experience in dealing with newspapers and had been used by the Hussman family in the past. He was not as confrontational as Houston. By this time, Walter had made some positive changes at the Democrat: putting in a profit-sharing plan and expanding space and salaries at least slightly.

There was obviously some dissension at the Gazette because during this period the Democrat hired two excellent people from the Gazette (that didn't happen often), and they said they were unhappy with how *the* Gazette *was handling the union effort. They were Julie Baldridge,* *who later worked under Bill Clinton when he was attorney general and* *then governor, and Sheila Daniel, who later worked for the* Chicago Tribune *and the* Los Angeles Times *and was a foreign correspondent for the* International Herald Tribune, Business Week, *and the* Economist.

Julie Baldridge: I was able to find a job at the *Arkansas Gazette* and worked there for three years until the newsroom became involved in an attempt to form a newsroom union. I left in the middle of that process and took a job at the *Arkansas Democrat* as a columnist. I was a copy editor for the first three years or so that I was at the *Gazette.* Jerry McConnell, who was the managing editor at the *Democrat,* had been the assistant sports editor at the *Gazette,* so we'd known each other. He called a couple of times about jobs, and he just happened to call about a column proposal that appealed to me, and, also, it was a time when I was unhappy with the atmosphere at the place that I was working, the *Gazette.*

Mel White: Because you were upset at the *Gazette* management, because of this union business?

Baldridge: I was upset at the management because of the owners, because the editorial page professed one thing, and their behavior toward their employees was quite a different matter.

White: Yes, that's pretty funny, because the *Gazette* was the liberal paper. The *Democrat* was the conservative paper, and yet the *Democrat* had women and African Americans before the *Gazette* did, at least in any numbers.

It was not long after the election that Hussman decided to install computers and computerized typesetting. These were huge advances for newspapers, helping cut costs and giving editors and reporters direct control of what went into the paper. However, it was not an easy switch at the Democrat. *Hussman brought only one mainframe computer to the* Democrat. *There was no backup, which meant that when the main computer went down (as they always do), there was a problem. He also bought only four terminals on which to make the final edit of stories, affix the headlines, and then send the stories to the typesetting machine. This wasn't nearly enough. But the* Democrat *was short on money and had to do it the hard way.*

Staff turnover was still a problem. The Democrat *was still some-*

what a revolving door. The upshot was that it now took more copy editors than ever before to put out the paper. So the Democrat *slowly began to increase the number of copy editors and reduce the number of reporters, which made it more difficult to compete with the* Gazette *in the breadth of coverage, and the* Gazette *already had an edge there anyway. Hiring new people was a problem because as time went on we seemed even more constricted in our salaries. And as time went on we began to hire more and more women. If I was allowed to offer a certain salary, I thought the women I could hire for that salary were often better than the men I could hire. I had always questioned the idea that women weren't as good as men. Nor did I hold to the old idea that women weren't tough enough to be good journalists. Whatever the reason, there weren't many women in daily journalism for a long time. When I first went to the* Gazette *in 1955, there was only one woman, Matilda Touhey, in the newsroom. At one time women comprised at least 48 percent of the* Democrat *news staff. These weren't just warm bodies. For the most part, they were excellent journalists. They included Julie Baldridge; Sheila Daniel; Carol Stogsdill, who went on to the* Rocky Mountain News *and the* Chicago Tribune *and then became senior editor at the* Los Angeles Times, *perhaps the highest position ever held by a woman in American journalism (other than inherited ownership) up to that time; Teri Thompson (hired by Fred Morrow as a sportswriter), who became the Sunday sports editor at the* New York Daily News; *Amanda Singleton Allen, who became travel editor of the* Atlanta Journal-Constitution; *the late Nancy Miller, who was the lifestyle editor at the* St. Louis Post-Dispatch; *the late Connie Hoxie, who obtained a doctorate in journalism and taught at Wisconsin and Penn State; Patti Cox, who later worked for the Fort Smith paper for several years, became a member of the State Board of Higher Education, and is now (in 2015) the chief fundraiser for the law school at the University of Arkansas; and Mara Leveritt, now an esteemed freelance journalist in Little Rock and a best-selling author. This list also includes Deborah Mathis, whom the* Democrat *hired fresh out of high school as a clerk but who was so bright she was soon promoted to reporter. She was the first African American woman reporter hired by either the* Democrat *or the* Gazette, *and she went on to a distinguished career as a television journalist and later a nationally syndicated newspaper columnist and author.*

The Democrat *kept hiring some excellent young journalists, men as well as women. It hired David Terrell, Mark Oswald, Garry Hoffmann, Steele Hayes, Gerald Koonce, and John Brummett, who all wound up at* the Gazette *en route to other jobs. Then there was Mike Kirkendall, who went on to the* Chicago Sun-Times, *where they soon made him editor of their Sunday magazine, and ended up at the* Los Angeles Times; *Al May, who became a top political reporter for the Atlanta papers and then head of the Journalism Department at George Mason University; Collins Hemingway, who became a top aide to Bill Gates at Microsoft and ghost-wrote one of his best-selling books; Gary Rice, a great investigative reporter, who now has a doctorate and is head of the Journalism Department at California State University, Fresno; Dan Farley, now head of the Arkansas School Boards Association; Mel White, an excellent freelance journalist in Little Rock who sometimes does articles for* National Geographic; *and Jim Allen, who went on to the Associated Press and became head of public relations for a major trucking firm and then for Hess Oil.*

Ralph Patrick directed the city desk staff, which produced some excellent work, including an exclusive by James Scudder on attempted block-busting by real estate salesmen in mid-Little Rock. The paper covered racial disturbances across the state, even though once a mob of whites chased two Democrat *reporters and a photographer out of Marianna.*

When the Hussmans bought the paper in 1974, they quickly learned why it had not been gaining in advertising and circulation, even though the people in the newsroom were working like Trojans and had made many changes trying to improve the quality of the paper.

Walter Hussman: The first thing I did after we bought the *Democrat* was that I went around and talked to various people who had been at the *Democrat* but who had left. One of those people was Gene Foreman, who was managing editor of the *Philadelphia Inquirer.* And I talked to a number of other people. And they said, "Man, have you got problems in your circulation department." The circulation manager played golf about three afternoons a week and would even wear his golf shoes into the newspaper.

Hussman immediately fired the circulation manager, Frank Simpson, and hired a new one, Gerald Doty, who had been circulation manager of the Dallas Times-Herald.

Gerald Doty: It was a total disaster [at the *Democrat*]. To say the least. The morale was as low as it could get. No one was doing their job. No one was paying their bills. The turnover was bad. It was just a complete, total disaster. Well, the first thing I did was try to get the confidence of the people that we could turn it around and get the job done—serve the readers. So we made some changes in midmanagement. We just worked at it. We had an awful lot of down routes [routes with no carriers]. The district manager did a lot of down-route delivery until we got to the point we had them all covered. Just a matter of organizing and doing some good delivery service, which was in bad shape. And we also convinced Mr. Hussman that we needed some consistent press runs.

Paul Smith took over as head of the advertising department, and he discovered things were just as dire there.

Paul Smith: I came down after the press conference [announcing the sale] and started going through sales records in the ad department. I discovered, for example, they had a salesperson—I think he was about twenty-four years old—that in November, December, and January had averaged selling less than forty inches of advertising per month. That's less than a quarter page a month. At an average rate of less than $3 an inch, he was bringing in about $100 a month, and they were paying him $125 a week in salary. It didn't take a rocket scientist to know that this guy's not even bringing enough in a month to pay a week's salary. And he had been here several years. That's generally what I found. Very, very poor performance in the ad department. I found their strategy in trying to sell advertising was to try to appeal to the advertiser's sympathy and tell advertisers that, "If you don't buy an ad from us, then we'll go out of business, and the *Gazette* will raise your rates."

What I found was that probably out of the sixteen retail salespeople, four or five were competent. The biggest problem we had was that the vast majority of the salespeople didn't believe that we had anything valuable to sell. And if a salesman doesn't believe in his product, it's hard for him to convince anybody else to believe in it. A real defeatist attitude. However, I didn't find people who thought this newspaper might go out of business. They felt since the paper had been here for more than one hundred years, somehow the owners would keep pouring money into it. I didn't see any concern that the paper might fail and they might lose their jobs, but I also didn't see any confidence that they could compete head-on with the *Gazette.*

Allen Berry, no relation to Stanley or to the Allen Berry who ran War Memorial Stadium, was the chief accountant for the Hussman operation, headquartered in Hot Springs, and immediately started working in Little Rock when the Hussmans bought the Democrat.

Allen Berry: I thought the *Democrat,* at that time, was about fifteen years behind the times. Everything they did was very manually oriented, and computers were not thoroughly integrated into accounting at that time. The only computer operation that they had involved at all was the First National Bank did their payroll, and they had only done that for a couple of years.

Here's a view of the two papers in that era by some of the top journalists who worked at the Democrat, *including several who later switched to the* Gazette.

Jim Allen: Bob Lancaster, Fred Morrow, and David Terrell were, I thought, the best pure writers on the *Democrat* during that time. And I always marveled at that scrappy little newspaper that had such talent. You remember we didn't get paid a lot of money back in those days. We had a good crew when I was there. I loved it. I liked the scrappiness of the paper. I loved working with the people. We all got along well. We literally partied together every night after work. We'd all be back the next day, and then we'd party all weekend together as a group.

Gerald Koonce: I said I didn't have a very high opinion of the *Democrat* when I first interviewed with Jerry. Working at the *Democrat* was like a huge eye-opener for me. It was actually a very good product —even then—understaffed, you know, short on resources. I would tell my friends, "Don't laugh, the *Democrat* is one of the better half of the newspapers in the country." I still didn't think it was as good as the *Gazette,* but I thought it was a good newspaper, and I was actually proud to work on it.

Mara Leveritt: In some ways I thought that it was a nice alternative to the *Gazette's* inclination toward [being] stuffy at times. You just would get some things that were refreshing in the *Democrat* in terms of local reporting that I think that the *Gazette* would have been just a bit too proud to have put in. That was actually, in my view, really nice. While the *Democrat* [staff] was so young, one thing that I noticed

about the *Gazette* was it seemed that everybody had been there forever. There was a staid quality to the paper and the staff.

Al May: I remember what I thought, and I still think, it was a
jewel of a little newsroom—and I think I was really fortunate to go
to a newspaper where I had really good editors. And a very talented
but small, scrappy staff. It was small enough that a beginner could get
good stories and get a lot of attention from the editors. I wasn't lost in
a cog. There was a scrappy feel to the place. At the time, the paper was
still an afternoon newspaper. It was bleeding circulation. It was not a
place where you looked for a lot of future, necessarily. I had planned
to move on. As it turned out, it was a terrific opportunity. But there
was the sense, you know, that we were up against the big *Gazette.* The
Gazette had a huge—a much larger staff. And I highly admired the
Gazette.

David Terrell: When Hendrix graduated me . . . I wanted to go
to the *Gazette,* but I was not offered a job there that I wanted. I had
thought that the *Democrat,* as the afternoon paper, and the less prestigious of the two by far, would be not much of a place to work. I was
encouraged, I think, probably by John Ward, who had for awhile been
managing editor of the *Log Cabin* in Conway, to apply there. He said
he thought it would be a good fit. So I wound up at the *Democrat* for
a period of a couple of years. That would have been in 1974. [Then
he left for the *Gazette.*] Well sure. You made a little more money at
the *Gazette,* but there were lots of other reasons. The *Gazette* was a
much more prestigious paper. It was a hell of a lot easier to get news
when you worked for the *Gazette* because people came to the *Gazette*
rather than the *Democrat*—because it was the bigger paper. I want to
say about the *Democrat* that I think we did great. They didn't have the
budget to pay people, and people were leaving all of the time. We had
this problem with the news cycle and the short hours. Under those
arduous conditions, I think all of us were darn well proud of what
were able to do. Newspapers are always called a daily miracle. The
Democrat was more of a miracle than most.

Carol Stogsdill: I knew almost right away that I was going to love
this. That it was just fun. That these people, by the way, become your
life. They become your family. You live with them. Especially when you
work for an afternoon newspaper, the god-awful hours that we kept.

I mean, how many times did you get up at three a.m.to be at work at four o'clock [a.m.]? Often. No one else in the universe was doing that; so we worked together, we ate together, and we played together. And these people really became a family. Also, I think that we were lucky that we were working with people who went on just to do great things. It was a good time to be there. The [Vietnam] war was going on, Watergate was going on, [and] newspapers were undergoing just radical changes. All of that was being played out in the newsroom. There were so many historical moments.

Then there came the time for Carol, and others, when it wasn't so much fun anymore.

Stogsdill: The paper was as fully computerized as it could be back then, Again, Walter Hussman was kind of out in front on many of those things in terms of newspapers. He was a great experimenter. I think one of the frustrations for me was that, having started out there, the focus was all on journalism. It was all on the story. By virtue of making a change so radical on the technology side, it became a lot about technology. At the same time, you had people leaving because they clearly could get paid more almost anyplace else. The *Democrat* was still losing circulation. It was a tough place to work, and people were doing it for someone that they had not really warmed up to. I think in terms of morale and the actual practice of what we did, it became a tough place to be. "Tough" may be the wrong word. That may be too strong. It was harder to find pleasure in a day's work. You looked up, and sometimes all you did was spend time fixing some freaking machine. It was rewriting how newspapers were going to be published, and that had its moments of "wow" like any new miracle will. But, if you're right in the middle of it and the reason you went to work for a newspaper was because of the thrill of the news cycle and that thing that we all had that we could all make a difference by doing it, then suddenly you realized that sometimes your ten-hour day would be just totally taken up with just learning how some piece of equipment worked.

CHAPTER 5

Democrat Coups

OVER THE YEARS, the Democrat *had its share of major news stories and scoops, many of which might not have been reported by the* Gazette. *Perhaps the* Democrat's *greatest coup came with its coverage of problems within the state highway program in the early 1950s. The* Democrat's *coverage led to the legislature's creation of a Highway Audit Commission, to probe allegations of corruption in awarding road-building contracts and in the location of roads. Many people had long suspected that the highway program was run as a gravy train for the reigning governor and that contracts were awarded to the people who made the biggest political donations. The Highway Audit Commission proved that supposition by subpoenaing the principals to testify under oath, and the* Democrat *gave heavy coverage to those hearings.*

Those hearings and the resultant publicity led to the passage of a constitutional amendment in 1952, the Mack-Blackwell Amendment, which provided for a new method of appointing the State Highway Commission, which would theoretically prevent any one governor from appointing enough members to the commission to give that governor control. The amendment provided for the creation of a highway commission with five members, each appointed to staggered ten-year terms. Almost sixty years later, that amendment is still being credited with major improvement in the state highway program.

The hearings also led to the creation of a high-profile Pulaski County grand jury to consider whether there had been criminal violations within the highway program. While problems within the highway program may have been going on for years, the hearings and jury scrutiny mainly covered the period during the administration of Governor Sid McMath, who was elected to a first term in 1948 and was reelected to another two-year term in 1950. The probe did also cover a few months in the administration of former governor Ben Laney.

After studying the evidence for five and a half months, the grand jury was abruptly dismissed by Circuit Judge Harry Robinson, who had been appointed to his post by McMath. Two days later the jurors met and composed a stinging response to Judge Robinson and then delivered their statement in person to the Arkansas Democrat. Fourteen of the sixteen jurors made the trip to deliver their statement to the Democrat, and all sixteen of them signed it. The trip to the Democrat was clearly a sign that the grand jury had been much more impressed with the Democrat's coverage than that of the Gazette.

Before the week was out, Judge Robinson had been censured by the Pulaski County Bar Association and the executive committee of the Arkansas Bar Association, both of which said Robinson should have disqualified himself from the case and that a new grand jury should be appointed to renew the investigation. A special committee of the Pulaski County Bar Association then picked Circuit Judge Henry Smith of Pine Bluff to preside over a new grand jury investigation, and Pulaski County sheriff Tom Gulley was designated, under state law, to pick the new members of the grand jury. Prosecuting attorney Tom Downie disclosed that he would subpoena about sixty witnesses for the first week of the new hearing. Judge Smith told the jury to consider only violations of criminal law, in order to speed up the investigation.

One week later the grand jury indicted only four persons but said it found that firms that contributed heavily to the governor's campaign fund also received the bulk of the state's business for the highway program. The jury said this was not surprising in light of testimony by a former highway director that vendors had to be cleared by the governor's office and that his instructions were to do business with friends of the administration, price and quality being equal. The jury also noted that the director said this had been the practice of all the administrations under which he had served. The jury also reported that it found evidence that some campaign funds had been used for personal purposes.

Perhaps the most sensational story that helped bring on the creation of the audit commission was one by Roy Bosson, who reported in the Democrat in 1951 that the state highway department was planning to build a road in Madison County at a cost to the state of nearly $500,000 *and that if the state had chosen an alternate route, it would only have cost it about $65,000. Bosson said the highway commission had sought financial help from the US Bureau of Public Roads, which could have paid for 50 percent of the project. The bureau turned the state down but said it would provide help for a shorter and less expensive route that would have cost about $130,000, half of which would have been paid by the federal government.*

Bosson reported that the state had decided to go ahead with the more expensive route, which just happened to pass the farm of A. C. Mowery Jr., a member of the state highway commission. Mowery had been named to the commission by McMath to replace Orval Faubus, who had resigned to become secretary to McMath. In his original story, Bosson reported that highway commissioners are required by law to take an oath that they will not have any interest directly or indirectly in the location of a state highway and that violation of that oath would be a felony. That section had at first been in the third paragraph of Bosson's story. In one of those great journalistic imponderables, the editors apparently became worried about it being potentially libelous and so removed it from the third paragraph and placed it at the bottom of the story. The location did not make any difference when Mowery later sued the Democrat for libel. Ordinarily as the plaintiff Mowery would have been required to prove that the Democrat had in fact libeled him. Instead the trial judge ruled that by including that paragraph the Democrat had implied that Mowery committed a felony, which was libel per se, and therefore the Democrat would be required to prove that Mowery had committed a felony. It took the jury thirteen minutes to rule in the Democrat's favor.

Gary Rice produced more scoops in two years with the paper than any other reporter I know about. He just walked in off the street, looking for a job, and he wasn't yet twenty years old, but he had this great set of clippings of stories he had done at the Wichita Beacon. He was a bulldog. He hit the ground running and never stopped until he left to go to the Kansas City Star, because he said the paper wasn't paying him enough, which was true. Here are his accounts of some of the top stories he handled. He was interviewed by Denise Gamino, who had been a reporter for the Daily Oklahoman and the Austin American-Statesman.

Gary Rice: There are several stories I remember; one that probably is most remembered by people down there who were around at the time was the Larry Pritchard story. Larry Pritchard was kind of a flashy oil broker. He had all of his staff driving these silver Lincolns that had "Pritchard International" on the side of the cars. And he would throw these big society parties and give away door prizes that would consist of overseas trips. He was really putting on the dog. This guy was really immaculately dressed—the whole bit. Well, we got a tip there. The people at that paper probably got as many tips as any place I've ever been. Well, the tip came in that all was not as it seemed—that he had some questionable business dealings. The rumor was that he had been writing some very large hot checks. The thought was that he was selling oil that he didn't really own and had somewhat of a scheme going, but it could come tumbling down around him. So I was given this assignment to investigate Larry Pritchard. Of course, I didn't know anything about high finance or oil dealing, but that didn't bother me. I just jumped in there. I worked on it for several weeks. The city editor, Ralph Patrick—he'd come back—"Well, how's that Pritchard story coming?" I was having a hard time with it. People wouldn't talk with me, or I couldn't find what I wanted. I was actually getting a little bit depressed because I had been freed to work on this story. I had been used to cranking out a story every day and having my name on the front page, and suddenly I wasn't appearing in the paper, and I was working on this story that just was not panning out. I finally said, "Well, I think we ought to just give this up. I'm just not getting anywhere." And Ralph said, "Oh, work on it another week. Work on it another week." Suddenly, I started getting a few little tips that led to other things. I was able to find the person who got one of those hot checks and actually see the hot check, and suddenly we were getting somewhere. In the midst of this, I started getting strange calls at home and hang-ups. Somebody in the business department or the personnel office at the *Democrat* said somebody was calling up and asking all kinds of questions about me. Then we got a tip that it was this guy who was sort of a crackpot, self-proclaimed private eye. So me and another reporter went and confronted him. "Why are you asking these questions, because we were hearing it from a lot of people?" And he wouldn't say. We said, "Who hired you?" And he wouldn't say. He said, "Well, if you don't like it, why don't you just leave town?" It was a really weird thing. We didn't take it super seriously because this guy was kind of a nutty fellow. Well, it rocked on and on, and we were finally, I think, getting enough to publish on this. But it was a little scary because this guy [the oilman] claimed to be rich. We were basically going to be saying he was a crook, and we had to have it really solid. About that time, the newspaper got sold. The family that owned it sold it to WEHCO Media—Walter E. Hussman and Company. One of the editors said, "Well, we probably ought to put this on the back burner because the paper is in turmoil now and we can't really be doing this story." I said, "Well, fine." So it was just a worrisome story. Well, another editor, and that was Jerry McConnell—he started hearing, I guess, from some people in the community that he knew that we were really onto something here. He had heard that the district attorney's office was hot to trot on this guy, too, so he revived the story. He said, "We're going to do this story. We're going to get it in the paper." And we did. He kind of juiced that lead up there. He made kind of a feature lead on it, and then we did this long line of bullets saying the things the guy was accused of—stretched it across the top of the front page. Every single word—ran it past lawyers—they approved it, and we ran it. As far as the story causing things to happen, within a few days this guy had filed for bankruptcy. I remember going to bankruptcy court when he did it and sitting in that audience in that courtroom. His lawyer said, "That whole thing is a lie, and there's going to be a big lawsuit out of it," waving it [the newspaper] around. And the judge said, "Well, was *this* a lie?" He'd ask him about specific things in there. And they got to something about a big, giant hot check. This thousands-of-dollars hot check. He [the lawyer] said, "No, it's not true. Absolutely no hot check." Well, the guy who he wrote it to was also sitting in the audience there in bankruptcy court, and his lawyer was there. His lawyer opened up a folder of some sort, and in that folder was the hot check. I remember looking over there, and the guy had a smile on his face as Pritchard's lawyer said it was all a lie. And the lawyer for the guy that he wrote the hot check to was waving it at me, and he was smiling at me.

Denise Gamino: I think you're referring to an $87,300 hot check that's listed in your story. We're talking about an *Arkansas Democrat* front-page story that ran April 18, 1974. At the top of the page with the headline, it says, "Questions Are Raised about Flamboyant Oil

Man." The story continues on the back page and takes up half of the back page.

Rice: Well, in any event, that's one of the stories that I will always remember. There were probably things in there that weren't 1,000 percent solid, but it was solid enough to force him into bankruptcy. A little while after that, the prosecutor filed a bunch of felony theft charges against him. Again, after our story—and, of course, their investigation had been going on, too—but we were out there in front with that one. We laid it out there in front of the people. That was the first thing that had been written about Larry Pritchard's business dealings. It ended up ruining him. He lost his company, went bankrupt, and ended up going to jail.

I was in a rush to get the story in the paper, so I called our libel lawyer immediately. At this time it was Richard Arnold, who later became a federal judge on the Eight Circuit Court of Appeals. At the time he was married to Gale Hussman, Walter's sister, and his office was in Texarkana. He said he would need to see the story. I told him we didn't have time, so I read it to him over the phone. He approved it, and the only thing he changed was the headline I had written for it, which was a little stronger than the one he wrote.

Rice: We felt we could beat them [the *Gazette*] on the big stories, and I think we did a lot of times. One example that I'll give, and I was pretty proud of this one. [In] 1975, [after] the fall of Saigon, thousands of refugees from South Vietnam were flown to the United States. They went to several different places in the US. There were refugee centers set up. One was at Fort Chaffee, Arkansas. When they were on the way, I got sent up for that along with another reporter and my favorite photographer, Robert Ike Thomas. We basically stayed there for about a week, covering breaking news out of that evacuation of refugees to Fort Chaffee. That was one where we were vastly outnumbered, but it was sort of by choice, in a way, because we just basically functioned better. The other paper might send half a dozen people, and we'd send one or two. We got over there and got into a pretty good sort of routine. The first day it was a media mob scene, with all the national people there—all the networks, all the big papers, all the Arkansas papers. Everybody was sticking microphones and notepads in front of this first group of frightened refugees. So I did that story. Then I said, "Well, we need to get in with the refugees. We've got to talk to some of them at length." The next morning I got up early. I got one of those army PIO [Public Information Officer] guys on the [phone]. I said, "Well, what time are you going to start serving breakfast?" "Five o'clock," he said. I said, "Well, I want to go over there at five o'clock." So me and Robert Ike Thomas showed up at the barracks and walked in there. Lo and behold, the one reporter that I really respected from another paper, a guy named John Bennett, who worked at the *Memphis Commercial Appeal* paper, was already there. Anyway, we went over there, and we were just kind of working the tables. Robert Ike had said, "Well, let's bring some film along because most of these refugees seem to have cameras. They may need film." And we'd give them some film. That was sort of our entree with talking with people. We sat down at one table with a family—father, mother, a bunch of little kids—and I started talking to the guy. It turned out he was an assistant mayor of Saigon. He was telling us about all the gold wafers that had been brought out by refugees, including himself, and he went into great detail about that. We broke that story, at least from Fort Chaffee, about the gold wafers that were brought out by fleeing refugees, and the fact that they had converted anything they could into gold. That was a story that went national. I recall going to the daily press briefing, and one of the national network guys was bitching at the army PIO officer because they had not put out a release on this. So the officer said, "That's something I just don't know about." It ran in our afternoon paper and beat everybody. Another one along that same line—the *Arkansas Gazette* ran some kind of national column, and buried deep in that story it said among the refugees to flee was this guy who had the reputation as some sort of a thug. He was in the secret police in South Vietnam. Well, we were able to verify that he was one of the refugees who had been brought to Fort Chaffee and had been given a little special treatment there. But we got that. They wrote about that guy in a column in their paper, but they hadn't bothered to check and verify that he was in the refugee camp, but I did, so I got that story.

Gary had his own "Deep Throat" on a story about a switched bullet.

Gamino: This is a story in the *Arkansas Democrat* on Saturday, March 22, 1975, across the top of the front page, by Gary Rice. The headline says, "Officials Think Bullets Switched," and the subhead is,

"The One Removed Did Not Come from Mother's Gun." What's that about?

Rice: This story was one that I still tell in journalism classes and tell reporters when I'm sitting around telling war stories. This involved a situation where a mother and her teenage daughter were at home alone, and they were in their beds at night. The young girl had her window open, or at least it was not locked. A guy climbed into her bedroom and started to attack her in her bed. Well, she was screaming, and the mother in the adjoining bedroom heard the commotion. She kept a revolver in her bedroom. She came into the [girl's] bedroom, and there was enough light [that] she could see this guy who was attacking her daughter. So she fired at him. She thought she hit him, and there was blood found. The police responded to that. Well, at the same time, an off-duty policeman named Monty Montgomery showed up at the hospital and said that he had been checking some of his rental property, surprised an intruder, and the intruder shot at him and hit him. Police examined him, but Monty Montgomery didn't want the bullet removed. It lodged into the fleshy part of his lower back. Police put two and two together and thought that Monty Montgomery might be a suspect in this case involving the attack on the teenager. Well, Monty Montgomery had a lawyer, and they did not want the bullet removed. Of course, the police and the district attorney wanted the bullet removed because they wanted it as evidence. They went to court and sought a court order, and this rocked on for several months. Finally, they got the court order. All of us in the media were waiting to see what the removal of the bullet showed. It was either going to show that he *did* it, or it's going to show that he *didn't* do it. The story came out that they removed the bullet, but the district attorney would not say a word. In fact, the *Arkansas Gazette* reported that they were not going to reveal what the removal of the bullet showed. I had an excellent source at the time. He was a state legislator. In fact, this wasn't long after the whole Watergate thing, and talk about Deep Throat and meeting in underground parking garages. We actually did that a time or two. Sometimes he would say, "Let's meet in the underground parking garage," and we'd go there, and the thing had exhaust fumes in it and it was dark and it was dank. I said, "Why don't we go upstairs to the restaurant?" So we'd eventually go up to a restaurant or a bar. But he just sort of did this for dramatic effect. He told me—this was one of the damnedest stories he'd ever heard—that they believed that Monty Montgomery, or someone for Monty Montgomery, operated on him before the police got to him and switched the bullet—took out the original bullet and put another one in. And I was just dumbfounded. I said, "Well, how did they *know* that? How can they be sure of that?" And the guy says, "Well, the original X-ray shows the bullet was going this way, but when it came time to take this bullet out, it was going the other way!" They had switched the bullet but had them going different directions. I said, "My God, that's a hell of a story!" I said, "Are you sure?" He said, "Oh, yeah, I got it from somebody in the DA's [district attorney's] office." This guy had always been reliable before. I put in a call that afternoon to a source of mine, an assistant district attorney, who I had met covering municipal court. He didn't return the call that afternoon. I went on home, but I left my home number. That night the phone rang, and it was my source in the district attorney's office. I said, "Say, isn't that really *something* about that Monty Montgomery bullet being switched?" And the guy said, "Yeah, isn't that something?" Then he proceeded to basically tell me everything that I had heard earlier. That was confirmation for me. I wrote this story up the next day. We just told what happened and got it ready to go. I went and called the district attorney. Of course, they didn't want to talk about it at all, and they were *livid*. We told them we were going to run this story. And, lo and behold, we did. It was a fun one because it had such a bizarre twist. We *really* nailed the *Gazette* on that one.

Gamino: What's another story you remember?

Rice: Well, this was a little bit different kind of story—the Nearly Home story. The Nearly Home was the center for homeless boys that had been funded by charities, and I think there was a federal grant involved in it. It basically was a place for runaways or homeless boys to stay while they were getting themselves back on the ground or getting relocated. It had mysteriously closed. This was one that they assigned to both Bill Husted and me. We started calling around. It's one of those kinds of things, you know, you'd call and call and call, and never get anywhere with it. Finally, I said, "We need to talk to this guy who had been on the board of directors." We made an appointment to go see him at night. We went over to his house—a pretty swanky part of town. We arrived, and the guy was drunk. He was literally drunk. We started asking him questions, and he basically spilled the beans on the whole operation—that the board of directors had caught this guy on several occasions and that they had decided to hush it up. They gave him another chance a time or two after he had been caught molesting boys. Finally, they just closed it down, but they were mostly interested in keeping it quiet rather than trying to do anything for the boys who had been molested. He was obviously troubled by the whole thing. Well, we got back to the office, and we reported that to our boss here. Then we gathered a few more things that pointed in this direction. A lot of people would not talk to us on the record, and other people flatly denied any of it. We had people who were saying it happened, and others who flatly denied it. And this got to the point that this was a hot potato because many of the people on the board of directors were well-known people around town—that is, money people who might sue. At one point, the editor of the paper, a guy named Robert McCord, called a meeting with us and the paper's lawyer, and I think there might have been some other editors in there. I remember to this day going to the meeting, and the lawyers had read everything we were trying to get in the paper. The lawyer's words were, "Well, my advice as a lawyer is not to run this." And I remember McCord standing up and saying, "It's not your job as a lawyer to tell me what I can run and what I cannot run. It's your job as a lawyer to tell me how I can run what I want to run without getting sued." I thought, "My God, that's all right!" So the decision was made. They set the bar pretty high. They said, "Well, if you're going to run this kind of stuff, you're going to need to get some notarized statements. That is, take a notary public with you and type up what they told you and have them sign it in front of a notary." I said, "I don't know if they'll do it." They said, "That's what you're going to have to do, or we're not going to run it." So Bill Husted and I did that. We typed up what these guys told us in kind of state- ment form, at least on two cases, including the drunk guy. We took it back when he was sober. He looked at it and didn't change a word and signed it. And we got that, I think, from either one or two other sources, and that was enough to get it in the paper.

Before it was going to go in the paper, we have to have the confrontation with the guy. We were trying to figure out how to do this, and we both were a little bit nervous, too. This was kind of a touchy story. So we went over to the guy's house. We went into the guy's house, and we were very cordial, and he was very cordial. He invited us down into his basement, which was pretty swanky. It had a bar down there and the whole bit. We went down, and we basically were lying to him all the way. We were saying, "We're just doing a story about different homes that have worked with young people. We're just trying to do kind of a comprehensive look on all those different homes in Little Rock, and which ones had worked and which ones didn't." And that was going to be our plan. We were going to kind of lead him on there and ask all these questions, and then I was going to put the drop on him with a tough question. We rocked on there about an hour—all these softball questions back and forth, back and forth. And then we sort of glanced at each other, and it was time for me to ask the question. It was decided ahead of time that I was going to ask the question. I was going to be the bad guy, and Bill Husted was going to be the good guy. I stumbled on it. I said something like, "Have you engaged in homosexuality relations with the boys at the home?" It wasn't a really grammatical question, but he got the point. I was almost stumbling with that because the tension had been building for an hour and a half. It was really intense. It makes me a little tense just talking about it now—it's been all these years. Anyhow, I got the question out, and he absolutely denied, flatly denied it. Said it was not true at all. So I started hammering him. "Well, we have this and this and this." "No, it's not true. It's not true." Then, after a few minutes of this, he yelled upstairs to his wife. "Dear, come down." She came marching down the stairs, and I say marching because it sort of looked like a march. And he said, "Dear, these two men are accusing me of having homosexual relations with boys at Nearly Home." And she started *screaming*. "Not true! Not true! It's all a lie! Why are you saying that?" And she just spewed this stuff, and we didn't even say anything. And he said, "Thank you, dear." Then she went back upstairs. Very odd. Very strange scene that was. We keep hammering away. I think at that point, you know, the initial tension had been broken, so we were determined we weren't going to leave until we got what we wanted.

Gamino: I wonder why he didn't throw you out of his house.

Rice: I know. That's what I thought, too. But he didn't. I kept asking the question over and over again. He kept denying it until he switched at one point. Instead of denying it, he said, "No comment. No comment. No comment." I saw that as a little chink in this. It was a subtle switch in his attitude, and we kept hammering on him. Finally, he broke down in tears and admitted it. He said it was true, and we packed up and left. I remember we went to a diner. I remember ordering a chicken-fried steak. Bill Husted ordered a full dinner, too. And once it came, we couldn't even eat it. We just picked at it because we were still so wound up and tense. And then we went back and we wrote the story, and it ran. The only thing that I was upset about that—the lawyers would not let us use the guy's name. And my contention was, "Well, if it's a libel issue, there's no doubt that we've identified him by position and everything." But the lawyers didn't want to use his name.

I thought this story would bring some reactions because we'd mentioned that all these prominent people in town had let this happen. We had laid all this stuff out there. I thought there would be all kinds of outrage out of this. I got one obscene phone call—[a] hang-up. That was all we ever got out of that. Before it ran, though, one other aspect was the guy had called up several times threatening suicide. He called me up on the phone and said he'd kill himself if the story ran. And I passed that along to the editors, but we went ahead and ran it. We didn't really give it a lot of thought, and he didn't. He didn't kill himself. As far as I know, he may be out running other homes to this day.

Rice also had several other scoops, but these are a good example of what he did and how he did it.

Gene Foreman and Ralph Patrick had a pleasant surprise one day when Lynda Zimmer walked in off the street and applied for a job. (Lynda was married to Bob Zimmer, also a newsman, who died young from a heart attack. She has since remarried.) She had a journalism degree from the University of Arizona, had studied journalism at Northwestern University, and had worked for the Associated Press in Tucson when there were a lot of mafia killings going on there. She was hired immediately, and before long she was assigned to cover the North Little Rock City Hall. Then it was Casey Laman's turn to be surprised.

Lynda Zimmer-Straw: Early on I met the infamous [William F.]

"Casey" Laman, who was mayor at the time. I guess he thought I would just be like another daughter of his. He was just so sweet at first, and he wanted to take me on a tour of the city. He took me all over and showed me this and showed me that. Even early on, he was very interested in creating parks. I was pretty naive, and I'd say, "Well, how do you get permission to do this or that?" And several times that day, he'd say, "Well, I'm just the head nigger here! I can do whatever I *want*." And being a non-southern girl, I went right back to the office and quoted him as saying he was "the head nigger" in North Little Rock. So, from then on, he didn't like me—he didn't trust me. He never expected me to write that. I just started right in doing kind of investigative things. I had a very good source early on who told me to check out things in the financial records. I found out, for example, that they were buying furnishings for city hall out of Casey's family furniture shop across the street without any bids. After I did a few stories like that, Casey just forbade me to talk to any of the department heads. And he forbade any of them to talk to me.

Brenda Tirey: Did Casey ever get more kindly toward you again, or did his hostility just continue throughout the time you were there?

Zimmer-Straw: No, it just got worse and worse. I was able to break the story when they were trying to rebuild a lot of things in North Little Rock with federal money. HUD [Housing and Urban Development] got wind of some of his deals and cut North Little Rock out of all the funding for that. I broke that story. One of Casey's best friends, John Blodgett, was on the planning commission, I believe. One time Casey and John went off to a convention of some sort for "city business," but there was word that they had spent a lot of city money doing other things. I learned a very important lesson in journalism that time. I called up John Blodgett and said, "Well, what did you do while you were at that meeting?" And he said, "Well, you know, we went to the meeting one day, but after that, boy, we just played golf. We went out to swimming pools. We had a condo on the beach." He just told me everything they did and the city money they spent. So that was another rough time with Casey, who was really upset and didn't want all that in the newspaper, of course.

Tirey: How did you get along with John Blodgett after that? Did he regret telling that to you?

Zimmer-Straw: Well, I don't believe he ever spoke to me after that. It was amazing. These officials just didn't expect their comments to be in the newspaper. Well, talking about scoops at the courthouse, I remember one story. Roger Mears was head of the election commission. Georgia Sells was working for him, and she was a social friend of mine. Roger was running for county judge, and he got all of his employees on the election commission one time to spend their lunch hour outdoors at the courthouse handing out political material for him. So I wrote a story about that because as public employees they weren't supposed to be doing that. Georgia told me years later that Roger came up to her and said, "Why did that get in the paper? I thought Lynda Zimmer was a *friend* of yours!"

Martin Kirby: In the early months of 1970, I started covering the major crisis in the Union National Bank in Little Rock. A guy named Harlan Lane had come in and bought controlling interest in the bank and was making various reforms that were being resisted by the pre-existing directors of the bank. There was a major vote of the board of directors to fire Harlan Lane, but he stayed on for a while after that. I managed to get the lineup for who voted for him and who voted against him on the board of directors, which was considered a coup at the time. Gene [Foreman] had instituted a policy of paying little cash awards for good work every week or so. As I recall, I won fifteen dollars and a complimentary note on the bulletin board for that. I just continued to cover that for a good while and got a lot of good information that they would rather not have had public, apparently. Eventually, I won a prize for that reporting. It was a prize administered jointly by the University of Missouri and a natural gas association [that] had the initials of INGAA. It was for one thousand dollars, which was a pretty good prize then. I went up to Columbia, Missouri, to get the prize, and I had to give a talk or two. I was sort of lauded and feted there. My father matched my prize money, so I had two thousand dollars, which enabled me to buy a new piano and pay off my psychiatrist in New Orleans.

Kirby also reported that the state had awarded a contract to a consulting firm in which four current or former members of state law enforcement organizations owned stock. Attorney General Ray Thornton later ruled that the contract was unenforceable because of conflicts of interest.

I reported in 1952 that two notorious killers had been released from prison on furloughs granted by Governor McMath on the recommendation of the state parole board. One of them had escaped from the state hospital by killing a guard with a gun smuggled to him by his brother. The other had killed a sheriff who was trying to serve a warrant on him for forging a check. The state had never announced they were being released, although it did announce when someone was granted parole. Only a few days after my second report the state changed its procedure and also started announcing it when a prisoner was being furloughed.

This is only a small sample of exclusive stories reported by the Democrat *over the years, but it is some indication that we did more than wait around to rewrite the* Gazette.

CHAPTER 6

The Hussman Method

THE CLYDE PALMER and Walter Hussman families had decades of experience in the newspaper business when the Hussmans bought the Arkansas Democrat in 1974. That experience involved operating several small- to moderate-sized dailies in south Arkansas. It did not include operating a paper as large as the Democrat or facing competition with a paper like the Arkansas Gazette. It did, however, include a background of innovation, including a predilection for using new technology to cut the costs of newspaper operation. That turned out to the advantage of Walter Hussman Jr. when he took over as publisher of the Democrat, because at that time the newspaper business was in the midst of some of the greatest technological changes in history.

Palmer, who started in the newspaper business in 1894, always used modern press equipment and was the first newspaperman in the country to hook up his papers (six altogether) with automatic teletypesetters, which meant stories could be transmitted to all the papers at a fairly high rate of speed. He did this in 1942, during World War II, which enabled his papers to share news items without having to hire additional staff.

Walter Hussman Sr. had married Clyde Palmer's daughter, Betty, and took over the chain after Palmer died in 1957. That year Hussman started a profit-sharing plan for all employees. In 1963 Hussman launched the first terrestrial microwave high-speed, high-definition facsimile network to connect a group of papers. That allowed him to transmit camera-ready copies of ads and news stories from one paper to all his other papers, thus enabling them to switch to cold type and get rid of the labor-intensive, high-cost linotype (hot lead) machines.

Walter Hussman Sr. was born in Bland in central Missouri, and he met Palmer's daughter, Betty, in the journalism school at the University *of Missouri. They were married on Christmas Eve in 1931. After a turn selling insurance, Hussman went to work for his father-in-law in the newspaper business. He was the business manager of the* Texarkana Gazette *from 1936 to 1942.*

Walter Hussman: In fact, my dad was best friends and roommates with Don Reynolds. Don Reynolds wasn't in the newspaper business then, either, but they maintained a lifelong friendship and corresponded with each other for years. And both ended up leaving the University of Missouri and both striking out and getting into the newspaper business. My dad kind of married into it, anyway. But my dad has devoted his whole career to newspapers from 1931. He retired in 1981. Fifty years. So he went to World War II in 1940 or 1941 [1942]. When he first came to Little Rock he was at Camp Robinson as the press information officer. Don Reynolds was in the military in Europe, and Don got a request for my dad to transfer over to Europe with him. And my mother always said she just never forgave Don for getting that transfer. Anyway, they were copublishers of the European edition of *Yank Magazine* [the most widely read GI magazine ever published].

Anyway, my dad came back from World War II in 1945, I guess. And he decided, "You know, I really love the newspaper business, but I really don't love working for my father-in-law. I'd really like to own my own newspaper." That was his dream, to own his own paper. So after a few years he found a newspaper that was for sale in Midland, Texas. By then he knew a lot of people in Texarkana, and they obviously regarded him highly on his business and publishing abilities. So he got an option to buy the paper in Midland. He got enough local business people there who said they would back him if he bought the paper. So he went in to see his father-in-law, C. E. Palmer, and said, "You know, I've always wanted to own my own newspaper. I've got an opportunity to buy one in Midland, Texas." My grandfather thought, "Midland, Texas!" And he thought, "You're going to take my only daughter all the way out to Midland, Texas. I'll hardly ever see her." So he finally came around and said, "Look. Here's what I'll do. I'll sell you one of my newspapers if you won't go to Midland." And so he did. He sold him the second-smallest paper he had, which was the paper in Camden, Arkansas. My dad said, "That's fine." It was eighty-three miles from Texarkana. In 1949 he bought the paper in Camden, which probably wasn't expensive to buy, Anyway, when I was two years old, which was 1949, my whole family—my two sisters, myself, and Mother and Dad—moved over to Camden and [took over] the *Camden News*. I grew up in Camden. I had a great experience growing up in Camden, I loved it. One of my Sunday school teachers was David Pryor. Of course, my brother-in-law, Richard Arnold, ended up running against David Pryor. You know, small-town Arkansas.

By the time I was ten years old, my grandfather died. And at that point my dad took over operating all the newspapers—Texarkana, Hot Springs, Magnolia, El Dorado, [Camden], and a CBS-affiliated television station which had been on the air five years at that point. That was in Texarkana. And then it actually became a Texarkana-Shreveport station. And my dad spent a lot of time on that. He really was instrumental in putting that TV station on the air. He kind of talked my grandfather into doing it. Anyway, after that my dad spent a lot of time in the car driving around to the various other properties. You know, my sisters ended up having summer jobs at the paper. I ended up working every summer at the paper. I was ten years old. I had my first job working in the mailroom inserting papers at fifty cents an hour. I'd go down there and work on Saturday mornings. And then I think I was a proofreader when I was thirteen years old. I had a lot of summer jobs like that. When I graduated from high school after my senior year, I had my first forty-hours-a-week job. And I worked at the *El Dorado News-Times* as a reporter. I'd get up every morning and drive down there. It was thirty miles to El Dorado. I think my dad told me, "Well, I got good reports from the editor down there on how you did, and I'm proud of that. But what I'm really proud of is that the whole summer you were never late to work a single day. " Anyway, that was a good experience for me. I guess the most important lesson was my dad was always not only saying but living the fact that the newspaper comes first. The newspaper is more important than anything in our family, than any family financial considerations. And we just all kind of absorbed that and believed that, and it was sort of a creed.

[When] my grandmother died, my mother inherited most of the stock in the company. Through a reorganization in 1968—I was just getting out of college at the time—the *Camden News* ended up giving stock to shareholders, and they turned in their stock in Texarkana,

Hot Springs, and El Dorado—the *Camden News* ended up, technically, being the parent company of all the other operations. But it was kind of odd. Here you had this small paper in Camden, which was owned by Camden News Publishing Company, which also was now the parent company for our other newspapers.

And then, I guess, in 1973 my dad came up with WEHCO—for Walter E. Hussman Company—WEHCO Media. The *Camden News* owned WEHCO Media, which, in turn, owned all the newspapers. A few years ago we decided to name the parent company WEHCO Media. So in 1974 we owned all those newspapers [Texarkana, El Dorado, Hot Springs, Camden, and Magnolia]. We put KTAL-TV, which was the NBC affiliate in Shreveport/Texarkana—on the air in 1952. And in the 1960s—probably 1963 or 1964—my dad had this idea of getting into the cable television business. My dad invested in a company called Midwest Video that obtained franchises in towns like Greenville, Mississippi, and Bryan/College Station, Texas, that had almost no TV reception. They were quite far from any large cities.

When I got out of school and was working in New York, my dad was sixty-four years old. He was thinking about retiring, and here he's got a twenty-three-year-old son who's going to be working and living in New York. He was wanting me to move back to Arkansas because my two sisters had married professionals, an attorney and an architect, and they were not involved in the business. One was twelve years older [than me], and the other was eight years older. Anyway, I said, "I'm really enjoying my job here in New York. I'd really [like to] stay here a while." He said, "Well, think about this. If you move back to Arkansas and try this family business for a while, and if you don't like it, you can always move back to New York. You might not get the exact same job, but you'll get another job, and you can do it. But if you decide you want to stay up there for a long time, we'll probably sell these businesses. And because I'm retirement age—I don't want to wait until I'm seventy or older to decide whether someone in the family is going to run the business." So he said, "If you stay up there and don't come down here and give it a try, you've probably given up that option because the business would be sold. But if you come down and try it for a year or two, you can always go back to New York." And I thought, "That makes a lot of sense. This might be an opportunity I'll want to pursue. I'll never know if I don't go ahead and try it."

So I moved back to Arkansas. I worked with him the first two years, and an interesting thing happened during that time. We had to fire the general manager of the newspaper at Camden. My dad said, "All right, your next assignment is to find a general manager for the *Camden News*. So go out and interview people and search for them, and let me know who you'd recommend." So I started looking for a general manager for the *Camden News*. You know, this fellow had done it for over twenty years, and I found it was hard to find somebody to run a newspaper in a small town like that. So after a month or so, he said, "How are you coming on this?" I said, "I'm not having much luck. I'm looking. I'm talking to people, making phone calls and interviewing." He said, "Well, this newspaper can't run itself. I'm tied up with a lot of our other companies in Shreveport and Texarkana. Here's what we'll do. We'll make you the acting manager, and you'll keep that job until you find your replacement." I said, "I don't really want to be the manager of the *Camden News*." I was more interested in the journalism side.

Well, at the time that newspaper wasn't doing very well. It wasn't making very much money, and it was still printed on an old press. Gosh, we'd crank up that old letterpress—it was a flat-bed press—and you could feel the whole building shake. We really needed to convert to offset lithograph printing. We weren't making much money. Buying another printing press to put in Camden made no sense. El Dorado had a really fine printing press that they had bought probably six years earlier. It was an Urbanite, and I said, "Why don't we print the *Camden News* in El Dorado? It's a morning paper, and we're an afternoon paper. They could print both of them and we could just truck it up here in thirty minutes." So we decided to convert the paper to offset and print it in El Dorado. While I was manager—I did find a good ad manager. I recruited him from the paper in El Dorado, our other paper. I got him to come to Camden and help me because he knew a lot about selling advertising. I knew nothing about selling advertising. That experience was fascinating. I started thinking, "This is really fascinating. I'm really enjoying this." I didn't think I'd enjoy this. And I thought, "What am I enjoying about this? What I'm finding is that you can really bring creativity into trying to solve business problems. You not only accomplish objectives, but in this case we started producing a better-looking newspaper with better content, more interesting journalism, more advertising that's valuable to you as well as the community and the merchants. And I thought, "This is interesting. The journalism side, I know, is creative, but it can't be more creative than this, can it?" I was really surprised. I thought, "Gee, I'm really having to rethink what I thought was going to be so interesting in coming down here to work in the family business."

So after about two years in Camden, my dad and I decided it would probably be a good idea if I worked at another one of our newspapers. So I moved to Hot Springs, and by that time my dad said, "You have done a great job, and you've really got a lot of potential. You're good enough right now to manage our five newspapers. I'll continue to operate the TV side and cable side, but we'll let each of the general managers report to you." I had my office in Hot Springs, so I moved up there in 1973 and lived there for about a year running the other newspapers. And in 1974 the *Democrat* came up for sale.

I was living in Hot Springs at the time and running these newspapers, and they were all doing fairly well. We were making a lot of progress. Not just financially. I had hired Mike Masterson to come in as the editor of the *Hot Springs Sentinel-Record*, and we significantly improved the quality of the paper—the journalistic quality. So things were going well. But, you know, I had this business degree from Columbia University. Back in those days I was anxious to use a lot of the ideas I had learned. I had used some of it in our business. But what was really exciting to think about was turning around a business. We had turned around the *Camden News*. It was a very small business, you know, but that was really exciting. And I thought it would be great to turn around a larger newspaper. I said, "As long as we're in the business of journalism in Arkansas, then the ultimate would be to have a newspaper in Little Rock. You know, that's the capital of the state. That's the center of the state—the largest city in the state. That would be a wonderful thing if we could own a paper there, and if it could be a really well-regarded and financially successful paper, that would be terrific." And we thought about it, and we looked at it. But we saw a lot of problems with the *Democrat* in evaluating it. We saw continuous declines there. And we had a high regard for the *Arkansas Gazette* as a newspaper. My dad read it every single morning. And when I went to New York and lived up there a couple of years, I subscribed to it by mail and read it every day. My dad said, "This is a well-packaged newspaper. It's got a lot of good in-depth reporting, high story count," a lot of attributes that were positive about newspapers. He said, "You know, if we buy the *Arkansas Democrat*—it may have gone down too far. We may not be able to turn it around. And we may not be able to succeed with it." And I kind of think we came to the conclusion that if we decided to buy it, it was going to be because it was in Arkansas. If we had found the same opportunity in Jackson, Mississippi, or Shreveport, Louisiana, or somewhere else, we probably wouldn't have done it. But because our whole family had been in Arkansas in the newspaper business for decades, it was worth a try. And, of course, I think if I hadn't been back into the business and my dad had looked at it, my dad probably wouldn't have done it. At his age—he said, "If we buy the *Arkansas Democrat* I can't go up there and run it. I'm past my midsixties now. If we buy the *Arkansas Democrat*, you're going to have to go over there, and you're going to have to take on the challenge in running it. And besides, you're the one who feels the strongest about doing it, so that's probably the way it ought to be." But I was only twenty-seven at the time. Anyway, my dad said at the time, "We've got to be able to decide now. We've got to pick out a point in time," and we picked three years. He said, "If this thing hasn't been successful after three years, we need to set that date now and revisit it at that time."

Roy Reed: Successful—meaning what?

Hussman: Meaning that we've turned the business around, advertising has been turned around, circulation has been turned around....

Reed: So it was losing money in 1974?

Hussman: Well, yes, it was losing money. It wasn't losing a lot of money, and it had been profitable several years prior to that. And it had been profitable for many, many years, so it had lost money only four or five years by the time we bought it. And turning it around also meant moving it back into the black—making money and reversing the advertising and circulation trends and getting those on the upswing.

Reed: Yes. So how did it go?

Hussman: Well, the first thing that happened when we were buying the newspaper, there was a union organizing attempt at the *Democrat* and at the *Gazette*, also, but different unions. We had the

ITU—International Typographical Union—trying to organize the *Arkansas Democrat* newsroom employees, and the Guild was trying to organize the *Gazette* employees. So when we bought the newspaper the first thing we had to do was work on this union organizing attempt because we were a nonunion operation. We perceived the newspaper unions with all their archaic work rules as an obstacle to improving the newspaper. It was something that was really holding back the *Democrat*, and we were going to try to convince the employees that they didn't need to belong to unions, that we had good healthcare plans, a profit-sharing plan, and lots of benefits. And, over time, hopefully, we'd become a nonunion operation and a more efficient operation.

There were four unions at the *Democrat*. There were the printing pressmen, there was the ITU for the composing room, there were the stereotypers, and there were the mailers union. So the first thing I did was spend almost every morning with Jerry McConnell, who was managing editor, and we worked on a strategy to try to win the union election. And that was wonderful. I really enjoyed working with Jerry, and I got to know him really well. All of a sudden, I was down in the trenches. We ended up winning that election thirty-one to fifteen, which was good because the majority of the employees had signed cards. But with new ownership and explaining how we operated our other newspapers and the fringe benefits, the employees decided to give us a chance. The *Gazette* ended up winning their election, also, fifty to fifty. In the case of a tie, management wins, but it was as close as you could get.

The vote will also tell you something else. Thirty-one to fifteen, if you add those numbers together, you get forty-six. If you add fifty and fifty together, you get a hundred. So that tells you something about the sizes of the newsrooms. The *Gazette* newsroom was over twice as large as the *Democrat* newsroom. Anyway, we won that, and the first year we operated the newspaper we did really, really well by this criteria: number one, our circulation losses stopped, and we started gaining circulation.

We sold it better. We delivered it more efficiently. Advertising turned around. We brought in a lot of new ad salespeople. We brought in a new ad manager. We got a new circulation manager. And, all of a sudden, with new ownership, and also an ownership that had decades of experience in the newspaper business, the employees and community perceived us differently than the two nephews. Maybe they thought highly of them. But with us, they thought, "They've operated newspapers for decades. They know what they're doing. Let's give them a chance." So a lot of people in the business community in Little Rock started advertising with us. I remember going to lunch with Finley Vinson [president of First National Bank]. And he said, "We're going to get back in the newspaper." Billy Rector said, "We're going to start giving a lot of our classified real estate advertising to the *Democrat*." And it was amazing because all of a sudden all this additional advertising that the *Democrat* hadn't had for years was now in our paper. So things were going great in advertising. I made Bob McCord the editor, and Bob started doing a good job editing the newspaper. We had a lot more interesting stories in the paper. And we started running some color, which the paper hadn't done in a long time.

But it dawned on us that as we went on month after month there in 1974, that something was wrong. I remember in September I went on a trip to Russia with Hodding Carter—there were twelve of us young journalists who went on this trip. I remember coming back from the trip, and Paul Smith said, "We had a twelve-thousand-inch gain in advertising in September." It was fantastic to have a twelve-thousand-inch gain. But every month I looked at the profit-and-loss statement, and the more business we did, the more money we lost. And I thought, "This is crazy. Something is wrong with this picture." And it turned out that [with] our operating expenses—mainly because of all the union work rules and restrictions—we couldn't make money by bringing in more business. It just didn't make any sense. I mean, here are some examples.

We would print more pages. We'd print a bigger paper. Well, because of the pressman's union, we had to hire *Gazette* pressmen to come over here and work at the *Democrat* because of these manning requirements on the press. I went back to our pressroom on a Saturday night one time—Saturday night was when we usually had to bring more people over—it was the biggest paper of the week, with more advertising—there were people asleep back there on cots to fulfill the manning requirement. And people were starting to send ads in that were already engraved. The ad agency would send us an engraving. Well, you know, the typesetters' union would say, "But we've got to reset that ad." So they would reset the ad, and they'd throw it back into the hot metal. They'd call that "bogus type." And the engravers said, "But we've got to reengrave that page." All these restrictive and costly work rules—we weren't used to this in our other newspapers. And so after about the first year, about March of 1975, we said, "We've proven we can turn things around, advertising and circulation wise, but there's no hope of making any money doing that unless we can solve our internal problems." You know, we had success externally with readers and advertisers. "We've got to solve our internal problem in order to be able to streamline now so that when we go out and get a lot of additional business, we can make money doing it." So we retrenched at that point. We retrenched externally from placing a lot of effort into selling circulation and selling more advertising. I said, "We need to reorder our priorities so that cost efficiencies are emphasized." And we did. From 1975 through about 1977, most of the unions decertified. Eventually, all of them. The members themselves said that they no longer wanted to be represented by a union. I mean, to me it was a tremendous vote of confidence that they would do that. And I think they were beginning to realize, you know—I told them honestly, "We can't make any money the way things are set up now. And if we can't make any money, none of us have any hope. Me, you, and all of us don't have any hope of having a job here." They all came around. They eventually all decertified. I think maybe the last union to decertify was the ITU in 1978. Maybe by 1977 three of the four unions had decertified. And what happened was our losses started getting less and less. We were still losing money. We lost money in 1974 and up through early 1975. But then once we started really focusing internally, our losses started shrinking. And we had reduced the losses down to a fairly small amount by 1977.

In general, it had cost us over one hundred dollars per page just for labor to generate a page of news content or advertising content, which was way out of line with what our other papers cost. And so we had to sit down and really negotiate with all the unions, and we reached a point where we just couldn't agree, which, I guess, they say in labor terminology, you've reached an impasse. And once you've reached an impasse, then at that point whatever changes you wanted to implement, you can go ahead and implement the changes. And, of course, the union—if they don't like the fact that you've done that, they can go on strike or have a slowdown or a sit-down or whatever they want to do, you know?

And so, anyway, that happened with four unions, we'd got to an impasse. We went ahead and started operating with our new procedures. One of those unions went on strike, which was the pressmen. And we did get a few people that worked at our other newspapers to come in and help us, but they didn't have to work very long because several of the guys who went on strike, within a day or two they were back working for us. The other three unions crossed the picket lines.

Hussman had also been making other preparations to get ready to switch to cold type, as Jim Shuemake, the head machinist in the composing room, remembers. He said he had heard the Hussmans were anti-union, and he thought about leaving when they bought the paper.

Jim Shuemake: At that time, I didn't have any kids. I was free and could've gone anywhere. But then I decided, "What the heck, I'll just stay and see how far I can go with this." And I did, and it's the best thing that ever happened to me. In July [1974], he called me down and offered me everything that I ever could want, but he had a stipulation—I had to get out of the union. This was to go to school on the computer. This was to take over and share in the profits from not having to have a service policy on the computer. Everything that I had ever even *dreamed* about wanting, I was offered—except I never thought about having to get out of the union. For the last five years, I had made more in overtime than I had made in straight time. And, you know, after a while—when you first start working overtime, it's gravy, but after a while it gets to be—if you're making it all the time, it gets to be just part of your salary. Well, it was part of my salary. I guess he had decided if he was going to be able to keep me, he was going to have to put me on salary. I was still going to have to put the same hours in. I was putting in a lot of hours, even when I was in the union, that didn't go on the payroll. That was the hardest decision I ever made. I mean, I had worked with these guys for fifteen years, and then I was going to have to be ostracized by them. And I thought I was the only one. Well, it turned out there were two more, and they really were ostracized. I mean, they really were. I was not because of what I did and the way I had been doing—I had been carrying the union. I had been doing a lot more for the union than the union had been doing for me. And everybody knew that. So I was not as ostracized as the others.

Jerry McConnell: Who were the other two people?

Shuemake: Fred Campbell and Ronnie Henson.

McConnell: Fred had been the foreman of the composing room, and Ronnie Henson—what did he do?

Shuemake: He was doing the cold type for the ads. He was in charge of the computer coding of the cold type ads. He was going to be instrumental in taking over and putting everything on cold type and going to this new computer.

McConnell: Both Fred and Ronnie did take Walter's offer and dropped out of the union.

Shuemake: Right. I'm sure it was just as hard for them as it was for me. We were all going through this, and each of us thought we were the only one. But we all decided that we didn't have any other choice but to do it, so we did. They both still had to work there—to work with these people. They both had to do jobs that were being done by union people—had *always* been done by union people, and now they were not union people.

I went to school for I guess a year and a half. Just every part of the computer school to the photo comp machine schools—just every-thing. The longest I was gone [at a time] was a month. I went to two two-week schools back-to-back at one time. That only happened once. Another thing happened after I was named production manager. I had had problems with getting out of the union because of these guys I had worked with for fifteen years. Now I was production manager, and they were cutting the force. I mean, cutting the force to the *bone*. I had to fire those people knowing they were never going to come back. They were the same people that I had worked with for fifteen years. But, as I said, the handwriting was on the wall. Everything was going to be done by computer and machine that the old typesetters and printers had done in the past, except pasting up the pages. And, of course, that was going to go by the wayside [eventually]. They may not have known it then, but when pagination came in, that went by the wayside. And some of those old printers walked out the door saying,

"Those computers will *never* work. They'll never take our place." As they were walking out the door they were still saying that.

McConnell: Yes. But they voted to decertify, isn't that correct?

Shuemake: Well, that was the ones who were left. When Walter bought the paper, there were seventy people in the composing room. Seventy printers. When it finally got down to decertifying—I can't remember how many there were, but there weren't but twelve or something like that.

McConnell: How did you get by with letting all those people go? Did the union not file a complaint over that?

Shuemake: Well, no, because that was just part of it. These were jobs being cut out. They weren't being replaced by nonunion people.

Hussman: But what had happened—while we were focusing internally, the *Gazette* was just getting stronger and stronger, gaining more advertising, gaining more circulation, and we were losing market share. I think when we bought the paper we may have had 65,000 daily circulation, and maybe by 1978 we were down to around 56,000. And the *Gazette* during that time had grown from 116,000 to 126,000. They were continuing to gain market share on us. And they were becoming more and more—which they already were, but even more so, they were becoming the primary buy.

You know, I remember the first time after we bought the newspaper that the *Gazette* had an advertising rate increase, and it was a big one. I mean, it was a double-digit rate increase. And we said, "Oh, boy, this will be great for us. We'll tell all the advertisers we're going to hold our rates steady." And what happened was when the *Gazette* raised their rates, we lost business. Now, why would we lose business when they raised their rates? The problem was that they were the must-buy, and we were considered as a complementary buy, like radio. We were not really an essential buy because we weren't a substitute. We were a complement. Anyway, soon, 1977 had rolled around. We had accomplished great things, I thought. We had been able to show that we could turn around circulation and advertising. We had shown we could reduce our losses. We got our production and operating costs—labor costs—down from over one hundred dollars per page down to around twenty dollars a page. A dramatic improvement internally, you know. But we weren't making money.

So my dad reminded me, "Hey. Three years are up." My dad was seventy-one years old. So we sit down and start talking about it, and he said, "I think it was a valiant attempt. It was a good try, but we're still losing money, and we've lost market share. It's time to come to grips with that reality." And at that point we decided that it hadn't worked, and we'd try to get out of this investment.

Of course, it was clear to most people that afternoon newspapers were having major problems in 1974. By 1977 no one wanted an afternoon newspaper. And it was better to sell the *Democrat* back when the former owners had owned it, but once an experienced newspaper operator had come in and operated it for three years and now they wanted to sell it, well, that made it more difficult to sell. So we thought, "This thing is going to be tough to sell. Maybe the best way out is to do a joint operating agreement [JOA]. And let's not make any bones about trying to get a good financial deal or the best deal or whatever. Let's just try to get out." So I called Hugh Patterson and set up an appointment with him to talk about trying to do a JOA. I had a couple of meetings with him. At least two, maybe three. I can't remember exactly how many. And I would meet with him, just the two of us, one on one. I had known the Pattersons—Ralph Patterson had gone to the University of North Carolina where we both were in college, and we even rode back to Arkansas once together. And I've stayed with the Pattersons in their home. Back in those days we were just a family that owned some small newspapers down in south Arkansas.

Anyway, I told Hugh, "We got into it for laudable reasons. We wanted to have a voice in Little Rock. We had been in the newspaper business for years, and we hoped to make money. We haven't been able to. We had hoped to be more competitive with the *Gazette*, and we haven't been able to do that successfully. It's time for us to recognize that, and we're willing to do a JOA. We're willing for the *Gazette* to be the dominant newspaper and the *Democrat* to be the secondary newspaper. We're not asking for fifty-fifty or anything like that. We will agree to whatever terms you think are reasonable." He got back in touch with me and said he didn't really think they were interested. I thought, "Gosh! You're not interested? Just about everybody would be interested in eliminating the remaining competition." And I couldn't believe he wasn't interested. So I told my dad, "They're not interested.

We've got to make them interested. Let's come up with a proposal, an offer he can't refuse." So that's what we did. We came up with this offer that basically said, "Look, we'll distribute the paper wherever you want us to distribute. If you want to distribute the *Democrat* in Pulaski County only, we'll distribute in Pulaski County only. If you want to deliver it in Pulaski and Saline County only, or if you want us to deliver it in Little Rock only. Whatever you decide is our geographic boundaries, that's okay. We'll be the afternoon newspaper, and you be the morning paper. You'll be the only Sunday paper if that's what you want. And what we'll do on the profit-split is that on the first $600,000 in profits—" Now, the *Gazette* was making $2 million a year and the potential was to make far more than that. The first $600,000 a year we would split that fifty-fifty, and the reason we wanted to split that fifty-fifty was that when we bought the *Democrat*, we gave the old owners a note for about $3.1 million. And our note payment was $295,000 a year for twenty years. So we said, "At least we'll cover our note payment." And after that, we said, "You get 90 percent of the profit and we get 10 percent of the profit." Basically, they said no to that. And he came back and said, "I think this joint operating agreement would be a drag on us, and I'm not sure we'll make as much money if we have to subsidize you guys and carry you along." And I thought, "Well, okay. He may legitimately feel that way. I don't think he realizes quite what the potential is, but maybe he legitimately feels that way." So I went back and said, "Here's what we'll do. We don't get anything until you earn as much as you made last year. You'll get 100 percent of the profits until you get that—then we'll split $600,000 fifty-fifty. And then you get 90 percent and we get 10 percent." And I thought, "That way he's guaranteed—he'll always make as much as he did last year, and that will address that concern." His response: "Not interested." So at that point, I went back to my dad and said, "Gee. They definitely don't want to do this JOA." And we thought about it, and thought, "Why don't they want to do the JOA?" And we thought, "Patterson probably perceives that we're about to go out of business. He had good reason to believe that. And if we go out of business, then he is better off than if he has to share 10 percent or $300,000 or whatever." And we said, "So what do we do now?" So at that point, what we said is, "Well, we need to find out how we close the newspaper." We didn't want to talk to any attorneys in Arkansas because there was a concern about word getting out. We talked to our Washington attorneys that we generally used for FCC broadcasting and cable TV, so we could keep it very confidential.

Reed: Was any thought given at any time, or was it even an option, to just sell the *Democrat* outright to the *Gazette*?

Hussman: We talked about that with Hugh Patterson. He said, "I might be interested in buying the paper." And we said, "Well, okay. How do we do that?" And he said, "First of all, you need to create a public monument to the fact that you've been a failure." I thought, "Okay, a public monument. Do I need to go build something down here in the Metro Center Mall?" [laughs]. I didn't really know what he meant. And I guess what he was trying to say there is that we not only had to admit to being a failure, but we had to convince the Justice Department that we couldn't sell the newspaper to anyone else. And if we could show them we couldn't sell to anyone else, then he would take it. That gets into federal antitrust law. [To avoid setting up a monopoly, the *Gazette* could not buy the *Democrat* if any other entity was willing to do so.] But then we thought, "Well, if we did that—if we've got to do that in advance of him telling us what he'd pay us for it, then how do we know he'd pay us anything?" So maybe if he said, "Well, I'll pay you x-y-z if you'll go do that," we might have sold it. But he said, "No, no. First you've got to go prove that you've been a failure and create a monument to your failure."

Well, it was more of a financial consideration. I mean, we were going to admit we had failed when we shut the newspaper down. It was more of a question of, "Well, if we prove that no one else would be willing to buy it, then haven't we just—from a negotiating standpoint with him—hadn't we lost any kind of leverage we would possibly have with him?" So we really didn't think that was a viable way to proceed.

Bob McCord: One day, Walter called me down to his office and said, "I talked to Hugh about combining," and he said, "He just is—was not even polite." I said, "Well, let me try." I knew Hugh Patterson saved the Arkansas Sigma Delta Chi chapter [of which McCord had been national president]. The organization from the beginning was always without money. Patterson was very generous. I didn't go over to the *Gazette*, I went out to his [Hugh's] house, and I just put it to him as straight as I could. I said, "You know, Detroit is doing it." I ticked off all the different towns that you'd never think would consolidate newspapers. I said, "I think this would be the greatest thing in the world for Arkansas, to put two papers together and still have two newspapers in this town." But Patterson said, "Bob, I just can't do that. The Hussmans came in here and attacked me." He took it all personally. He said, "I never liked those people, anyway." One day when I went to his house to talk he followed me out in his yard. I'll never forget it. He said, "I know you think I'm making a mistake. I can't do it. I don't want any part of consolidating." And he said, "Bob, we're going to win this war, and you'll be back over working for me." I said, "Hugh, I don't think that's ever going to happen." And he said, "Well, we'll see."

Barbara Day, who had left a position with Dillard's to join the Gazette *staff in the business office, recalls hearing about the JOA offer.*

Barbara Day: I was at the *Gazette* when he [Hussman] went back and made the second proposal to Mr. Patterson about having a joint operating agreement, and Mr. Patterson asked him to leave his office because he wasn't interested. Later, Mr. Patterson came down to the advertising department and was telling us about it and said that he really wasn't worried about the *Democrat* [and] that he didn't think they'd ever make it, so he was not going to do a joint operating agreement. He really didn't acknowledge the *Democrat* as a newspaper. [Day later was fired by the *Gazette* and went to work for the *Democrat*.]

I was unaware that all this was going on behind the scenes, but by 1978 I was aware that things were getting tighter. Salaries seemed more constricted. Because of problems processing copy on just four terminals, and the pressure that put on the copy desk, we had added some copy editors, but we had to cut out some reporters. That made it even more difficult to match the Gazette's *coverage.*

At some point in 1978, McCord told me that he had the feeling that Walter might want to try someone else as managing editor at the Democrat. *Walter never told me that himself, nor did McCord ever say that Walter told him that specifically, but I considered the information good enough that I started looking around for another job.*

At about this time I received word that Walter Hussman Sr. wanted to talk to me about a job at his flagship paper at Texarkana. We had been together on trips to newspaper exhibits and expositions. I thought he had a lot of poise and class, and I found him very personable, so I agreed to go to Texarkana to talk to him.

I remembered hearing news people at the Gazette *run down the*

Palmer and then the Hussman chain. The criticism was that the chain was virulently antiunion and that it cut costs to the detriment of good journalism. Palmer had pioneered the system of having one paper capture all the wire news and then ship it to the other papers.

As we began to discuss the job, I asked Mr. Hussman to describe how they operated, and I eventually raised some objections about the microwave service and perhaps some other practices. At any rate, he eventually said he would change them the way I wanted and offered me the job. I told him I would have to talk to my wife about it.

The next day I received a call from Gene Fields, who was the general manager of the paper. He said he needed to meet with me urgently and suggested that we meet in Malvern, and I agreed. Fields said he had heard what Hussman promised me and was astounded. He said he told him, "Mr. Hussman, you know you won't follow through on that. It will cost you a lot of money." He said Hussman reluctantly agreed and said that perhaps Fields had better talk to me about it.

"The problem is, Jerry," Fields said, "Mr. Hussman likes you so much he was willing to promise you almost anything to get you to take the job. But I know he couldn't do this."

I thanked Fields and told him that under those circumstances I could not take the job. In retrospect, I think I may have been a little condescending about small-town newspaper practices. I had only worked on metropolitan dailies and perhaps had developed some purist expectations that might not be possible everywhere. I also didn't know much about newspaper finance and profit margins. For all I know, those savings may have kept the other Hussman papers afloat. They were all located in south Arkansas, where the partial demise of the oil industry had left many areas facing tough times.

So I continued on at the Democrat, probably for several months, until one day Jim Standard called me, seeking advice on a new executive sports editor for the two jointly owned dailies in Oklahoma City, the Daily and Sunday Oklahoman and the Oklahoma City Times. So I flew over to talk to him and was hired.

I left the paper in August of 1978 and missed out on all the ideas Walter was hatching and the start of the war.

Walter Hussman Jr., then only twenty-seven, announces on March 4, 1974, that his family has bought the struggling *Arkansas Democrat*. Looking on is Marcus George, one of the former owners. He was a nephew of K. August Engel, who was connected to the paper for fifty-seven years and ran it for forty-two years. *Courtesy Walter Hussman.*

Bob McCord, still a college student, snapped this picture for the *Democrat* in 1949. It shows President Truman (in a white suit) and Arkansas governor Sid McMath (in a dark suit) on Main Street in Little Rock, leading a parade down Main Street in Little Rock of the Thirty-fifth Division, Truman's World War I outfit. The picture was named national picture of the year by the Associated Press. *Courtesy Butler Center for Arkansas Studies.*

Wilmer (Will) Counts always seemed to turn up at just the right place, which led him to go to work for Bob McCord at the *Arkansas Democrat Sunday Magazine* in June 1957. He was sent to Little Rock Central High School that September when Governor Orval Faubus called out the National Guard to stop nine black students from entering the school. Counts wound up in the area when Elizabeth Eckford, one of the black students, inadvertently turned up on her own to try to enter the school. Counts snapped away as Eckford ran the gauntlet of jeering whites. He made this picture as Hazel Bryan, who later apologized, shouted racial slurs at Eckford. The photography subcommittee unanimously recommended this picture for the Pulitzer Prize that year but was overturned by the Pulitzer board. It was later named one of the one hundred most significant news pictures of the twentieth century. *Courtesy Indiana University Press.*

Besides having a great eye, Counts had another edge. He used a 35-millimeter camera, which allowed him to take thirty-six shots without reloading, while most of the
main news photographers then used 4x5 Speed Graphics, bulky cameras that had
to be reloaded after every shot. Thus Counts was able to follow and snap away as a
crowd of angry white men harassed and beat Alex Wilson, a black newsman from
Memphis. This shot of Wilson being kicked by a man carrying a brick was named
"News Picture of the Year" by the National Press Photographers Association and
was selected by the *Encyclopedia Britannica* as one of the most memorable pictures
of the past fifty years. Counts wound up starting a photojournalism program at
Indiana, from which he had a doctorate, and remained there for thirty-two years.
Courtesy Indiana University Press.

Attending the 1940 convention of the Southern Newspaper Publishers Association are (from left) K. A. Engel, publisher of the *Arkansas Democrat;* Donald W. Reynolds, publisher of the *Fort Smith Southwest Times Record;* an unidentified man; and Walter Hussman Sr., general manager of the *Texarkana Gazette. Courtesy Walter Hussman Jr.*

The two Walter Hussmans at Walter Jr.'s wedding reception in 1975. Walter Sr. approved Walter Jr.'s urge to buy the *Democrat* in 1974 and then backed him when he switched the paper to a morning publication and opened an all-out competition with the *Gazette* in 1979. *Courtesy Walter Hussman Jr.*

Bob Starr, who later became known as John Robert Starr, perched on a *Gazette* newspaper box in his own declaration of war in May of 1979. This type of activity was almost unheard of in the newspaper business, but Starr later did a lot of things that weren't common in the newspaper business. *Courtesy Alan Leveritt, owner of the Arkansas Times.*

Walter Hussman Jr. (far right) celebrates with employees outside the *Democrat* building on March 28, 1986, after learning that a federal jury had found the *Democrat* not guilty in an antitrust suit brought by the *Gazette*. *Courtesy Arkansas Democrat-Gazette.*

Starr leaves no doubt how he feels about the verdict. *Courtesy Arkansas Democrat-Gazette.*

Palmer Hussman, age three, prepares to start the *Democrat*'s new offset lithography printing press in 1986 with the help of his father and mother, Walter and Robena (Ben) Hussman. Looking on are general manager Paul Smith (far left) and circulation manager Larry Graham (far right). *Courtesy Arkansas Democrat-Gazette.*

In one swoop, Hussman tells his staff on October 18, 1991, that he has bought the assets of the *Gazette*, which will close, and reveals the new name for his newspaper. *Courtesy Arkansas Democrat-Gazette.*

Phyllis Dillaha Brandon is surrounded by past covers as the paper celebrates the twentieth anniversary of the successful "High Profile" section in 2005. *Arkansas Democrat-Gazette photo by Staton Breidenthal.*

The Farkleberry Follies became a popular biannual spoof of politicians and the press put on by the Little Rock media. This skit features me (with the gun) shooting Bob McCord, while Bob Starr sits at the table, being kept in check by Jerry Rush. *Democrat photo by Robert Ike Thomas.*

The *Democrat* circulation leaders (from left), director Larry Graham, state manager Bill Taylor, and city manager Dale Enoch, in front of the maps where they track their progress. *Courtesy Arkansas Democrat-Gazette.*

In April 2006 Paul Smith, hailed by his cohorts as one of the real architects of the victory of the *Democrat* over the *Gazette,* was named president of WEHCO Newspaper, Inc., as well as president of the *Arkansas Democrat-Gazette.* He had been vice president and general manager of the paper since 1981. *Courtesy Arkansas Democrat-Gazette.*

Lynn Hamilton, vice president of operations, speaks at the retirement party in 2001 for Jim Shuemake (at right, joking with Hussman). It was Shuemake's job to keep most of Hussman's numerous new machines running. Hamilton said that when Shuemake retired he found a bunch of notes from Hussman saying "see me about this" that he had never had time to open. *Courtesy Arkansas Democrat-Gazette.*

Executive editor Griffin Smith (at left), reporter Andrew Davis, photographer Michael Marshall, and Susan Scantlin, editor of the Northwest Arkansas edition, head to a Fayetteville courtroom on May 25, 2000, after the paper was fined a maximum of one hundred dollars for violating a judge's gag order. The Arkansas Supreme Court overturned the decision in late June by a 6–0 vote. *Courtesy Arkansas Democrat-Gazette.*

Roy Bosson reported many of the stories in the *Democrat* that led the legislature to establish a Highway Audit Commission, whose hearings sparked passage of a constitutional amendment in 1952 to change the method of appointing highway commissioners. *Courtesy Arkansas Democrat-Gazette.*

Gene Foreman (left) and the bearded Ralph Patrick were excellent newsmen who tried to resurrect a moribund afternoon *Democrat* but had too many built-in handicaps to overcome. They went on to bigger things. *File photo of Foreman; Robert Ike Thomas photo of Patrick.*

above left: Jon Kennedy was an excellent artist and cartoonist who worked for the *Democrat* for forty-seven years. He may have been slightly hampered as an editorial cartoonist because he was a liberal who worked for two conservative publishers. *Democrat photo by Robert Ike Thomas.*

Amanda Husted Allen (above right) and Carol Stogsdill (right) became friends in journalism school at Arkansas State University and were aces on the copy desk at the *Democrat.* Stogsdill later was named senior editor and vice president of the *Los Angeles Times,* Allen became travel editor of the *Atlanta Journal-Constitution.* *Democrat photos by Robert Ike Thomas.*

above: Bob Lancaster
typically waiting for
inspiration, which came
often enough to win him
a prestigious Neiman
Fellowship to Harvard.
*Democrat photo by
Robert Ike Thomas.*

right: Gary Rice (right)
and Bill Husted on their
way to work. They were
two of the *Democrat*'s
best reporters, Rice
the better reporter and
Husted the better writer,
and they made a great
team. *Democrat photo
by Robert Ike Thomas.*

Reporter Dorothy Palmer sits in front of financial editor Bobbie Forster in 1972. Forster had a messy desk that could only be matched by that of *Gazette* sportswriter Jim Bailey. They both had organized minds and could find stuff on their desk in a hurry. *Democrat photo by Robert Ike Thomas.*

The *Democrat* newsroom in 1973. Nearest the camera is James Scudder, a former Methodist minister, an excellent writer, and the assistant city editor. Just beyond him is Mable Berry, the city desk clerk extraordinaire, who wrote obits, tracked down the weather and river reports, and took dictation over the phone. *Democrat photo by Robert Ike Thomas.*

News editor Si Dunn looks over a typewritten story while beyond him Mike Kirkendall sits in the slot of the horseshoe-shaped copy desk. Kirkendall moved on to the *Chicago Sun-Times* and eventually ended up at the *Los Angeles Times*. Note at the right the conveyer belt that took stories on paper up to the composing room, where they were set into type. *Democrat photo by Robert Ike Thomas.*

Fred Campbell (center), only the third composing room foreman in *Democrat* history, looks on as corrections are made in a page of hot type. When computers took over setting type and making it up on the page, the composing room became superfluous. *Courtesy Arkansas Democrat-Gazette.*

This is the newsroom that Hussman built on the third floor, the site of the old composing room, in 1991 or 1992. Note all the computer terminals and the lack of stories written on paper, which had been scattered all over the old newsroom in the early 1970s. *Courtesy Arkansas Democrat-Gazette.*

Frank McDonald announces that he is selling the *Chattanooga Free Press* to the Hussmans in March 1998. It was Frank's late father, Roy, who had suggested to Hussman that running more news than his opposition had worked for him. *Courtesy Arkansas Democrat-Gazette.*

CHAPTER 7

A Plan of Attack

AFTER HUGH PATTERSON refused to enter into a joint operating agreement with the Democrat *and left little hope he would buy the paper, the Hussmans started to seriously consider how to close the paper. Walter Jr. had a lot of trouble with that idea.*

Walter Hussman: We were talking about what the financial implications were and how you went about it. We had never closed a business. Anyway, our Washington attorneys were giving us advice on that. I said, "Dad, we've been really successful at newspaper publishing. We've been successful in radio broadcasting. We put the first radio station on the air in Texarkana in 1933. We've had successful radio stations. We've been successful in the television business. We've been successful in cable television. This is the first unsuccessful business we've had." At that time, we were kind of mulling this over. I just started thinking, "Is there anything else we could possibly do to revive and resuscitate the *Arkansas Democrat*?" So I started on my own doing a little investigating, and I thought, "Who has ever been in the shape we're in today? And if they have been in that shape, have they ever made a comeback?" So I started doing some research, and I discovered a paper over in Chattanooga [the *Free Press*] that had been a distant number-two newspaper. In fact, it had started out as a shopper. It eventually passed the established morning paper over there, and it was an afternoon paper. And it had started out with far less circulation. And I thought, "Maybe I ought to go over and talk to those guys." So I went over there and talked to the owner, Roy McDonald. "What did you do? How did you accomplish that?" And he was very inspiring. He was telling the story of how he had done it. [He did it by publishing a lot more news.] He started asking me a lot of questions. He started saying, "Yes, you know, you could do a lot of these things in Little Rock. It might work. It might just work." His story is probably one of the greatest in the newspaper industry as far as a business success story. It's incredible what he was able to accomplish. So I became inspired by going to Chattanooga. And I thought, "Well, you know, if we were going to do [only] that, it would be hard to convince my dad by saying, 'Let's give it another go.'" If we were going to try to do this, we would need to try not only what they did in Chattanooga but anything anyone tried anywhere else that worked. Because this was really like the last-gasp effort to save the *Democrat*.

So we went down to Dallas. The *Dallas Times-Herald* had switched their state circulation from afternoon to morning. They were an afternoon paper, and they had started publishing a morning edition. And they had had a lot of success doing that. And they said, "Our circulation has gone up. The people are much more receptive. They were giving up on us because we're an afternoon paper, and Texas is more of a morning newspaper market." So we thought, "Well, there's an idea. Roy McDonald didn't switch to morning, but maybe we should do what Dallas did and deliver the circulation outside Little Rock in the morning. Circulation in the Little Rock area would still be in the afternoon." We got to talking, and we said, "You know, the most basic problem is how we have been operating the *Democrat*, just trying to edit it more cleverly, carve out niches, in areas that the *Gazette* wasn't covering." Our niche was a more intensive level of local coverage. And Bob McCord had done a fairly good job of that. But I said, "You know, the basic problem is that we're not seen as an alternative to the *Gazette*. People almost have to read the *Gazette*. It's a far more complete newspaper. It's got more national, international, state, and local news. It's got more advertising. It's got more display advertising. People who are going to shop at Sears or Penney's or Dillard's that day, it's got the information. It's got the classified advertising." So we started looking at every section. "How could we get more retail advertising in the paper to appeal to readers?" And we started coming up with, "For the *Democrat* to survive, we've got to become an alternative, and we've got to increase our circulation. So everything has got to be focused on 'how do we get readers back in the newspaper?'" So one of the things we looked at was retail advertising. We said, "We could go to the major retail advertisers and say, 'Look, you operate in Tulsa. There's a joint operating agreement in Tulsa. If you run an ad in one Tulsa paper, you pay seven dollars. If you run an ad in both Tulsa papers, you pay eight dollars an inch.'" So it's a no-brainer. They ran in both newspapers in Tulsa. With these alternatives, they forced the advertisers into both newspapers by making it uneconomical to run in only one paper. We said, "Well, we don't have a joint operating agreement in Little Rock." The *Gazette* didn't want to do one of those. But we can make the economics the same. We could say, "We'll just charge you a dollar an inch if you'll duplicate your *Gazette* ad in the *Democrat*. Not if you run different ads." So our newsprint cost, I think, was seventy-two cents an inch. We said, "Hey, to be an alternative, we've got to put out as big a paper as the *Gazette*. If they put out a forty-page Monday paper, we've got to put out a forty-page Monday paper. We can do it because we've got tons of wire service. We're going to get more reporters, but even if the reporters can't fill it up, we can put in more wire service copy. But wouldn't it be better to have a Dillard's ad in there than having just some more wire copy, because there are people who want to read the Dillard's ads?" That's local content. It's advertising. And if we had a full-page ad at one dollar per inch with newsprint cost of seventy-two cents per inch, wouldn't we be better off than another page of wire service copy with no revenue? So then we said, "Really, these are kind of loss leaders. If we go to the four major retailers—Dillard's, Sears, Penney's and Ward's—and get those people to duplicate their ads, then we'll have a large amount of display advertising. We may not have the Mr. Wick's ad, or we may not have some of the smaller ads, but maybe those people will come along after we get more readers." Then we said, "What are we going to do about classified advertising? There are four people who make the decisions on where Dillard's and Sears and Penney's and Ward's run their ads. There are thousands of people in Little Rock every day who decide where they're going to place their classified ads. We can't make thousands of sales presentations. So what can we do?" We heard about this newspaper in Winnipeg, Canada, that had gone to free want ads. So we went to Winnipeg. We flew up there. And several of us went up there, including Paul Smith, our classified ad manager Dave Reddoch, and our circulation manager. Dickie Langford went with us. He had an ad agency, because we were already starting to develop a plan for advertising if we were going to do this. So we went up there, and they said, "It's incredible what happened when we started offering free want ads. About 15 percent of our classified advertising was transient ads, and about 85 percent was commercial accounts." And they said, "So we gave up that 15 percent of our revenues when we went to free want ads. We just forfeited it." They had about 70,000 circulation. Their competitor had about 130,000— not exact numbers, but close. And they said, "Within about three or four months, we went to 90,000 circulation. And the really amazing thing was our classified revenues went up." I said, "How did your revenues go up after you lost the transient ads?" And he said, "Well, all of a sudden, now we had all these free ads. We had all these bargains in the newspaper. People were looking for the bargains. So all of a sudden the auto dealers started saying, 'Hey, there's a lot of readership over there. Let's start running some ads in that paper.' They ran ads and they got good results. And they ran bigger ads. So their classified revenues went up despite the free want ads. Of course, the free want ads were costly because of the newsprint and other costs in producing the ads. But by then it was becoming economical to produce the ads with computerization and cold type compositing."

So we had picked up numerous ideas. From Roy McDonald— put out a bigger news hole with a big emphasis on local news. *Dallas Times Herald* published a morning edition outside their city zone. Winnipeg—do free want ads. Duplicating the big retailers' ads was an internally generated idea. We didn't find anybody who had come up with that idea. Running more color on the front page. And, at that point, we started thinking about this as an overall marketing plan. I went down and talked to my father about it. I said, "You know, I think, given the fact that this newspaper is failing, and we're about to close it down, what if we give it one last shot and try to really become an alternative to the *Gazette* and just see if that will work? And if it won't work, I, for one, would feel much better about saying, 'We tried everything.'" If we did, it was like, "We can try this for ninety days. And if it isn't working, we can say—or we can try it for six months. We don't have to set a time limit of three years on this." This was 1978. And I said, "To do it, we really need to convert to a morning publication out in the state. And that seemed to be the most dramatic thing we were considering doing. But part of the plan was to double the size of the newsroom and get more local reporting, and start covering the same stories the *Gazette* was covering. I said, "It's going to be costly, but it might work. And if it works, then we can resuscitate the newspaper." Anyway, that's what we did. We came up with this plan to do this. He gave me the go-ahead to start the morning edition.

So we started our plan in December of 1978, when we came out with the free want ads. That was the first thing we did. And Bob McCord and I sat down and talked about this. Bob McCord thought it wouldn't work, and he had good reason to think it wasn't going to work. I'm not saying he should have thought it would work. Everybody was skeptical. This was sort of an unheard of—there were little pieces of precedents all over, but nowhere had anyone done anything quite like this. It was a pretty bold effort. Anyway, we started with the free want ads. Bob McCord told me, "You know, you need to get somebody in here who would really believe in this, who could think they could really challenge the *Gazette* and really put out as good a newspaper as the *Gazette*. They can't do it from day one, but eventually they could." And he suggested John Robert Starr. So I went to see Starr. He was in Knoxville, Tennessee: I think he had obtained his master's [degree] in journalism, and he was working on his PhD. So I went to see Starr and talked to him, and Starr was intrigued with the idea and would even consider postponing completing his PhD to come back and do it.

Roy Reed: He had a background here—old reporter, Associated Press.

Hussman: Yes, and to me, if we could find somebody from Arkansas to do it, there was a big plus there. And I think McCord realized that, also. Anyway, we hired Starr. The first year, 1979, we increased the news hole 60 percent. We went from about fifty people in the newsroom to about one hundred people in the newsroom. And we started running color every day. We intentionally tried to publish a few more pages than the *Gazette* every day. If they published a forty-page paper, we'd publish a forty-two-page paper. We had to guess what they were going to do because we didn't know until we picked up the paper. So that way we could call ourselves Arkansas's largest newspaper. That was sort of a stretch. We weren't the largest in circulation, but we were the largest in page count. We were literally a larger paper every day.

And we really had to promote anything we had because we didn't have much to promote. And we were promoting the free want ads and running color; we really promoted the morning edition.

Bob Starr and I went to a marketing seminar in Arizona, and it really dawned on me at that point that the experience here in Little Rock in 1979 had taught me that marketing really is about taking limited resources and maximizing those to try to accomplish some market objective, that no one has infinite resources. And case studies about Xerox or Exxon getting into the office equipment business [illustrated that]. They were the best-financed and the biggest company and all, and they were miserable failures. Why? Because they had too many resources, basically. And you need to focus your resources to maximize what you're doing. And I sat out there and I thought, "That's what we're doing. We've got these limited resources. We've got so many pressmen, yet we're using half the pressmen to put out the morning edition. We're using half the pressmen to put out the afternoon edition, and we don't have enough good pressmen to put out either one of them. And that was just duplicated throughout the whole operation from production to circulation. And I thought, "We ought to just give up on this afternoon edition and then we can focus all of our resources on one edition, the morning edition."

And we came back, and about a month or two later, in October, we switched completely to morning, because the morning circulation was what was going up out in the state, and afternoon circulation was going up some, but not much. Anyway, that's when we became all morning. So that's where we were in 1979.

Well, what happened is immediately our circulation just jumped. It went up significantly, and everything was helping. The morning paper, the free want ads. And all of a sudden the people in Arkansas responded—there were people who didn't like the *Gazette*. Maybe they didn't like their editorial policy. Maybe they didn't like it from years ago in 1957, or maybe they felt they were a little bit arrogant, which they were a bit because they were so dominant. I'm not talking about news, I'm talking about the business operations and advertisers. All of a sudden, people started saying, "Well, hey! These people are really going to challenge the *Gazette*." So a lot of people started taking subscriptions. A lot of advertisers started coming in. So our circulation was going up. But we started losing more money. We had lost more money in 1979 than we had ever lost. In fact, it drug our whole company into the red. We lost, I guess, $5 million in 1979. That's a staggering amount of money to lose. I mean, by 1977 I think we lost $500,000, and that was down from maybe a million our first year. So we really started getting the losses back down where they were more reasonable, and all of a sudden, you know, my dad was, like, "Good grief! Look at the amount of money we're losing." My mother would say, "Look how much money we're losing." I'd say, "I know! It just makes you ill to see that much money being lost. But look at the circulation. It's going up. Look at our advertising. It's going up. We're really having to force-feed this thing to resuscitate it."

Anyway, what happened after the first full year, 1979, was the reality of how much it was costing. We said, "We can't continue to lose this amount of money. We've got to get our losses down. Circulation is still up. Advertising is going up. Great. But this is just too much to lose, so we've got to raise our prices." When we became a morning paper, I think we were charging about $3.60 a month for a seven-day subscription. The *Gazette* was charging about $4.95, about $5.00 a month. So in early 1980 we said, "Okay, we've got to start raising prices. We're going to raise our subscription price from $3.60 to $4.25." And the circulation people here just about had a fit. "We can't raise our rates! We've gained all this circulation. People will stop taking the paper." And I said, "Well, you know, if they stop taking the paper and circulation goes back down, then we'll go out of business. But, you know what? If we don't raise our prices, we'll go out of business. So we don't have any choice. We have got to raise our prices, and if it works, great. And if it doesn't work, then there's no hope." Anyway, we raised our rate. And you know what? Circulation didn't go down. It kept going up. And the next year, 1981, we came back, and we said, "You know what? We've got to raise our prices again." We went from $4.25 to $4.95. We went up and we matched the *Gazette*. We're going to charge $4.95 just like the *Gazette*." Again, our circulation people protested, saying "We can't charge [the same rate] as the *Gazette*. The *Gazette* has been so dominant here for years, we'll never be able to do it." That's what our circulation people said. And I said, "Same reasoning. We have to." We went up on our prices, and again, circulation did not go down. People were willing to pay for a better-quality newspaper. And we're publishing a better newspaper every year—a more interesting newspaper. A lot of hard news. A lot of local news. Anyway, the real acid test comes up the next year. We said, "We've got to raise our prices again." The circulation people tell me, "We can't raise our prices. We'd be higher than the *Gazette*." And I said, "Guess what? We're going to charge more than the *Gazette*. We've got to raise our prices because we've got to have more money to compete." The various departments were always saying, "Well, we need to do this. The *Gazette* is doing that." Anyway, we raised our prices. We wanted to make so many improvements. In 1982 we did an offset conversion on our press. That cost us money. The *Gazette* was still printing letterpress. We started printing by offset lithography. We started printing our "Style" section and some of our "Advance" section down in Hot Springs, where we could print them offset. And they were printed in advance like most Sunday papers. Now part of our Sunday paper was offset. The colors were fantastic. The *Gazette* didn't have it. All that costs money. We had to start getting more revenues—we just didn't have the money as a company. We were a smaller company than the *Gazette*. Our whole company was a smaller company than the *Gazette*. That's one of the myths that's been perpetuated, that we were a much bigger company than the *Gazette*. It's really not true. Anyway, we said, "We've got to have more money," so we raised our price to $5.75 in March 1982. The *Gazette* was $4.95. Well, the *Gazette* wouldn't take that. They raised their price the next month to $5.85. And neither one of us lost circulation. So we realized at that point that there wasn't a lot of price elasticity there. People were willing to pay for a newspaper as long as it was a reasonable price. So as we started raising prices, our revenues started going up even more. The *Democrat*'s revenues from 1974 until about 1978 were fairly flat. They were between about $5 million to $6 million a year. We really couldn't increase our revenues. The *Gazette*'s revenues were going up. From 1974 to 1978, the *Gazette*'s annual revenues increased over 50 percent. In 1978, the *Gazette* revenues were $22.5 million compared to $23.6 million for all our companies. And what happened in 1979 when we really came out with the free want ads and the bigger paper, our revenues started going up. And they really went up significantly. And not only did they go up significantly, but our share between the two newspapers went up. By 1978 our share of revenues was down to about 20 percent. Of course, you can see under our ownership from 1974 to 1978 our share continued to decline. But once we came out with a more competitive product, in 1979, our share of revenues went up. It went up almost every year. It went up every year until we had over half the advertising revenue. So raising our prices helped. The other thing that was amazing was on classified advertising, our classified revenues were, I think, in 1978, about $800,000 a year. Some six years later, by 1984, which was the year the *Gazette* filed a lawsuit against us, our classified revenues were up to almost $4.5 million. It increased more, and it was because of the free want ads. The free want ads brought tremendous additional readership to our classified section, lots more commercial advertisers wanted to run with us. We were able to raise our classified rates by larger percentages—than we could raise our retail rates, because our classified section really gained a lot of readership. And readers would even look in our classified section before they'd look in the *Gazette*'s classified section, even though the *Gazette* had more circulation. So the free want ads were tremendously successful. So we were able to raise prices. By the time the *Gazette* sued us in 1984, we were up to $18 million in revenues. We had taken our revenues from $5 million to $18 million. That's why our share of revenues had gone up, because our revenues were going up faster than the *Gazette*'s revenues. The *Gazette*'s revenues still went up while we were competing with them, but they weren't going up as fast. When we started raising those circulation prices and the advertising rates, our losses started coming down. So I said, "Well, this has a familiar ring. We've been through this in the mid-1970s. We got in and streamlined things. But now our losses were coming down because our market share was going up. We've got an efficiently run newspaper." So in 1984 we made our first profit. I think it was in April. And I think we made, after interest and depreciation, I think we were still paying interest on our note—we had to pay for ten years—and I think we made $14,000. So we took that $14,000 and divided it by three hundred plus employees we had, and everybody got a check for about $42. What was $14,000 to us when we had years when we had lost $5 million? So our losses had started coming down. And then we made money again in May. We made $50,000 in May, and that was after everything—depreciation, interest, et cetera. We made money two months in a row. And we publicized the fact. I mean, we put buttons on. "We're in the black." I've still got my button that says, "We're in the black." We were all so proud of that. Here, we had come from virtually going out of business to actually publishing a newspaper that was an alternative to the *Gazette*. It is still argued that the *Gazette* was a better paper than the *Democrat*, or some people might say the *Democrat* was better. But by then, many people felt like they really needed to read both papers. There were things in the *Democrat* that you just couldn't get in the *Gazette*.

Reed: Was the circulation pretty close to the *Gazette's*?

Hussman: No. We were still behind them. We were really getting close on Sunday. We were at about 80,000 and they were about 120,000 daily.

The first big success had come in classified advertising, and it had been somewhat controversial and set something of a pattern for relations between the two papers. The Gazette *did not immediately respond, except to make fun of the new policy. Paul Smith, the* Democrat's *advertising director, and Dave Reddock, the classified advertising manager, saw immediate results.*

Paul Smith: The first big change we made was in December of 1978. We announced that we were going to run free want ads for anybody in Arkansas who was selling something that they personally owned. No commercial advertising, but if you owned a car, personally, or furniture, or a motor home, or whatever, you could sell it in the *Democrat* with a free want ad. Within a week we had more classified volume than the *Gazette,* not revenue, but volume. We had more pages of classified. Circulation started going up almost immediately. But you can't attribute all of that to free want ads. A month after we started offering free want ads, we switched to a morning paper—a morning publishing cycle—and we increased the news volume in the *Democrat* 60 percent to 70 percent, enough that we started publishing more news than the *Gazette*. So, I think, it was a combination of free want ads, more news, and switching to a morning newspaper that affected circulation. We also became much more aggressive in selling subscriptions. People go to the classified ads because they're trying to find a bargain. And while they're looking for a bargain, they're exposed to the commercial ads that are not free. Initially, the auto dealers and the realtors were upset because we were running free want ads. The auto dealers said we were competing with them by allowing individual owners to advertise their car with a free want ad. But it didn't take long for them to realize their ads were working better in the *Democrat* than ever before. Their ads were working better because we had more people reading our classified section. In fact, it wasn't long until our ads were more effective than ads were in the *Gazette*. People would go to the *Democrat* if they were looking for a car because they knew we'd have ten times as many as the *Gazette*.

Reddock had long been sold on the importance of individual ads, and he had some influence in converting Hussman and Smith to that idea. He had learned of this approach while selling classifieds at the Houston Post.

Dave Reddock: There was where I got my newspaper education. They had begun the *Post* want ads, and they knew the value of private party ads. They had what they called three lines for three days for three dollars. They were catching up with the *Houston Chronicle* in circulation and in classified ad count, because of these private-party ads they were getting in the newspaper. You might have all the big display ads you want, but without those little reader ads—those little private-party ads—you don't have the readership that you need. And that really stuck with me and became really valuable, even more so when I made my move to Arkansas and went to work for the newspaper here. That was in 1975. I took over as classified ad manager in 1976. We averaged about three or four pages of classified daily and maybe six pages—maybe sometimes seven pages—on Sunday. I could see right away that the main problem we had in the classified section was the anemic condition of the ad count we had. The main count you need in classified is ad count. Ad count is more important than measuring space. The more readers you bring into the paper, the more people have to buy the paper. Your circulation goes up, so everything ties in from the classified perspective. I had to actually sell management on this theory—talking to Paul Smith and then him relaying the messages to Walter. Well, it was Walter who heard of a newspaper in Winnipeg, Canada, that had free want ads, and, man, they were getting a bunch of them. So he called up there and made the arrangements [to visit them].

[When we started] Dick Lankford drew up a half-page ad—big, bold—if I remember right, it was either color or at least all-black reverse. And all it said was, "D-Day is here! Call 372-FREE." And we ran it in the *Arkansas Gazette*. He called the *Gazette,* as an agency can, and reserved a half-page space—didn't give the client's name and purposely brought the slick in—the ad in—right at the deadline. When everyone was gone he took it to the pressroom. They pasted it down at the last minute. So the *Gazette* promoted in their *big* Sunday paper our free want ads. So that was kind of the shot that was heard around the world, so to speak, in the newspaper war. A business couldn't use the ads free, but any private party could run an ad—five lines for a week, absolutely free. We set up a separate room at the *Democrat* with a phone bank. I think we initially set up twelve phones and operators. We wound up having to pretty much double that. We just didn't know [how the people would respond] because this had not been a private-party market. But I'll tell you what, *did they respond.* People *loved* it. The telephone lines *lit up,* and they *stayed* lit. In fact, there was a problem—people trying to call in and they couldn't get through and they were put on hold for too long, so we had to put in more phones. We had to hire more people. It was just absolutely amazing. So, just right away, we jumped up from about three or four pages of classified a day to twelve to fourteen pages of classified, with literally thousands of reader ads in there. We were up to twenty pages and over on Sunday of classified. All at once, the *Gazette* had the little, small classified section with hardly *any* private-party ads. Jerry, we had people who would come before daylight to the *Democrat* pressroom trying to get a copy of the classified section because they knew if they didn't get that classified section *early* and go through and circle those ads on the items they wanted, if they waited, they might be gone. And it was just amazing. The people were so hungry for an avenue to sell items that it became like one giant central Arkansas garage sale. The readership went up, and as readership went up, circulation went up. Then our classified display advertising went up. As the readership went up, classified went up. Walter and Paul were happy. And the *Gazette*—you know what they did? They *laughed* at us. They mocked us. They thought we were crazy.

Smith: We realized that if we had more news than the *Gazette* but didn't have the advertising that they had, there would be a serious deficiency. People buy newspapers for all the information in them. With our free want ads, we had corrected the imbalance in classifieds to the point that we actually had more classified information than the *Gazette*. We were publishing more news because the owners were willing to beef up the staff and buy the newsprint necessary to publish more news than the *Gazette*. But we still had a problem in retail advertising. At that time, the *Gazette* had about 95 percent of the department store advertising—Sears, Montgomery Ward, J. C. Penney's, Dillard's, Cohn's—so we went to the department store advertisers and said, "If you will duplicate your ads from the *Gazette* into the *Democrat*, we'll sell this advertising to you for one dollar an inch." The plan wasn't designed to try to create a lot of revenue, because the newsprint was going to cost that much. It was designed to give us the same department store ads as the *Gazette*, so that if someone decided to subscribe to the *Democrat* instead of the *Gazette*, they would have the same advertising information. It really wasn't designed to hurt the *Gazette*. We didn't go to them and say, "Give us more advertising," or, "Give us advertising the *Gazette* doesn't have." We asked for the same ads that were in the *Gazette*. It was designed to try to eliminate a deficiency that readers would consider that we had.

Jerry McConnell: Did you pick up quite a bit of department store advertising?

Smith: We didn't with Cohn's. We didn't get much of their business, but we were successful in getting Sears, Dillard's, Ward's, and Penney's to duplicate their ads. We only offered this to department store advertisers, but we offered it to *all* department store advertisers. This was starting, I believe, in January of 1979. And it continued for several years. Having the department store ads probably didn't help us get new readers because the *Gazette* had the same ads. It just somewhat negated the advantage they had.

The other major development in early 1979, and it was a major development, was to get more news into the Democrat. *When the* Democrat *started running more pages than the* Gazette, *that created a huge hole for news. While the* Democrat *had started getting more advertising, it still didn't have as much as the* Gazette, *so that meant all that empty space had to be filled with news. Starr was given the authority to hire a lot more people, and he delegated some of that to his department heads. Bill Husted was the city editor at the time, and he remembers it vividly.*

Bill Husted: I'll never forget meeting John Robert Starr and sitting down with him. He said, "What do we need to beat the *Gazette*?" I thought of it in terms of bargaining with a car salesman, so I gave him an overly inflated list of things we needed, as far as the number of reporters and some other changes. In what must be a really great management technique, after I gave him that long list, he said, "Okay, it's all yours. Now you've got to beat them. You have no excuses."

Wally Hall: Sports was the first place we put an emphasis on in the newspaper war. We became the largest sports section in America on Sundays. It was huge. And, you know, in retrospect, we burned out some really good newspaper people putting that out because we didn't increase staff. We went from a sixteen-page section to twenty-four, and we began to really make inroads.

Rex Nelson started at the Democrat *as a sportswriter; left to become editor of the daily paper in his hometown, Arkadelphia; and then returned in 1985 as assistant sports editor to Wally Hall.*

McConnell: When you got back in 1985, how was the competition between the *Democrat* and *Gazette*?

Rex Nelson: It had tightened up. I mean, there was still a *big* gap when I was there in 1981 and 1982. By 1985 the *Democrat* had started to pretty seriously close the gap—[we were] still in the old second-floor newsroom, but the equipment had gotten a little better. The travel budget had gotten a little better. And you felt by then, just in those few years that I'd been gone, that you were suddenly on a little more of an even playing field. We still considered ourselves—again, the blue-collar, number two—"We try harder." I think that's part of what we used to drive our staff.

McConnell: At what point did the *Democrat* and the *Gazette* get in the mode of trying to decide who could send the most people to cover things?

Nelson: Oh, yes, flooding the zone. That had started by then. I mean, we sent a huge number of people. I remember when I was assistant sports editor in 1985, Arkansas played in the Holiday Bowl in San Diego. Big expense because it's a long way, and San Diego's not a cheap trip. And I remember, it seems like we sent half the staff to

San Diego. It got even bigger the next year when Arkansas played Oklahoma in the Orange Bowl. Now, that wasn't the famous one where [Arkansas] won. This was when they got blown out at the end of the 1986 season—January 1st of 1987. I was already in Washington at the time, but Wally called me in Washington. Congress was out of session anyway, which was what I was covering by then. He said, "Look, Walter wants to print a special section *every day*." He basically needed somebody who could write a lot *fast*. He said, "I'm going to need some *help* down here." I said, "Look, if the paper wants to pay my way to Miami for a week during the middle of winter, that sounds great." We had a special section every day leading up to that game and then had eight open pages the day after the game, and that was a night game. So a lot of those we had to put together with advance features and so forth. But it had an eight-page, wide-open section on the Orange Bowl, actually, on January 1st of 1987.

Jim Bailey clearly remembers that thrust in sports and its repercussions. Bailey wrote sports for the Gazette *from 1956 until it closed in 1991. He was a great sportswriter and the confidant and friend of his boss, Orville Henry, who hired him. When they started an Arkansas Sportswriters Hall of Fame, Henry was the first person inducted, and Bailey was the second. Bailey later went to work for the* Arkansas Democrat-Gazette, *where he says he was welcomed and treated admirably.*

Jim Bailey: Yes, they did [expand their sports section greatly]. In the football season—I don't have any idea how many sports pages they had, but it seems like it was two or three or four times as much as the *Gazette* had on Sundays. Virtually every college football game in the country, even Ivy League—if the Associated Press ran fifteen inches on the wire on Army and Lehigh, or whatever, they'd have all fifteen inches in there under a big headline. Starr was always shooting at Orville [Henry] in his columns about his affinity for the Razorbacks and this, that, and the other. But the *Democrat* was also pouring tons of copy on the Razorbacks, of course. They were covering it heavily and, at the same time, blasting Orville for covering it too much. Obviously, they thought sports was the *Gazette*'s strong point, and that's where they attacked both with increasing their own sports coverage and Starr's constant yammering in his columns about Orville. I told Orville once that it's strange that if he [Starr] thought the *Gazette* had such a weak point, he'd go to such pains to warn them about it.

I think everybody in the state pretty well understood that [sports was the *Gazette*'s strength] except the *Gazette* ownership. Orville was one of the rare assets who could single-handedly sell papers.

McConnell: Did they [the *Gazette*] open up much space or hire extra people in the sports department?

Bailey: They would replace people who left, but they didn't really expand the number of people that much. And the space was, of course, almost always at a premium. The things the *Democrat* was doing—opening up a lot of space—and I'm speaking now specifically of sports—opening up a lot of extra space, doing a lot of extra things—the *Gazette* did not in any way respond in kind.

The failure of the Gazette *to respond to the* Democrat's *big change in sports coverage led to the first cataclysmic change in the* Gazette *sports department, which had dominated sports coverage in the state for at least forty years. That was the decision by sports editor Orville Henry to move to Fayetteville and relinquish his chance to maintain direct control of the sports department that he had created. Here's how Henry described his decision in an interview by Bailey for the* Gazette *oral history project.*

Orville Henry: I said, "Mr. Patterson, you won't let us hire this person," or "You won't let us have this much space," or "You won't let us have this little money to compete with them. Do this for me then, let me go to Fayetteville, where I don't have to wear myself out traveling and a lot of other things, and we can compete better with them if I am up there." He said, "Fine. Okay." I remained sports editor, but I went to Fayetteville.

The extra space soon had an impact on regular news, as well as sports. Similarly, the Gazette *did not respond. Here's how it was viewed by Max Brantley, an assistant city editor and then the regular city editor, in an interview by Ernie Dumas for the* Gazette *oral history.*

Max Brantley: Hussman made the commitment to publish the biggest newspaper in Arkansas, that is, the most number of pages, and beefed up his staff. The *Gazette* never, never, never, in the Patterson era, made the commitment to newsprint expenditure that Hussman did. And even if we had covered the same stories, even if we had done the same thing, we had no place to print them. It got worse and worse until the late 1980s.

The people at the Democrat *were delighted. Several* Democrat *veterans say that the* Gazette's *inaction, the lack of response, gave the* Democrat *a chance to learn how to compete, that they were to a degree flying blind in the early stages. One of those was Larry Graham, who took over as* Democrat *circulation director in June 1980.*

Larry Graham: In the early 1980s we were learning how to compete. I had never been in a competitive market. We were learning how we should sell. In the early 1980s we weren't a very good newspaper. Many mornings I would come in at eight a.m., and we would still be printing that day's paper. Our production wasn't very good. We were printing the paper late. We were producing a large paper with the free classifieds, as you know. The paper was substantial. I think as a newspaper we were all learning how to do our jobs. I think we were lucky in that the *Gazette* at that time was such a dominant competitor they basically ignored us. In the circulation department, they weren't selling. They didn't have a sales staff. They didn't have a telemarketing operation. They didn't have door-to-door salespeople. They didn't have to sell, because they were the dominant paper. We were trying to figure out how to sell and service our subscribers. We were not doing a good job servicing our customers, printing the paper, or selling. We started trying to get better. We started trying to sell our paper. We experimented with different structures to try and improve our circulation. I think that one of the things that Walter and Paul allowed me to do was to experiment. When I arrived here, we didn't have any district managers. They had these part-time home counselors that they paid three hundred dollars a month that delivered papers and would take care of the ten or twenty papers in their neighborhood. They were not employees. I think I was here about a year, and we eliminated that system in Pulaski County and went to twelve district managers. We hired a telemarketing outfit to sell for us. We contracted with a company to sell door-to-door with a bunch of kids. We were learning how to do this stuff. We would do some direct mail. We had some early successes in the 1980s. We had some small circulation gains in the early 1980s. Not substantial, but we started to get better. Our production department was getting more consistent. We converted our presses from letterpress to offset, so our paper started looking a little better. We bought more racks to put out—I don't know how many—in a two-to-three-year period. We generally bought about two hundred a year, so over a two- or three-year period we increased our locations by five hundred or six hundred. I decided to hire adults to sell the paper. We hired a couple and had a little bit of success. Sometime in 1984 I hired a new sales manager by the name of Jerry Reeves. He was from Joplin, Missouri—and had been the circulation director up there. Prior to that, I think Jerry had sold insurance door-to-door and managed salespeople. I hired him, basically, to hire a bunch of door-to-door salespeople. We were trying to figure out how to sell subscriptions door-to-door. We converted to an employee telemarketing operation. We decided we wanted to do it ourselves, so we cancelled the contract. [We] hired our own telemarketing supervisor [and] our own employees. We thought we could do it better ourselves [and] have more control over it. We were doing a lot of things in the sales department. Over here in service we were also trying to get better. Walter and Paul let me experiment with several different things. We went from these twelve district managers—we went from, like, twelve to twenty people overnight. We were experimenting over there with several different types of structures to improve our service. It didn't work very well. I guess every time you experimented it may have improved service a little bit. We used that structure for about a year. Then we eliminated that, and we went to an assistant district manager and a district manager. We had about twenty-five of those people trying to improve service. In the sales department, we were trying to figure out how to sell there. I guess we had a little bit of success because—I guess it was in 1984 that the *Gazette* filed their lawsuit against the *Democrat*.

One other innovation the Democrat *tried was having the carriers place the* Democrat *on the porch at each house, rather than throwing it in the yard.*

Graham: We were trying to figure out in west Little Rock how to make inroads into this area where they [the *Gazette*] were so strong, so we started testing porching the paper. One of the areas I remember doing myself [was] Pleasant Forest Drive that runs off Rodney Parham in west Little Rock. We sampled six hundred homes every day, putting the paper on the porch. The very first morning we went out there, [we] tied a balloon to the paper and put it on the porch. We probably had about thirty people out there blowing up balloons and delivering papers on porches. We delivered a free paper to everybody for a month, and then at [the end of] that month we went back and asked how many people wanted to keep taking the paper. I forget how much circulation we grew. We grew quite a bit, and we started delivering papers on porches in that area.

We had also been experimenting in some other areas, but we decided to go hog-wild putting papers on porches. So we started trying to put the papers on porches in these areas of town where we thought we could grow, which was mainly west Little Rock, the Heights, and Lakewood in North Little Rock. It was, like, a four- or five-year project from 1984 to 1988 or 1989. In fact, at one point we had a hard time keeping papers on porches because the *Gazette* was in the driveway. My carriers would ride by and see the *Gazette* in the driveway and throw ours in the driveway. It was a real struggle trying to condition our carrier to walk past the *Gazette* and put it on the porch. At one point we had four or five people that all they did every morning was go out and ride behind our carriers and see if they put them on the porch. We called these people "porch monkeys." That wasn't our official title for them, but I think that's what our district managers called them. We terminated a lot of carriers who refused to put them on the porch.

Then by the late 1980s, we did it. We aggressively, in most areas of the town, put papers on porches. Just like the tube project—about a year and a half after we did that, the *Gazette* came in and tried to— started putting up tubes. Well, when we started putting papers on porches, they tried to put papers on porches. We just did a better job than they did. We did a better job with the tubes. We did a better job putting papers on porches. Our people were just good at it.

Apparently the people at the Patterson Gazette *weren't convinced it was such a great idea.*

Bob McCord: When I went to work at the *Gazette* I begged Hugh to do that, but Leon Reed, who ran the circulation department all those years, said, "Bob, that's ridiculous." And, to my grave, I will tell you I think that it was important in choosing the *Democrat* over the *Gazette*.

The Gazette's *unwillingness to get down into the trenches with the*

Democrat *led to the first big staff raid in the war when the* Democrat *hired away Randy Moss from the* Gazette *in 1984. Now a horseracing analyst for ESPN and ABC, Moss worked as a sportswriter for the* Gazette *from 1979 to 1984 but handicapped the horses (picked the Morning Line) during racing season at Oaklawn Park. Both papers sold a lot of extra copies during racing season at Oaklawn, but the* Gazette *at this time was really selling because of Moss's success. He was unusually successful in picking winners because he was one of the first handicappers in the area to use a speed rating.*

Randy Moss: During that 1984 horseracing season, toward the end of the season in April, Wally Hall came up to me in the press box and started sort of half-jokingly asking me when I was gonna come to work for the *Democrat*. And finally about the third or fourth time he said something, I said, "Well, when are you gonna make me an offer?" And he said, "Well, I tell ya what, just put down on a sheet of paper what it would take for you to come to work for the *Democrat*." I had no real desire at the time to do it. I was making $15,000 a year for the *Gazette*. Back then in 1984. You know, nobody's gonna get rich working in the newspaper business, so I decided to just sort of call their bluff and I doubled it. I put $30,000 down on a sheet of paper, and I handed it to Wally, and Wally took it—you know, didn't say anything. The next day, which was Arkansas Derby day, last day of the racing season—he came up to me in the press box and he said, "You got a deal." And I said, "You're kidding." And he said, "No, you got a deal." And I said, "Well, I'm gonna need to talk to the *Gazette* about it. I'll get back to you early next week." So Orville was gone the first of next week, and so I needed to talk to somebody. This was before cell phones, so I couldn't reach Orville. So I called Carrick Patterson and I told Carrick what the situation was, and that the *Democrat* had made me a pretty generous offer, and he said, "I'll get Orville. I know where Orville is. I'll get Orville, and I'll call you back." So Carrick called me back a little later in the afternoon and said he had reached Orville on the phone, and Orville advised him not to match the offer. And, you know, he said, "We'd like you to stay at the *Gazette*. I would be very disappointed if you went to the *Democrat*. I always thought if you left the *Gazette* it would be for some place like the *Daily Racing Form* or something like that. I never really thought you'd, you know, sink to the level of going to the *Democrat.*" So I called Wally back and told him I would take the job. I would later see Orville in press boxes—Razorback games, primarily, and he wouldn't speak to me for the longest time. [Moss had been doing the Morning Line for the *Gazette* ever since he was in the eleventh grade and did it under someone else's name. Henry hired him right out of college, and they had been close all that time.] And I want to say it was about 1988, maybe, and we were in the press box at Texas Stadium covering an Arkansas-SMU game, and I was in the food line in the press box, and suddenly behind me I hear somebody making a horse whinny sound. And I turned around, and Orville's standing right behind me with this big grin on his face. We started talking again at that point, and it wasn't until years later that I found out what exactly had happened. Orville told me. He was playing golf at Augusta National with Jack Stephens. It's very difficult to be able to play a round of golf at Augusta National, that is something that very few [outsiders] get to do, and Orville got to do it every year—one round every year with Jack prior to the Masters. [Stephens was president of the Masters at the time.] He was on the course, and Carrick Patterson called him off the course. And Orville was furious at being called off the course for any reason. And he got to the phone, and he found out that Carrick wanted to talk to him about some horseracing handicapper kid making $15,000 a year, and Orville said he was so angry at being pulled off the golf course at Augusta National, he just said, "Let him go. Let him go."

Moss said the Democrat *never told him how many papers they were selling in Hot Springs, but they were really promoting him.*

Moss: The newspaper war was going pretty hot and heavy at the time, and the *Gazette* had begun to advertise the Oaklawn handicapping and advertised me and put me in half-page house ads and things of this sort. And I remember one of the very first things I did when I came over to the *Democrat* in 1984—they hustled me over to a TV studio and taped a TV commercial, in which they gave me a script and everything, and I basically was saying on the TV commercial that I essentially "saw the light and switched from the *Gazette* to the *Democrat,* and you should, too." And you can imagine, as someone who was given his very first newspaper job by Orville Henry and still felt a great deal of affection for the *Gazette,* it made me very uncomfortable. It was sort of like they wanted me to thumb my nose at the *Gazette* while I was walking out the door. But in the end I did it. I guess I had to have some allegiance to the people that were now paying my salary.

That was during the heyday for Oaklawn, when there were no other race tracks within hundreds of miles open at that time of the year, and the Arkansas Derby might draw as many as seventy thousand fans. That had changed by 1989, when Moss was hired by the Dallas Morning News, *which had been engaged in a newspaper war of its own.*

The Democrat *had launched the newspaper war on December 3, 1979, when it started offering free classifieds, and the* Gazette *never responded in any major way until 1983, when it came up with a classified promotion of its own, offering classified ads for three days for three lines for three dollars. It widely promoted its program as three-three-three, and the* Democrat *quickly responded with an ad that said, "Who needs three-three-three when you can get free-free-free?" The* Gazette *was obviously feeling an impact by this time. The* Democrat *had only $796,535 in classified revenue in 1978, while the* Gazette *made $3,831,242. The* Democrat *took in $1,162,886 in 1979, and kept growing each year, while the* Gazette *income went down slightly each year through 1982, when the* Democrat *earned $2,423,762 and the* Gazette *took in $3,434,977. The* Democrat *still had a lot more classified ads, which was helping its circulation to grow. After the* Gazette *started its promotion, its classified revenue started growing again.*

Hussman: When they came up with this three, three, three—look what happened to their classified revenues. It went from $3.4 million in 1982 to $4 million in 1983 to $5.6 million in 1984 to $6.4 million in 1985. That's when they really started getting more competitive. And it paid off for them.

Walter's point was that the Gazette *would have fared better if it had been more competitive. While the* Gazette's *classified earnings went up to $6.4 million in 1985, the* Democrat's *take was still growing even faster, having reached $5,457,996 that year.*

Smith: The *Gazette* should have reacted to free want ads quickly. Their three lines for three days for three dollars didn't work. And they kept changing it until finally they went to three lines for fourteen days for three dollars. But it still didn't work. When the *Gazette* introduced their three-three-three classified plan, they promoted it with the largest multimedia campaign ever for a local company in this market. They had a massive television schedule of very elaborate commercials. We countered with a ten-second commercial featuring an elderly actress from Dallas. We chose her because our commercial was very hard-hitting and somewhat sarcastic. We thought a grandmotherly type would get more acceptance from readers for this type commercial. In the commercial, she first held up copies of both papers and then asked, "Who needs three-three-three, when I've got free-free-free? Where were those other guys when I needed them?" The *Gazette*'s massive advertising campaign created interest in selling personal merchandise with classified advertising, but most of the people who responded ran their ads in the *Democrat* instead of the *Gazette*. The *Gazette*'s advertising greatly increased our volume of free want ads, thus increasing our classified readership.

McConnell: They still weren't getting as many classifieds as you had.

Smith: No, and their pride kept them from going to free. They lost more money by running a three-line ad for fourteen days for three dollars than it would have cost them to run a free ad for three days. But they had laughed at us when we announced free want ads and they just were not going to swallow their pride and go to free want ads. And it helped us greatly.

If the Gazette *was not doing much to challenge the* Democrat *financially, some* Gazette *staffers wondered why it didn't do more to respond to* Democrat *claims about how it was gaining ground. The* Democrat *was not shy about making such claims and in fact, at the behest of Paul Smith, set up its own in-house advertising agency to extol its gains and also to save money and react more quickly to any counterclaims. Smith hired Estel Jeffrey, who had a life-long background in journalism, away from the* Conway Log Cabin Democrat *to be marketing director for the* Democrat.

Estel Jeffrey: My job was to help the *Democrat* with not only image but to combat anything the *Gazette* was doing at the time. I'd match them step for step and contest any step they might make. So I was in charge of doing all the TV commercials, the radio commercials, the billboards, all the newspaper ads—anything that required promoting the *Democrat*. Also, I had to do reader contests to get reader involve-ment—pull readers away. I supported circulation in their marketing efforts at the time, editorial also, and advertising. My job was to sup-port them. We took care of everything in-house because we could do it faster. We could turn quicker, and in a lot of cases that made a big difference.

When it [the *Gazette*] was still privately owned [by the Patterson family], I think the main thing that we pushed that I can remember is that we were growing. Our theme was more. Everything was more, more, more. More pages, more news. We'd get ABC [Audit Bureau of Circulations] reports, and we were always growing faster than they were growing. We were showing how their circulation on a graph was going parallel and ours was coming straight up at them.

Paul Smith told me one day when I was still at the *Log Cabin*. He said, "Boy, I hope that big old' dog doesn't wake up over at Third and Louisiana because we're in trouble." But I think that was every-body's feelings here—we would do something—sometimes we'd get a response. But, Jerry, I really felt like they felt it would be beneath them to respond to us because I think they felt if they responded to us, then people would see that as a sign of weakness.

Ron Robinson had become the executive for the Gazette *account in 1978 while working for the Cranford and Johnson advertising agency. He later became president of the firm.*

McConnell: When this all happened, what was the reaction of the *Gazette* hierarchy to all these moves by Walter?

Ron Robinson: By the *Gazette* senior management, I think, there was a feeling that the *Gazette* was the *Gazette,* and how dare they think that they were number one? I mean, and why shouldn't they feel that way to a certain degree after being around for so long? I always felt like management thought that the Hussmans would just eventually run out of money.

McConnell: Did the *Gazette* utilize Cranford [and] Johnson to do some of their ads for use in the competition with the *Democrat*?

Robinson: Yes and no. Yes, from the standpoint that the *Gazette* had a larger advertising budget, but the management of the *Gazette* simply did not want to go in a head-to-head defensive posture. I constantly was trying to get the *Gazette* to debunk the *Democrat*'s claims. The publisher and I disagreed about that, and he won. But, you know, it was very hard to get him into a posture of really using all the weapons we could to debunk those claims because he just didn't think the *Gazette* should lower itself to get into a newspaper fight like that. There were many different kinds of ads that were very effective. I was also very close to lots of people on the staff of the *Gazette* as well, being a former staff member myself, and I can assure you that as the competition heated up, the staff was thinking one way, but management was thinking another. "They'll eventually run out of money, they'll eventually give up, they'll eventually run its course, and we've been here since 1819."

During this particular period, the *Democrat* was sponsoring virtually anybody who wanted to do something in this town from a community service standpoint. The *Democrat* wanted to sign on to do it. Well, it was hard to get the *Gazette* to do it unless *Gazette* management had a personal interest in it. There was also a reluctance of the *Gazette,* unlike the *Democrat,* to be a co-media sponsor with anybody. They didn't want to be in there with those television guys, those radio people. You know? Please! And there was no reluctance whatsoever as far as the *Democrat* was concerned. "We'll do anything with [Channels] 7, 11, and 4 and KRAY and KARN, or anybody else who wants to ride." One of the things that finally made a difference, I think, was that the *Democrat* was able to convince people in Little Rock, at least, that the *Democrat* was the community newspaper of Little Rock. And that the *Gazette* was an Arkansas newspaper with its offices in Little Rock.

McConnell: At this time you were making recommendations to the *Gazette,* were any of those written, or were those mostly verbal?

Robinson: They were written. Absolutely. In 1984, when the *Gazette* v. *Democrat* antitrust suit came down, the records of the *Gazette* at Cranford [and] Johnson were subpoenaed. I remember that Annabelle Clinton Imber, who [became] a judge, was one of the attorneys who was in charge of this particular aspect at the Wright Lindsey and Jennings firm (which represented the *Democrat*). She and her people came over one day, served that subpoena, and made eight thousand copies of the records—of the *Gazette* proposals and everything out of our records. Mostly my files. and then I went through a three-day deposition. Based upon that. And one of the things I particularly will never forget is that some of those that I wrote were internal staff memos that basically had to apologize to the creative staff over and over again to the fact that they'd done fabulous work as far as trying to create proposals for the *Gazette* to run, but the publisher had decided that he didn't want to. We certainly provided the ammunition; there was just a reluctance to fire the gun. I can tell you this: that I have never discussed it with him directly, but I have had people tell me that Mr. Hussman read every one of them. And had expressed the fact that he was glad the *Gazette* management decided not to do what we proposed.

CHAPTER 8

The Trial

THE BELEAGUERED LEADERS at the Arkansas Democrat *found a cause for optimism when the paper finally turned a profit, albeit a small one, in April of 1984 and then had an even bigger profit in May. They could finally see some hope after a period of consistent losses, and suddenly they were hit by a lawsuit by the* Arkansas Gazette *that, if successful, could have put the* Democrat *out of business.*

The Gazette *filed suit on December 12, 1984, in federal court in Little Rock, charging the* Democrat *with violating the US Sherman Antitrust Act, two other federal acts, and the Arkansas Unfair Practices Act. All of the arguments were hashed over in a twelve-day jury trial in March 1986, and the eleven-member jury (one juror had been excused) voted unanimously for the* Democrat *on all four counts.*

The trial turned into a battle between two celebrated lawyers and testimony from a battery of expensive expert witnesses, who differed sharply on the merits of the case. The Gazette's *lead attorney was Steve Susman of Houston, one of the top antitrust attorneys in the South. The* Democrat's *attorney was Philip Anderson of the Little Rock firm Wright, Lindsey and Jennings, who had represented the* Democrat *since the Hussmans bought it in 1974 and later was elected president of the American Bar Association.*

Philip Anderson: The *Gazette* was trying to stand the antitrust law on its ear if you will. The antitrust law exists to encourage competition. Competition makes you better, and that was our theme during that trial. Competition makes you better, and competition should be rewarded. The truth of the matter is that the *Gazette* had not ever had strong competition from the *Democrat*. The *Democrat's* contracts with the unions that were at the *Democrat* when the Hussman family bought the paper had been negotiated by the *Gazette*. The *Democrat* had just let the *Gazette* negotiate with the unions, and whatever the *Gazette* worked out with the unions was fine with the prior owner of the *Democrat*. It was not a serious competitor. Walter Hussman was the first real competition that the *Gazette* felt, and Hugh Patterson thought that it was unfair.

I was astonished [by the suit]. I learned about it on the afternoon of December 12, 1984, when Walter called me and told me that he had been served with a summons. It seemed crazy to me—just foolish, because it was all over [about] competition. A lot of people said after the news came out the next morning about the lawsuit—a number of businessmen around the city of Little Rock said to me, "I've faced competition every day, and Hugh Patterson is just not used to it."

The *Gazette* accused the *Democrat* of predatory practices. Those predatory practices included selling newspaper advertising to the major advertisers in Little Rock at one dollar an inch if they would repeat the program [ad] that they had in the *Arkansas Gazette*. We can get back to why that was done, although I'm sure other people that you've interviewed told you about that. It made perfect sense. There were free want ads. Free want ads were looked upon by the *Gazette* as a predatory practice. Price cutting on advertising—going off the rate card—was alleged to have been a predatory practice. Free newspaper delivery to our prospective customers—the *Democrat* tried to break into areas where it did not have high circulation. It was viewed at the time as a blue-collar paper. The newspaper was delivered free on routes [where] the *Democrat* would like to have subscribers in order to attract advertisers, because of the demographics of the neighborhood. The subscribers to the *Gazette* were generally more affluent than those who subscribed to the *Democrat* and were more attractive to the advertisers to reach. There may have been some other practices, Jerry. We can look at some of the documents we have to flesh that out. But, the one-dollar-an-inch advertising program that Walter Hussman came up with was because people read newspapers to read ads—to see the advertising as well as to get the news. They got the news too, but they also read the newspaper to see the ads. If the ads from Dillard's and the other large department stores were not in the *Democrat*, people would not read the *Democrat*. They would gravitate to the *Gazette*.

Well, the case was submitted on four counts to the jury—two counts under the federal antitrust laws and two counts under the state unfair competition statutes. The jury found for the *Democrat* on all four counts. Basically, the *Gazette* was claiming that the *Democrat* was trying to put them out of business, that its pricing practices were predatory, and that predatory behavior was unlawful under the federal statutes and unlawful under the state unfair competition statutes. But, in order to prevail, the *Gazette* had to show that the *Democrat* had market power. That was something, as I said, [that] could not be shown given the fact that the *Gazette* was profitable, had more circulation, [and] had more advertising than the *Democrat* did. It was clearly by every measure the dominant newspaper.

That's why the lawsuit seemed so foolish and ill advised, because it seems obvious that as long as it was profitable, as long as it was dominant in circulation, advertising, and revenues, then it couldn't show that the *Democrat* had market power. Because market power means the power to set prices, and the *Democrat* did not have that power. The *Gazette* itself had market power, because when it raised its advertising rates advertisers felt that they had to be in that newspaper. It raised rates and took advertising dollars from the advertising budget that could have been used to buy advertising in the *Democrat*. In other words, by raising its rates—which it had the power to do because advertisers had to be in that newspaper—it was making advertising dollars unavailable to the *Democrat*.

Whether it was foolish or not, the lawsuit shook up everybody at the Democrat, *including the general manager, Paul Smith, who had helped develop much of the* Democrat *strategy.*

Paul Smith: [I viewed it with] discouragement and apprehension. We had fought and clawed our way to the point where we were occasionally making a profit, and the trend lines showed that we should eventually be in a solid financial position. If you look at where we came from—market share, both circulation and advertising—the trend lines indicated that it was just a matter of time before we were a viable competitor in this market. Our share of advertising revenue had gone from 18 percent in 1978 to 38 percent in 1984. I believe that was the motivation for the lawsuit, I think our profitable months frightened them, and they took this extreme action to try to stop our progress. But the lawsuit certainly was a shock and a disappointment. We didn't think it was a legitimate lawsuit, but people sometimes lose lawsuits that are not legitimate. So there was a real danger. It cost us about $1.25 million just to prepare for it and to defend it. That was approximately one-third of what the company paid for the *Democrat*.

The documents produced by the discovery process were voluminous, and many of them were also presented at the trial.

Anderson: The document production started immediately upon joining issues in this case. Walter told me that he wanted me to get the case to trial as quickly as we could. He didn't want any delays. He wanted us to get a trial date and hold on to it. He wanted us to respond to discovery within the thirty days allowed for doing so on the various requests for documents. We didn't get any extensions of time. We were on a fast track. The case was filed on December 12, 1984, and was tried in March of 1986. There was enormous discovery on both sides. There was no protective order. We tried to work out a protective order to protect information that was deemed confidential, proprietary, competitive information. We wanted to restrict financial information from the *Democrat* just to the lawyers for the plaintiff and Hugh Patterson, and we would agree to restrict the information obtained from the *Gazette* just to Walter Hussman. They didn't want to do that. We were on a conference call with Judge Overton—that is, the lawyers were, and Walter Hussman was on the conference call with us. We were trying to work out a protective order to protect the financial information. Walter realized that he was not going to be able to keep his information completely away from people other than Hugh Patterson. He said, "We just won't have a protective order. Let's abandon the effort." So everything that was produced in discovery was available to everyone. About a month before the case went to trial, Walter and Paul Smith and the other principal people at the [*Democrat*] for advertising—the advertising manager [and] the circulation manager, came to our offices. At that time I was practicing with Wright, Lindsey and Jennings, and we had a large room set aside where all of these exhibits were kept. The people from the *Democrat* worked all day every weekday into the night going through the evidence that we had obtained from the *Gazette*. They started work I think around six a.m. at the *Democrat* and came over to our offices around nine a.m. or nine thirty. And they stayed into the night going through reams and reams of documents.

And they turned up numerous instances of off-the-rate-card deals that the *Gazette* had been putting together in recent years. That is to say, undercutting their statement that they [the *Gazette*] didn't sell off the rate card. They did sell off the rate card.

Those documents also contained other information that the Democrat *found useful and some that confirmed many of their suspicions about how the* Gazette *operated, particularly in its advertising department, as well as the attitude at the* Gazette.

Smith: Well, they were really arrogant. And they didn't want to react to things that we did at the *Democrat* because it would appear to their readers and advertisers that they were worried about us. They didn't really seem to have an offensive strategy. They wouldn't react to something that we did until they came to the conclusion that it was hurting them, and then they would react, but it was always defensive, and it was often too late to be effective. I'll give you an example. We had all of the coupon advertising. Tom Kemp, the ad director at the *Gazette,* had gone to call on the coupon advertisers and asked why they had switched their business from the *Gazette* to the *Democrat.* He came back and wrote a memo to Hugh Patterson. In the memo, he said that the previous *Gazette* ad director had insulted the largest coupon distributor. Back then the post office required that you show the names of the newspapers that carried the preprint on the front of the preprint. Preprint advertisers would sometimes list forty or fifty newspapers in their supplement line. Otherwise, when they got through printing the circulation for each newspaper, they'd have to shut the press down and replate the front page, and it would cost a lot more money due to drastically lengthening the press run. The *Gazette* wouldn't allow any other newspaper's name to be on a preprint that went in their paper. One of the preprint advertisers, Valassis, made a mistake, and the preprint showed up at the *Gazette* with multiple newspaper names in the supplement line, so the *Gazette* ad director called the person that scheduled the coupon insert at Valassis and told her that they needed to pick up these preprints. She said it was too late to get others printed and to the *Gazette* for distribution. She asked them to make an exception and go ahead and insert them, and he refused. She asked, "What are we going to do?" And he said, "Well, they're on our dock. If you don't pick them up, we're going to shove them off the dock." And she asked, "Well, what are we going to do with them?" And the *Gazette's* ad director said, "You can stick 'em up your—if you like, I don't care, but get them off our dock." This was all detailed in the memo from Tom Kemp to Hugh Patterson. The owner of Valassis was so angry he switched all of his coupon advertising to the *Democrat*. And News America, the other large coupon advertiser, quickly followed suit and switched their advertising. Part of the problem at the *Gazette* was extreme arrogance.

Reading their research was interesting. They had conducted some focus research sessions with their readers—they would throw out words like "fastest-growing" and "largest," and they would ask what the reader's impressions were. They went through the same process with other groups who were nonreaders, some new people in the market, and some groups in which they were all *Democrat* readers. In every case, the response was that the *Democrat* was the fastest-growing and largest newspaper. That was because we had promoted that we were the fastest-growing. And we were. We were the largest. We were. We published more pages; we had more news; we had more classified. That really bothered Mr. Patterson. It was very revealing to read some of the comments made in those meetings—they thought we were trying to mislead people by causing them to think that we had more circulation. We never one time said in any of our promotions that we had more circulation. We said we had the fastest-growing circulation in Arkansas. In fact, we eventually became the fastest-growing circulation newspaper in any metro in the country, from a percentage standpoint. We said we had the largest sports section. We published more news. We published more classified advertising. Never did we say we had more circulation. But it was interesting, because people who knew we were bigger in other areas often assumed that we had more circulation. But we never said that or implied that. One thing that surprised us was that they were claiming that there was a danger of our eliminating them from the market, and they had never lost money. Not in any year.

You know, the lawsuit really helped us. I mean at the time it frightened us, but it greatly helped us because it gave us credibility with *Gazette* readers and advertisers. We have always been aggressive in circulation, and generally we got 90 percent of the newcomers, and we were getting more of the young readers. One reason we got these readers was because we had a lot more classified advertising, and the younger people tend to be acquiring more and looking for bargains. But the *Gazette* had a solid lock on west Little Rock and the more affluent parts of the market. The perception was that the *Gazette* would never be challenged. In fact, during the first year I was here, I had several people make almost verbatim the same statement to me: "The *Democrat* doesn't have a chance. There are three institutions in Arkansas that will never be challenged: the Arkansas Razorbacks, the *Arkansas Gazette,* and Worthen Bank." Two of the three are gone. The lesson there is to not ever get so arrogant that you think you can't be challenged. When you do—I mean, look at Sears. Twenty-five years ago, people in the retail business thought Sears would take over the retail world. They never thought Wal-Mart would.

Jerry McConnell: So did you have access to memos on their board meetings that they had?

Smith: Yes. I read all of the board minutes. We had access to everything in their files. I spent several hours almost every day with one of our attorneys—I had to have an attorney with me. I did that for a year. I read the documents from the *Gazette* files and tried to explain the significance of the documents to the attorney. Many times they wouldn't recognize the significance of something as it related to the newspaper business. Walter did some of it too. Through that we learned a lot about their operation. As far as I know, neither Hugh Patterson nor George Van Wagner, the *Gazette's* general manager, spent much time going through our documents; they just left it up to the attorneys.

A lot of what they were saying was that we were hurting them and we were not doing it fairly. They cited examples such as our giving away free want ads and delivering free newspapers to readers. They were really paranoid about what our intentions were. They could have done the same thing. If they had, they probably could have negated some of our advantages. But they didn't want to do those things. They also didn't want us to do them.

McConnell: Did they ever say why they didn't want to do those things? Did they ever give you any insight into that?

Smith: At first, they didn't think they would work. Also, I think they really believed that if they reacted to us it would indicate in the market that they were worried about us. I believe that was a big factor in it. Now, when Gannett took over, they announced free want ads within thirty days.

When you sue a competitor for antitrust it can be a devastating weapon if you win. If you lose, it can backfire, like in their case, when they told their readers and advertisers that if the court didn't stop the *Democrat*, we were likely to take over the market and force them out of business. They lost the lawsuit and then had to come back and say, "We're doing great." When they changed their message after they lost the lawsuit and claimed they were doing great, we ran an ad showing their sworn testimony in court. We asked in our ad, "Are they not telling the truth now, or were they not telling the truth in court?" Well, when they swore under oath that they were in danger of failing as a business, it was hard to be convincing when they came back a month later and said, "We're doing great." I believe that's why they had to sell the newspaper. I think if they had never sued us, they might never have had to sell the newspaper, because we were really struggling to gain credibility in west Little Rock. I think they probably did for us with the lawsuit what we couldn't have done with ten million dollars in promotion.

Paul Smith wasn't the only one who developed the opinion that the Gazette *had been arrogant toward its advertisers.*

Anderson: The *Gazette* was imperious—if you will—in the way it treated advertisers. And it made some advertisers furious. I remember that movie advertising was particularly bad. The restraints and demands that the *Gazette* made with regard to advertising for the movie theaters. The movie theaters had to have advertising in the *Gazette* for the same reason that other advertisers had to be in the *Gazette.* The *Gazette* set demands on how the copy was to be delivered, how soon the copy had to be delivered prior to publication. It made rate increases at will. The advertisers felt like they had to go along. That rate increases weren't discussed with the advertisers. They were just imposed on the advertisers. There were many furious advertisers, and some of them testified at the trial. They testified that the *Gazette* was demanding and very difficult to work with.

Anderson said the Democrat *looked into the reports that Patterson had tried to sell the* Gazette.

Anderson: We had the documents that I showed you earlier today. Those were produced during the discovery process. We knew that Hugh Patterson had talked to the *New York Times* about selling the paper to the *New York Times*. We knew that he had talked to the *Los Angeles Times* about selling the paper. We knew that he had shopped around. The most we could glean from people that we talked to who were very closed mouth about the matter—that is, people in the industry—was that Hugh wanted too much for the newspaper—that his asking price was not reasonable. And I think that the *New York Times* matter fell through, because Hugh wanted to continue to run the paper after selling it to the *New York Times*. Now, these are old memories, and I can't tell you where I got them, but I can tell you that this was suggested to us during the investigation that we made of his efforts to sell the paper. We made an extensive investigation, and we could not turn up much that was useful in the trial.

He found other statements in the Gazette *board meetings that were more helpful.*

Anderson: The *Gazette* board minutes of April 1984 contained a report from an advertising manager that the *Democrat*'s response to the *Gazette*'s advertising programs was weak and ineffective. This was eight months before they filed their lawsuit saying that they were going out of business. The minutes also stated that 1984 was a very good year. There were minutes after the lawsuit was filed stating that 1984 was a very good year and minutes stating that 1985 was looking like a very good year. The minutes of the board meetings contradicted the testimony from the witness stand and the allegations that the lawyers were making about how dire the *Gazette*'s situation was.

So how did the Democrat *win the trial?*

Roy Reed: Did you have better lawyers? There was a feeling at the *Gazette*, I think, that their lawyers were just outlawyered. Is there anything to it?

Walter Hussman: I'll tell you who the lawyers were, and history can make that judgment. The *Gazette* hired a really highly recognized law firm and lawyer in Houston named Steve Sussman. Steve had a huge reputation in antitrust. He had won a huge verdict, I think—a couple of hundred million dollars, maybe, which was huge at the time. At one point I remember reading in *Texas Monthly* after our lawsuit that Steve Sussman was asked—he was representing the Hunt family down there—so they said, "Steve, you're charging $600 an hour. The top firms in Houston and Dallas only charge $300 an hour. You're charging double what the top lawyers in Texas charge. How do you justify that?" He said, "I justify it because I'm at least twice as good as any lawyer in Texas." Anyway, Hugh Patterson and the *Gazette* obviously found some really high-profile attorneys for the case. Our attorneys were Williams and Anderson. Well, it was Phil Anderson. He was at Wright, Lindsey and Jennings at the time. And Phil is a great attorney, but Phil also had a great passion for what we were doing. He had been our attorney since 1974, for twelve years by the time the trial came. And Phil was absolutely convinced that we were right, that what we were doing was procompetitive, not anticompetitive, that it had increased competition between the newspapers in Little Rock. It hadn't diminished competition among the newspapers. So I think the fact that he felt so passionately about it helped. I think Phil is a better attorney than Steve Sussman. He certainly didn't have Steve Sussman's reputation.

But I think there is a tendency to say that if you lose a case, "Well, we got outlawyered." The facts of the case really hurt the *Gazette*. First of all, to be engaged in predatory pricing, it's generally a bigger company that does it to a smaller company. This was the case where the smaller company was supposedly using predatory pricing against the bigger company.

Reed: Can you put dollar figures on those sizes?

Hussman: Yes, I can. In 1984, the *Gazette*'s revenues were about $32 million to the *Democrat*'s $18 million. But first of all you usually have to have the dominant market share to predatory price against the people with smaller market share because they're a nuisance, and they're nibbling away and offering these cheap prices, and "We've got to get rid of them so we can solidify."

It was a very maverick or unusual idea that someone with a smaller market share could predatory price against someone with a larger market share. So it was a very unusual theory of antitrust laws. We at the *Arkansas Democrat* never spent in any single year as much as the *Arkansas Gazette* spent to produce their newspaper. So if we were gaining market share, that's not the most remarkable thing. Companies gain market share against other companies all the time. The remarkable thing is that we were gaining market share and spending less money to do it. How can you spend less money and gain market share? Well, the only way you can do it is by being more efficient. And we were far more efficient than the *Gazette*. And we made better business decisions and a lot of times made some better journalistic decisions than they did. So that's the remarkable thing. And someone expressed the fact that it must have been very frustrating for the *Gazette* or for the ownership of the *Gazette* to have realized that they had the whole Little Rock newspaper market at one point, and they could have had 90 ... or 90-plus percent of the profits. They turned that down. [Hussman was referring to his offer to Patterson to enter a joint operating agreement.] We almost went out of business. And, literally, we did almost go out of business. But we didn't. And then, by the time 1984 had come around, not only were we not going out of business, we were making money. And we were gaining market share. And it looked like they'd never get rid of us now. So someone expressed the opinion that maybe what the *Gazette* wanted to do was win in the courtroom what they had not been able to win in the marketplace. So when they sued us for between $30 million and $133 million, our net worth at the time was, I think, $30 million or $40 million. And, of course, any judgment is tripled in antitrust. If they had won a judgment, then we wouldn't have been able to pay it. We would have had to file bankruptcy or sold our companies, or we could maybe have settled the case by agreeing to close the *Arkansas Democrat*. That's speculation. And I think maybe it was expressed by the *Gazette*'s attorneys at the time that—"Well, I can tell you, if they don't win this lawsuit, they're going to sell the newspaper."

Anderson: At some point during the preparation of this case for trial, Steve Susman told me that, if the *Gazette* was not successful in its lawsuit against the *Democrat*, the Pattersons were going to sell the paper.

There was another theory as to why the trial turned out as it did.

Anderson: Steve Susman, I am told, was on an antitrust program sponsored by the Anti-Trust Section of the American Bar Association in Washington [DC] a few months after this trial. He told the audience how he lost the trial. He had held mock trials outside of the state and in the state. He said that the plaintiff in the mock trials—the *Gazette* in the mock trials won in the trials that were held in Texas and lost in the trial—or trials—in Arkansas—because the *Democrat* was not seen in Arkansas as a credible threat to the *Arkansas Gazette.*

McConnell: Do you buy that theory?

Anderson: The theory that it was not seen as a credible threat, yes. The trial changed that. Looking back, I believe that it [the trial] was the turning point. I think that the lawsuit by the *Gazette* against the *Democrat* gave the *Democrat* a stature that it had not previously had. The *Democrat* was clearly taken seriously by the *Gazette* in the lawsuit. I think it caused advertisers to pay more attention to the newspaper than they had before. I think that they saw it in a different light. I think readers saw the newspaper in a different light. As you know, before the end of the year in which the *Gazette* lost the lawsuit, the *Gazette* announced the sale to Gannett on October 31, 1986.

In Anderson's view there was another factor in the Democrat's *win: Hussman himself. In his summation, Susman said that Hussman was the cleverest witness he had ever seen.*

Anderson: He said that in a book, too. There was a book that was published after the trial, and each chapter featured a lawyer, and the lawyer was permitted to write about his great cases. Steve Susman had a chapter. He referred to Walter Hussman. What happened was that Walter's [pretrial] deposition was a little shaky in some places. Walter had never given a deposition before. He was somewhat tentative. Walter underwent a change during the time we were working on this. He became less tentative and more forceful. He realized that he was going to have to win the lawsuit himself. That it was up to him. It was wonderful to watch. Steve Susman came at Walter expecting to find the tentative person whose deposition he took. He bored in on him immediately in cross-examination, and Walter roared right back and bit him. But what Steve was trying to get him to testify to was wrong, and Walter told him it was wrong. He said, "You should know that was wrong," and told him why. Walter was a tiger on the witness stand. Steve said in this book and also told people at the antitrust conference where he lectured after the trial that he had never seen such a transformation in a witness.

McConnell: I noticed at some point, and I never found a follow-up on it, that the *Gazette asked*—Judge Overton I presume—to order a new trial or set aside the verdict and enter a judgment for the *Gazette*. And I presume that he rejected those.

Anderson: I presume so as well. Those are normal motions that would be filed. At some point Steve Susman called me and said that the *Gazette* would not take an appeal if we would not seek to recover our costs from the *Gazette*. And we reached that agreement.

McConnell: Oh you did. I don't remember ever seeing that.

Anderson: That may not have been in the paper. We would have been entitled to costs. We wouldn't have been entitled to attorney's fees. I say "we." The *Democrat* would have been entitled to recoverable costs. The recoverable costs would have included the cost of depositions that were actually used in the trial, some other expenses, court costs, and the like—but not attorney's fees and not a great part of the expenses incurred in the preparation and trial of the case.

McConnell: How many attorneys did you use?

Anderson: I can tell you something about the trial preparation and working with the people at the *Democrat*. And I'd like to tell you about that, because that was an unusual experience for me. It was remarkable really in so far as the lawyers working on the case. Peter Kumpe was on the case. Leon Holmes, who [became] a United States district judge, was a young lawyer cutting his teeth on the trial of that case and sat with us at counsel table. Annabelle Clinton at that time—now Annabelle Clinton Imber Tuck, who [later served] on the Arkansas Supreme Court—was a member of the trial team. There may have been other lawyers with us, but my belief is that that's the lot. Annabelle Imber, Leon Holmes, and Peter Kumpe worked with me. They all had specific areas of interest.

McConnell: Even after they lost the lawsuit, if the Pattersons had buckled down and said, "We're going to fight this thing tooth and nail, and we're going to get in there and we're going to meet them toe to toe," could they have remained in business?

Smith: Absolutely. In fact, after the lawsuit, Walter said he thought this market could support both newspapers, even though neither would make as much money as in a typical one-newspaper market. He thought both newspapers could coexist in the market. Maybe they thought they couldn't.

Anderson: Yes, the minutes of committees of the *Gazette* reflected a thread of expressed concern about how they had to keep costs down. The costs were continuing to escalate. Statements were made—"We have too many people around here" [and] "We're going to have to stop hiring." Those complaints continued for several years going right up to the time of trial. Apparently, they couldn't get control of their—or didn't get control of their costs. They didn't do whatever they should have done in order to get control of their costs. They bought top-end equipment. The presses were top-of-the-line presses. The computer system used by the *Gazette* was absolutely top of the line. Walter Hussman had a computer system that I think he bought second hand for $25,000. [Walter remembers it as costing $50,000.] It was a rubber bands and chicken-wire sort of thing. He ran a low-cost operation. He knows how to stay on top of costs, and he kept them down. He competed on a shoestring.

Hussman: I mean, despite this myth that got perpetuated that we had [laughs] oil wells and all this kind of thing to use. We really didn't have as much money. The *Gazette* bought a new front-end [computer] system. They paid $1.2 million or $1.3 million for their front-end system. We didn't have $1.2 million to buy a front-end system. So what did we do? We bought a used front-end system from the *Raleigh [NC] Observer*. I think we paid $50,000 for it. We brought it [here], and it was so big, we took a part of it and we put it in the *Democrat*, and then we took the rest of it and put it in the *[Hot Springs] Sentinel-Record*. And for $50,000, as opposed to $1.3 million. That is really why we ended up winning the newspaper war. We were a lower-cost operator. And, you know, the day the *Gazette* closed, I looked at their balance sheet and they had $49 million as the original cost of property, plant, and equipment they used to publish the newspaper. We had $19 million to their $49 million—the original cost of our property, plant, and equipment. They spent $10 million a year more than we spent to publish their newspaper, and yet we published more news, more classified ads—you know, we were just a more efficient operator.

Marvin L Stone, a certified public accountant from Denver, testified that the Gazette's *operating expenses were higher than those of the* Democrat *and other similarly sized newspapers nationwide. He said the* Gazette's *salaries were 21.3 percent higher than similarly sized newspapers and 32.5 percent higher than those of the* Democrat.

Another prospective witness did not make it to the witness stand. That was Gale Hussman Arnold, an older sister of Walter. The Gazette *tried to call her on the last day of the trial to testify against her brother.*

According to the Gazette *story the next day, Franci Beck, a* Gazette *attorney, said Gale would have contradicted Walter's testimony that his family had not objected to his purchase of the* Democrat. *Beck said Arnold would have also testified that her brother threatened to quit in 1978 as head of the family enterprises unless he was given voting control over the various corporations and that by "forgiving" loans to the* Democrat *from other Hussman companies, he had adversely affected the interest of minority stockholders like herself. Judge Overton refused to allow her to testify.*

Anderson: Gale had been in the courtroom. Gale was not listed as a witness as I recall. She had been advising Steve's side. I think she inserted herself into the lawsuit. You will recall that the lawsuit was originally filed not only against Camden News Publishing Company, the *Arkansas Democrat,* and Walter Hussman Jr. but also against Walter Hussman Sr. and Mrs. Hussman. And they were not in good health. Gale tried to give the other side whatever information she thought would be harmful to her brother. At the beginning of the trial—the first day of the trial—Steve Susman on behalf of the *Gazette* dismissed claims against Mr. and Mrs. Hussman Sr. We had the rule on witnesses. That is, if a party is going to be a witness and the other side asks for the rule on witnesses, the witness will be excluded from the courtroom and would not be permitted to stay in the courtroom and then testify. The night before Steve was about to rest [his case], he called me. Walter and I had been working on documents. It was about ten p.m. at night. We were in the elevator hall, and the phone rang in our offices. It was Steve Susman, who said he was calling to say that he was going to call Gale as a witness the next day. He indeed tried to do so, and we objected because we had asked for the rule on witnesses, and she was present in the courtroom. Steve had some argument that she was the best and only person who could testify to something. She, presumably, was going to testify that Walter hoodwinked her father or something about buying the newspaper, but it was not helpful.

McConnell: Carrick [Patterson] in his interview said some very flattering things about your operation as a newspaper. But one point that he made, he said that he didn't think the *Gazette* could afford to compete with you and some of the things you were trying because they needed to buy a press. Is that logical?

Hussman: You know, first of all, let me say, I don't dismiss the fact that Carrick probably really does believe that. But the fact of the matter is that we were both newspapers in Little Rock, Arkansas. We both had older presses, you know? They had two older presses, and we had one older press. So, you know, they didn't need presses any more than we needed presses. We both hired from the same labor pool of people available to work in Little Rock, Arkansas. We were both in the same business and bought from the same vendors. And so, you know, I think the fact is if you go back and look at how much money did we spend to produce our newspaper back after 1978 when we put out as many pages as they did, we spent $10 million a year less than they spent. We were just a lot more efficient. They would've had to be a lot more efficient than they were.

Incidentally, when we decided we needed a new production facility—our circulation was just getting too large—we had been printing here behind this building [the *Democrat* building]. We bought the old Terminal Warehouse building for $1.8 million, which was about $8 a square foot. We converted it into a production facility with the tax-exempt financing—we were still losing money. We had to be economical. We bought new printing units, but we bought an old press. So the printing press was three stories high. The lower story is the reels. The upper story is the superstructure, and all the printing units are on the second story. Well, the quality is determined by the printing units. So we bought new printing units. We were able to finance those. And we bought this old press out of the *Wall Street Journal* in Palo Alto, and we got the substructure and the superstructure—we bought it for, like, $500,000. We paid $4.2 million for the printing unit. So we ended up at about $5 million. I think we bought a folder out of the *Boston Globe*. We put this thing all together. The superstructure and the reels don't have anything to do with the printing quality. So we invested about $5 million for what was essentially a new press. So we were printing offset. So the *Gazette* decided they better buy a new press, too. Hugh made the decision to buy the press before they sold the newspaper, so the press was on order. So their press came online maybe a year after ours did—six months or a year.

McConnell: Did it appear that maybe Hugh just wasn't willing to make those cuts, or was it clear whether he didn't know how? Or he just wasn't willing?

Anderson: I think he wasn't capable of doing it. Whether that's a lack of knowledge of what to cut or lack of will, I'll let others determine that. He was not capable of doing it.

Two publishers of smaller nearby newspapers also testified for the Gazette *and said the* Democrat's *practices had hurt their operations. They were James Canfield, retired former owner and publisher of the* Jacksonville Daily News, *and Thomas Riley of the* North Little Rock Times. *Canfield said his sale of personal ads dropped when the* Democrat *started free classifieds, and when it started delivering free papers on Wednesdays, he lost all Dillard's advertising, lost one furniture store account and all advertising from Wal-Mart, but got that back by selling Wal-Mart the space at cost. Riley said the free classifieds made it impossible for him to raise the price of his ads even though expenses were going up, and he said he also lost advertising from some of the major stores when the* Democrat *started giving them special deals. They apparently were not alone among other Arkansas newspapers in their views on the war. Estel Jeffrey, who joined the* Democrat *as promotions director in 1984, grew up around the* Searcy Citizen, *where his uncle worked, and later was advertising director for the* Conway Log Cabin Democrat, *had a lot of contacts with smaller state newspapers.*

Estel Jeffrey: There was a perception amongst the newspaper people in Arkansas—and back then, most daily papers and weekly papers were owned by families. They did not like the *Democrat* after Walter bought it, and it became apparent why. They were fearful, because Walter was changing the landscape. He was changing the way you publish a paper, the way you market a paper, and they didn't like it. I grew up in two privately owned newspapers, and it was like they had entitlement. It's like money wasn't that important to them. It was the fact, "I own a newspaper, and I am gentry." I don't mean to go overboard with it, but I'm telling you, it was there. Walter and Paul, back in the early stages, started doing things because they had to survive. They threw the "newspapers don't do it" philosophy out the window and started saying, "We're going to survive as a business. We've got to look at it like that." And this represented huge change—if he won, it would never be the same again. And I think it scared the living daylights out of them. Because newspapers did things the same way for 100 or 150 years, and nobody rocked the boat.

McConnell: They probably weren't really excited about giving away free classifieds.

Jeffrey: Oh, absolutely not! No. That scared everybody to death.

McConnell: Did you [Phil Anderson] ever consider whether or not the *Gazette* thought the cost of the suit itself would drive the *Democrat* over the edge?

Anderson: I didn't get the idea that they would [try to] put the *Democrat* out of business with a lawsuit.

That idea did occur to someone else during the course of the trial. Eric Harrison, a veteran Democrat *reporter, sat in on some of the trial.*

Eric Harrison: I remember particularly they brought in Roy McDonald, the old coot who ran the *Chattanooga Free Press*. He was their publisher. He was brought in as an expert witness on what would constitute unfair trade practices, which was what we were being sued for. I remember they got this guy on the stand and they said, "The *Democrat* does this—would you consider this an unfair trade practice?" And he said, "No." And they said, "Well, how about this?" And he said, "No." And the lawyer asked him one question too many, which was, "What would you consider to be an unfair trade practice?" And he said, "Filing nuisance lawsuits against your competition." I remember talking to the lawyer at the time, and he said he thought that really was the turning point.

One other interested observer who had to feel like he had a lot at stake was Allen Berry. He joined the company as an accountant at Camden, became comptroller when he moved to Little Rock when the Hussmans bought the Democrat, *and then became the treasurer for WEHCO Media. When the* Democrat *decided it needed more money from WEHCO, it was Berry who had to find it.*

Allen Berry: The whole time it was a very stressful situation for all of us here. My job—somebody had to round up the money when the *Democrat* needed money. That was my job—well, one of my jobs. It was quite difficult at times because this vast conglomerate that we were described as having was not—you know, it was just difficult sometimes to round up—to get money from those other operations.

McConnell: So you had to round up the money from the other parts of the operation to supplement the money over here?

Berry: Right. Of course, when they would have a good month and the *Democrat* didn't need money, we would invest it in something interest-bearing—a transaction like US Treasury Bills, probably. Then, when they needed money—when the *Democrat* would have a big newsprint bill or something, and it was very difficult to project their cash needs—they would hit me by surprise a lot of times. It would be very tough and quite stressful to round up the money. Terrell Strickland was the chief accountant and controller at the *Democrat*. I would always tell Terrell, "Hey, I know you're going to need money. Just try to give at least three days' notice—just as much as you possibly can." Terrell tried to do that, but he couldn't always do that. Quite frequently he'd come over here and say, "We got some bills due tomorrow." We kind of butted heads over it. We were actually very good friends and still are today. We laugh about a lot of those times when we were trying to have some of those meetings. They tried to portray us as a big company who was moving all this money from big places like Camden, El Dorado, cable companies, and Hope to Little Rock to run Mr. Patterson and the *Gazette* out of business. They really tried to portray us in that light. It was not a huge operation. The biggest newspaper—the *Texarkana Gazette*—had a circulation—well, a Sunday circulation of about thirty-four thousand. Hot Springs, the next biggest, was around nineteen thousand. It certainly was not a big media conglomerate. The cable companies at that time were doing fairly well. We didn't have to spend much on capital expenditures. The cash flow in the cable companies was pretty good, but we were anything but a big conglomerate.

Hussman said the cable TV money (WEHCO Video) did not become available until 1982, more than three years into the war, and that most of the money used by the Democrat came from WEHCO Media, which included the Democrat. The Gazette was bigger than WEHCO in those early years, he said. WEHCO did not become significantly larger until 1982. In 1984, the Gazette had revenues of $32,247,827, and WEHCO's revenues were $38,056,401. In that year, Hussman pointed out, the Gazette had operating expenses of $31,122,085, and the Democrat had expenses of $20,792,171.

The Democrat reported that about an hour after the jury's decision, Hussman and managing editor John Robert Starr led a celebration in the Democrat newsroom "This feels so good I'd like to get sued again,"

Hussman told the reporters, adding, "That's a joke." The publisher said the lawsuit had been "good for the Democrat, good for the Gazette—though they don't know it yet—and good for Little Rock." "Maybe they'll stop complaining and start competing," he reportedly said. As some of the four hundred Democrat employees gathered around, the paper reported, Hussman told them, "We have to put out an even better newspaper—it's a great challenge for us. It's great you all still have a job," he said. "It's great to still have a company, it's great to still have a future."

CHAPTER 9

The Starr Effect

EASILY THE MOST controversial figure in the historic and some-times histrionic Arkansas newspaper war was John Robert Starr. As the managing editor and acerbic columnist of the Democrat, *he was hated or loved by the readers and also by his own staffers, whom he sometimes berated publicly in his column and more frequently on the bulletin board. Some said he managed by fear. Some said he was fair to them and they admired his combativeness. Many of them detested him. He sometimes violated the way newspapers had done things for years, and he even shocked the man who hired him, Walter Hussman Jr., on a couple of occasions.*

Walter Hussman: Bob had a lot of common sense. He had really good news judgment. He realized that even though we were doubling the size of the news staff, we didn't still have the resources that the *Gazette* had. We really had to stretch a dollar. We had to get the most out of our people. There was deadwood, and he was trying to clean out the deadwood and trying to get more productive people who would write more. So in that sense he was great. And he also bought into the concept. He believed that we could do this, which was a lot at the time. So I was really pleased with him and what he was doing. Then I was at the grocery store [one day], and I picked up a copy of *Arkansas Times* magazine, and there's Bob Starr squatting on the [*Gazette*] news stand with a knife in his teeth, saying, "I'm Bob Starr. I'm declaring war on the *Gazette*." [*This was on the cover of the* Times's *May 1979 edition. Starr was also wearing a helmet. The headline read "Arkansas' Newspaper War," then in smaller type, "Listen you, I'm Bob Starr of the* Democrat *and I'm declaring war on the* Gazette.*"] And, you know, I saw that, and it really shocked me. He didn't even tell me he was doing that. First of all, that worried me. And I thought, no, no, this is not an alley fight or a knife fight. We're not out to kill the *Gazette* or maim the *Gazette*. We're trying to compete. We're trying to save a dying newspaper. This is not a message we want to convey." I remember thinking, "Maybe I need to fire Starr. This is crazy. We've got this guy, and he's almost the perfect person for it, but then he goes off and pulls some stunt like this. He might do something else like this. But if I fire this guy, then who am I going to get?" Anyway, we had a pretty serious talk. He was sort of contrite about it. Anyway, I didn't fire him. It was probably a good thing that I didn't, because I think he was very helpful to us in trying to continue to improve the newspaper and trying to catch the *Gazette*.

Anyway, the next unexpected thing that happened with Bob Starr was a couple of years later, and by then we were making real progress in advertising and circulation. We were incurring huge losses, but by then our losses started coming down. Then he wrote a column. He had never written a column before, so I sent him a little note that day that said, "This is a good idea to write an occasional column. I think it would really be good if you could kind of help explain to our readers some of the dilemmas you confront as an editor every day—some of the trade-offs, why readers are more important than friends of the newspaper, and why we have to alienate some of our friends sometimes." Then there was a column the next day and the next day and the next day. "What are you doing, writing a column every day? Nobody writes a column every day." And he said, "I can do this." And I said, "I didn't hire you to be a column writer. I hired you to run the newspaper." He said, "No, I can do both. I'll do the column in my spare time, and I can do it." He was a workaholic. And he wrote in a very simplistic style that people in Arkansas could relate to. So I guess I really sort of acquiesced and said, "Well, okay. Let's see how this goes. He'll get tired of it. He won't be able to write a column every day. He'll come over and say, 'I'm going to go back to three times a week,' or once a week, and that will be fine." And I also had concerns about news versus opinion, because my father had taught me, and I really believed there needed to be a complete separation of news and opinion in the newspaper. Well, here's the managing editor writing an opinion column. So that kind of crossed the line. That worried me. That always worried me.

Anyway, he said, "No, I can manage that." So what has happened was I still had misgivings about it, especially when he continued to do it for a year or two years. The thing that always worried me the most was about the news versus opinion separation. But, you know, what happened was his column got so incredibly popular, and it was one of the most popular things in the newspaper. And then it was kind of, "Well, how do we get rid of this thing if we wanted to?" So, frankly, it's a little easier to do something like that [get rid of it] if you're the only newspaper in town than if you're a struggling newspaper that's trying to make a comeback. You need things that attract reader interest. And he did attract a lot of reader interest. And a lot of times I would disagree with him, but I thought, "Well, that's okay. I don't have to agree with him. He's not the editorial page. I expect the editorial page to agree with me."

Roy Reed: Would it be his political opinions or some other kind of . . . ?

Hussman: Any kind of opinions. Some of them were political. Some of it was his style. I thought he'd be too caustic. He was a more caustic kind of guy than I was. I sort of came to realize that and understand that. But occasionally I would have to go say, "Bob, you're just beating a dead horse too much. I think you'd be more effective if you'd write something else. I'm not telling you not to write about that. But you've written about it fifteen times. Maybe it's getting a little overdone." And he'd say, "Well, thank you. I appreciate that. You're probably right."

Reed: I remember he would write a column now and then about the *Gazette*. And some of those were caustic, as you say.

Hussman: Oh, absolutely. And I would say, "Bob, I think it's too self-serving. It doesn't help us to be writing about our competition. Obviously, people see that as a self-serving—you're better off when you're writing about the governor or you're writing about other issues." It didn't deter him much. He was very, very competitive. That was very important to have an editor who was competitive. And he did want to beat the *Gazette*. If he got up in the morning and he saw a story that was in the *Gazette* that wasn't in the *Democrat*, it just made his stomach churn. It made my stomach churn, and I wanted it to make his stomach churn, too.

One of Starr's first tasks at the Democrat *was to hire a large staff and then try to direct them in competition against the* Gazette. *Alyson Hoge, who started as a city desk clerk and rose to be a city editor and deputy managing editor, could offer some insight into that.*

Alyson Hoge: All of a sudden we had people who were from all over the country who were working here in the newsroom, and they were people who he thought were really aggressive news reporters, or that maybe he taught them in a class at UALR [University of Arkansas, Little Rock], or something like that. If you didn't mind the wages, you could get a job here pretty easily because our turnover was pretty high. It was always a perpetual frustration. We had a lot of turnover through the entire newspaper war. You were getting up every day and trying to beat this competition, and when you were successful at it, you probably didn't get praised for it, which is so typical of the business world. But if you got beaten, you would certainly hear about it. After a while you get to a point, where you just say, "Well, who needs that? I'm getting paid a low salary. I'm getting screamed at every day. What's my motivation for doing it?"

He used to write a daily critique of the newspaper. He wouldn't hesitate to blast any member of the staff in this critique that was posted on the bulletin board. It was posted on the bulletin board every day, and you'd go read it, and your stomach would turn because you would see how badly you were criticized over something that you had handled.

Rex Nelson: Starr could be demanding—terribly tough. Some will tell you unfair in certain circumstances, but he was always fair to me. Starr would write these critiques of every day's paper and compare what we had to what the *Gazette* had and would post these things on the bulletin board, and you would see people go up—and, of course, people would get in line to read that critique when it would go up there and see what Starr had to say about that morning's paper. And you would see people literally in tears as they would walk away from reading that daily critique because Starr would obviously have pointed out how they got beat by the *Gazette* on their beat on that particular day.

George Arnold: Starr was always really good to me. I'd come up on the copy desk side, and he was *really* tough on the copy desk. I mean, even in print. When he started writing his column, he'd just complain about the copy desk and the dumb mistakes that got made over there and all that. I just didn't really think that was someplace that I wanted to stay under that kind of regime or that kind of outlook. I've heard it said, too, that he came up through the Associated Press, where they didn't have a copy desk, and never really understood the point of it or the value of it. So that could have had something to do with it.

Tim Hackler: Was there a lot of what people might term "creative tension" coming out of Bob Starr's office?

Arnold: Yes, I guess you would call it that. Certainly, tension. The creative part, I don't know. I remember markups of the paper going up—papers looking like they were bleeding. The toughest thing I remember back then was him just berating his own staff in his column early on. It seemed pretty severe and unnecessary, even for some of the errors that certainly did get made—just to air that in public seemed to be—well, it was pretty brutal on some of the folks who were there.

Hackler: Another person whom I've interviewed as part of this series was upset that Starr had made a habit of criticizing staff people publicly in his column.

Mike Masterson: Yes. Publicly and frequently. As a former editor of three daily papers in Arkansas, I would never consider doing that. I would never hold up one of my employees for public ridicule, especially if I'd had to discipline them. I don't feel that's the public's business. And besides, if I'm trying to redeem that person, or I'm trying to eventually restore them, or encourage them, to be what they can be to fulfill their potential, that's the worst thing you can do.

Hackler: Did that have any demonstrable effect that you could see on the staff at the *Democrat*?

Masterson: Well, what it does—you only have to do that about once or twice before it instills a climate of fear. And John Robert, to a large degree, I think, tried to manage by fear.

Starr demanded absolute loyalty to himself and to the Democrat. *Even among the favorites, it did not pay to challenge Starr or to perform what he might consider a disloyal act. This happened fairly early on to Amanda Allen and Bill Husted, who at that time were married to each other.*

Amanda Allen: I have great admiration for him as a newspaperman. He had a really good sense of what made news. He was very determined, he wouldn't let something go. He was quite difficult to work for because he had a cot in his office, and he slept there a lot of nights because he was working until midnight or one o'clock, and he thought all of the managers who worked for him should be as dedicated. A lot of us did try to keep up that pace. During the time that I worked there, we went to a twenty-four-hour operation. We went from being an evening newspaper to competing in mornings with the *Gazette* [but still putting out an afternoon edition], and eventually it became just a morning newspaper. But for a while, we were a twenty-four-hour operation. Well, during that time I was in charge of the copy desk. It was very, very difficult. There were days that were like seventeen-hour days, where I would get there at five in the morning and not be able to leave until well after midnight. I don't function well on five hours of sleep. This was not a rarity; it was pretty regular. One day after a marathon session, he [Bill Husted] had gotten in [to work] at five in the morning, and I had gotten in [to work] at five in the morning, and we were both still there at about two a.m. I mean, nearly a twenty-four-hour shift. We left work, and we met at an all-night diner that was near our house. And we looked at each other and said, "This has got to end. We can't do this." And that's when we started looking around for other jobs. So that was about late 1979. We found jobs and went in to tell John Robert, and he was not happy. He asked us to leave right then. I think he saw it as a sign of disloyalty, and I can see his point of view. But we had both at various times tried to talk to him about the hours, and he just didn't quite get it because the newspaper business was really his life, his entire life. He loved it. He breathed it. And I was only thirty years old at that time, but I had already come to the conclusion that even though I loved my job, I didn't want it to be a twenty-four-hour job. And if I have one regret about working at the *Democrat,* it's that I did let it become all-consuming for probably three years of my life. A twelve-hour day was a short day, and that's just too much. It's not a life. John Robert, difficult as he was, taught me a lot of things. I don't regret having worked for him. I regret letting him bulldoze me, but I don't regret having had that experience, because I did learn a lot from him, and I wish that during that period of my life I had been strong enough to stand up to that strong personality, which I was not.

Bill Husted recalls it much the same way, except for when they got the word of their firing.

Bill Husted: This is going to get a little bit personal. Starr sort of enlisted you into his army. I was married to Amanda Husted then, who ran the copy desk of the *Democrat*. We were two key employees for John Robert Starr. He began a friendship with us. It was an awkward time. Though he was an interesting person, on the other hand, he was also your boss. So, if [he] said, as he would—"I think I'm going to come over for dinner"—that he would literally invite himself over for dinner. He'd say, "We need to talk about this matter and that matter. I want to come over for dinner." And he started doing that. Then, along the way, he would say, "Let's go to the horse races in Hot Springs." Well, whether I wanted to go or not—I guess I did because it [was] better than being at work, maybe. You couldn't say, as you could with someone else, "Well, I have to work." So we would take off and go to the horse races. I'm going to follow this drift, since this is a logical place to do that—that the friendship grew. We spent more and more time together. Then, toward the end of the time I was at the *Democrat*—I was there eleven years, so this would have been ten years plus—I applied for a job at a company in Medford, Oregon, called Bear Creek Corporation. And because I regarded John Robert as a friend, I told him up front before I even flew out to interview for the job months ahead—things you probably wouldn't do without the friend relationship. Well, John Robert saw that as a great betrayal, and I think people who knew John Robert would understand that as part of his personality, that I was his guy. I was not only his guy as an editor; I was his friend. Within weeks of that, I was sitting there after about a fifteen-hour day, and I had my feet propped up on the desk. John Robert walked up and said, "Husted, if you're going to prop your feet up on the desk, why don't you get on home? You're not doing any good to us down here. You're lazy." It was within a week of that, John Robert called me in and fired me. And here's the great part of the story, I still didn't have the job in Oregon. This is a wonderful example of John Robert Starr. He called in Amanda, my wife, and tried to convince her to stay. He said, "Now, Amanda, I fired Bill because he's going to Oregon and he's also goofing off, but I'd like for you to stay on at the newspaper," which she didn't.

Bill did get the job with Bear Creek Corporation, and Amanda quickly got a job with the Medford paper. They both eventually ended up with the Atlanta Journal-Constitution. *Both were veterans when they left the* Democrat.

Steele Hays: How did you feel participating in that effort to beat the *Gazette*, or to match their coverage and beat it as much as possible? How did that feel at the time?

Husted: I didn't think of it in terms of putting the *Gazette* out of business, but it felt great because we had been the ugly sister of the two. It was my newspaper, and all of a sudden, we had parity, at least, in the number of people that we would send out on a story. We had parity in the budgets, to send someone out of town or, gosh, even out of state. So there was an excitement to it, and there was an excitement in people watching that happen. Now, I'm not sure that the quality of the work really was the key element in the eventual outcome of the newspaper war. I think that might have been more a function of the free classified ads. But the newspaper was definitely better, and there was a huge sense of pride in that.

Hays: As I recall, John Robert Starr was very critical of Governor Bill Clinton at the time and made very close and critical coverage of Clinton a big part of the paper's efforts and his own editorializing or his column. How did you feel about that?

Husted: I didn't like it—it bothered me. It's almost a two-edged sword. On one hand, I was embarrassed, almost, at times by the partisanship it showed. On the other hand, there was something about the fighting spirit—the fact that he did fight so hard, that you had to admire, in a way. So, you had two faces. On one side, you thought, "This is wrong. This isn't how newspapers operate. This guy is running the show. He has made his feelings clear, and the readers have to think that that's going to taint our coverage. How could we ever be objective?" On the other hand, without that kind of attitude, I'm not sure the newspaper would have prospered. He was the right man for the job.

Starr died in 2000, so obviously he can't respond to some of these critiques, but we can quote some of his thoughts. They were in a book he wrote in 1987 called Yellow Dogs and Dark Horses, *which is a history of Arkansas politics from the time he started covering it in 1958. It was published by August House in Little Rock. It is a breezy, interesting account* of the period, loaded with his opinions. His opinions seemed to veer more toward bias when he felt some politician wasn't giving him his due.

He was not always at odds with Clinton. He started off for him, briefly, then was against him, then supported him for several years, and then lambasted him at every turn after, he said, Clinton went back on his word to him not to run for president. He had an excuse for supporting him at the start. "Like everybody else, I expected Clinton to establish Camelot on Capitol Hill. Unlike some other reporters who covered him two years in the AG's office, I had an excuse for misjudging him. I didn't know him. I left the Associated Press shortly before he was elected attorney general in 1976. I didn't keep up with day-to-day politics in Arkansas during the nine months I was on the faculty of the University of Arkansas at Little Rock or during the 15 months I was a graduate student at the University of Tennessee-Knoxville. I got to know Clinton well during his first months as governor. We did not develop a warm relationship.... Clinton [had] surrounded himself in the attorney general's office with a group of young idealists whose inexperience in practical matters would not manifest itself until they moved with him into the governor's office. For one with so much political experience, Clinton was unbelievably naive in dealing with people. He gave more loyalty than he got. He protected underlings who should have been protecting him, and he did not get upset, at least in public, when it was obvious that some of his aides put self-interest ahead of the interest of the boss. To avoid embarrassing these employees, he often embarrassed himself by trying to defend their indefensible acts. He also had difficulty admitting mistakes, and he insisted on flirting with national office when his state office was in danger. A cardinal rule of warfare—political or otherwise—is that one makes sure he can hold what he's got before he goes after something else.... The revitalized Democrat broke story after story about mistakes and scandals in his administration. Some of these exposés were major, many were minor, but all made headlines larger than they might have in a noncompetitive newspaper situation."

Starr really took on the administration after, he said, "the Great Energy Department Retreat of 1980, which I credit for launching my career as a columnist. Paul Levy, whom Clinton imported from Massachusetts to direct the new Energy Department, spent $2,000 in agency funds to take 65 employees to the lodge at DeGray Lake to talk *about how they did their jobs. [Mike] Rothenberg [a* Democrat *reporter] wrote a story about it and I remarked, half-facetiously, that the retreat should be nominated for a Boondoggle of the Month Award for creative waste of public funds. That would have been the end of it if Levy had not called early on the morning the column appeared, asking with a laugh when he could pick up his award. I am sure he did not intend to make me angry, but he did. While his laugh was still ringing in my ears, I wrote a blistering column for the next day that took a lot of the humor out of his life. I was not prepared for the public reaction to that column. Fed up with a decade of profligate government spending, readers grabbed telephones and pencils to thank me for writing what they had been wanting to say for years. . . . This was heady stuff for a writer who had labored in near obscurity during a 20-year news service career. . . . Until then I had produced columns sporadically, never writing on the same subject for two consecutive days, never on a regular schedule, and only when I wanted to. From then on I wrote regularly—three times a week at first, six times a week after a couple of months, and seven times a week starting in 1982." Starr explained to his son, Rusty, also a newspaperman, why he switched to seven columns a week.*

Rusty Starr: Back in those days, I was a copy editor. And he loved telling me how he could blame this on a copy editor. But apparently at that time his column may have been running six days a week and did not run on Saturday. There was some kind of special "Voices" page that ran on Saturday, and some copy editor put his column into the Saturday paper by mistake. My dad claims that he got so many calls the next Monday from readers happy to see his column in Saturday's paper that he could just never go back. And he actually said the process of writing a column every day was much, much easier than the assignment given to a guy who had to write a column three days a week or one day a week. I mean, if you're only writing three days a week or one day a week it better be good. . . . The only reason you go to seven is his ego.

Perhaps encouraged by the reaction to his Boondoggle Award for the DeGray Lake episode, Starr soon provided more awards. He learned that at an energy conference in the Camelot Inn, the Energy Department had spent $37.50 of an $80,000 budget for fifty corkscrews to pass out with bottles of wine in the souvenir kits donated by the Wiedekehr Winery. He *used that to start a Boondoggle of the Month Award, which he named the "Sweet William" on a reader's suggestion, and then came up with a "Sweet Willie" award that he could pass out on the spot. He said the episode provided him with a rallying cry for his anti-Clinton campaign: "Remember the corkscrews."*

After Frank White beat Clinton in his bid for reelection in 1980, Starr wrote, "I'm sure I was the only happy person in a crowd of about 200 that gathered on the back lawn at the mansion two days after the 1980 election to hear a teary-eyed Bill Clinton say, 'With the grace of God, we will have the chance to serve again.'"

After White had served one term in office and Clinton apologized for some of the mistakes he made in his first term, Starr said, "I had changed my mind about Clinton since 1980. I expected him to be different if he became governor again, and he has been. . . . I suggested that voters who didn't like Clinton because they thought he was a radical could lay aside those fears. He is no longer a radical. He is still a bit of an idealist, but his idealism has been tempered by realism that one can learn only from rejection and defeat. . . . I discovered at Clinton's campaign headquarters during the primary . . . an attitude entirely different from the one that had usually greeted me in his office when he was governor. I no longer had the impression that they wanted me to leave as soon as I got there."

Julie Baldridge Speed talked about what it was like dealing with Starr during Clinton's first term, and she apparently was one of the few people on Clinton's staff that Starr liked. She had written the "Answer Please" column for the Democrat *for a few years before Starr arrived, and then she joined Clinton's staff in the attorney general's office and was his press liaison in the governor's office.*

Julie Baldridge Speed: I had to start dealing with Bob Starr, and that was interesting. I believe he really liked me, which was my very good fortune since I had to work with him. But he was very difficult to deal with—very scary. I remember one conversation when he called me [at] the governor's office in the middle of the day and said that he had reports of criminal activity by Governor Clinton. And he [said] if I didn't tell him something right that minute to refute it in a convincing manner—that he was going to run with it. It was really pretty close to deadline, as I recall. I just sort of held my breath and punted and said, "Have you ever met anybody that you thought was more politically ambitious than Bill Clinton?" Of course, he said, "No," and it was in sort of an angry tone, even though I knew he wasn't angry at me, but it was frightening. And I said, "Well, can you imagine he would do anything to risk his political future? Anything, anything?" And he said, "No." Then I said, "Then why would you believe this story?" And there was this sort of pause on the other end of the line, and he said, "That's the only thing that you could've said that would convince me to kill this story." Then he hung up the phone on me. And I don't have any idea if he was just having a little fun, or if he was really serious, because the subject never came up again. But there were episodes like that. I'll bet I spent an average of an hour and a half a day on the phone with him . . . just to keep him on an even keel.

Mel White: Well, he pretty much hated Clinton, didn't he?

Speed: He didn't start out hating him, but he always seemed to have it in for him. It was more of an edgy thing. I was there for the first year of his governorship, and, of course, I had talked to him [Starr] some during the two years in the attorney general's office. But the relationship just sort of built up. And when Maggie was born—the child that I had when I left the governor's office—he came to my house and brought me a baby gift. You know, we had—in his mind, I think—a cordial relationship. I mean, I can't imagine that he went around delivering baby gifts [laughs] to people very often.

There were some people who thought Starr injected himself into the way some stories were reported, which is supported by some of his reporters, like David Davies, who now has a doctorate and is head of the journalism school at the University of Southern Mississippi. Davies worked at the Democrat *in the early 1980s, left to go to the* Gazette *in 1985, and left the* Gazette *to go to graduate school in 1989.*

David Davies: Now the one time that I got pulled into some Starr stuff was whenever the [Little Rock school desegregation] case was in court. Of course, Starr took an intense interest in the school case and was very, very resentful of Henry Woods and had a lot to say about Henry Woods. About the time I got on the beat, Henry Woods had ordered the Little Rock School District to consolidate with the North Little Rock and Pulaski County School Districts. Starr was a huge opponent of that consolidation and—and therefore, a huge opponent of Henry Woods [the federal judge]. I covered the Senate campaign in 1984 in which Ed Bethune ran against David Pryor. Among the standard planks of Bethune's platform was to rail against the powers of federal judges. I was assigned to do a big Sunday piece on federal judges exercising all of this power. I interviewed all of my sources about federal judges, the judiciary, and the expansion of the federal courts into new areas over the previous decades. And essentially all the sources said the same thing, that Congress had expanded federal oversight in this area and in that area and that any increased power in the federal courts was simply a reflection of the federal encroachment into areas previously reserved to the state. It really wasn't that the federal judges were the bad guys. So I did this story, and it was a pretty even-handed story. I think I included some folks on either side of the issue. But it ran in the Sunday paper, and it was a full page or a half a page—with a really big graphic of a federal judge, as I recall it, pretty much dressed as Moses, handing down the law to the waiting masses. The graphic, of course, ran totally counter to the content of the story. But that was the *Democrat* in those days.

McConnell: Who was responsible for the graphic? Do you know?

Davies: The assignment was to do a story on federal judges overreaching their powers. And so they assigned a graphic to match that. But as was typical of the *Democrat*, they assigned a story that fitted their preconceived notions as opposed to saying, "Find out what's going on in this area." Now, I'm almost positive that assignment came from Starr. Actually, I know it came from Starr for that part.

The most sensational story of the era involved Mary "Lee" Orsini, who was convicted and sent to prison for the hit-man murder of Alice McArthur and was also convicted of killing her husband, Ron Orsini, although that conviction was overturned. Starr was in the middle of the coverage of that story. His frequent source was Sheriff Tommy Robinson, who kept trying to insert himself into the case, although Ron Orsini was killed in North Little Rock and Alice McArthur in Little Rock. The reporter caught in the middle was Cary Bradburn, who had just taken over the court beat when the story broke.

Cary Bradburn: For about a two-year period I wrote at least one story every day concerned with that case. I was still pretty much a young reporter and pretty green. There was a lot coming pretty fast at times [on] certain days. I believe it was July 2, 1982, when Alice

McArthur was murdered. There were three people ultimately convicted in that case, including Mary "Lee" Orsini. She was portrayed as the ringleader of that murder. We knew that there had been a confession made in the case by a man named Eugene "Yankee" Hall. Carol Griffee for the *Gazette* wrote a story. She appeared to have been getting portions of the transcript. I did not personally witness it, but, apparently, Starr went on a bit of a tirade and got Tommy Robinson to turn the entire transcript of the confession over to him. I don't know that firsthand. Starr was questioned at length in court about the source of the leak. I just believe that it was probably Tommy Robinson. [Starr never revealed his source.]

Anyhow, that confession was pretty interesting. It suggested in the confession that Mary "Lee" Orsini was promising to pay him some money to have Alice McArthur killed. She implied to—or Hall said that she implied to him—that the money was coming from Bill McArthur. Hall went out and recruited a man named Larry McClendon, who was identified as the actual trigger man. Lee Orsini was convicted in October of 1982. If I had imagined that things might slow down, I was wrong, because it seemed like they just picked up after that. Tommy Robinson drove much of our news coverage. And Starr, of course—he was writing columns quite often about the case, although his main source of information seemed to be the sheriff and not anybody else. I had far more sources than Starr did and was getting I thought more of a complete picture of what was happening. It did reach a point where I really believed—based on interviews and what I knew—that Bill McArthur really did not have any direct involvement in the murder. I don't know that Starr was ever exactly convinced of that, but he wrote more than once that . . . if there's a question, let's just put him on trial and have the jury decide. I didn't think that was right. I know the prosecuting attorney Wilbur C. "Dub" Bentley had to endure quite a bit of criticism from Starr in his column, but Bentley was always pretty firm in his conviction that there was not credible evidence that he could as a prosecutor ethically take to court and present a case against McArthur. Robinson would not give up trying to prosecute Bill McArthur. Before the Orsini conviction, Tommy was trying to get Dub Bentley to file a felony information in circuit court against McArthur, and Starr was trying to pressure Bentley to file that charge.

There were all these implications about the "good old boy" system and lawyers looking out for each other. In January 1983, and it was Super Bowl Sunday, and I'm sitting at home watching the TV and on comes Bill McArthur in an orange jumpsuit handcuffed. He's been arrested for allegedly plotting to kill Tommy Robinson. Tommy had some old boy who supposedly said that he met McArthur in a gravel pit in Malvern, Arkansas, and McArthur offered him money to get rid of the sheriff. The guy retracted any kind of confession. In fact, when he showed up again in David Hale's court there was about a three- or four-hour hearing on it, and it was thrown out. In fact as I recall, Tommy Robinson and Larry Dill were held in contempt of court for even bringing that before the judge. It's just a measure of how desperate Tommy was getting. But to my astonishment, Starr backed him all of the way. Starr even showed up for a Sunday-afternoon hearing when they arrested McArthur and then wrote this glowing column [about] how Tommy was standing up for what was right and all of this. I didn't have very many conversations with him about the case after that point, but I didn't know why he was so adamant in backing Robinson except the general public believed Tommy. It was sort of a populist position to take, and there was a newspaper war on.

I was summoned back to Starr's office one day, and he had a hot tip. Tommy had gone ahead and arrested McArthur in August of 1982 for the murder of Alice McArthur against the recommendation of the prosecutor, and that's what led to the hearing in Judge Hale's court in November of 1982. So it was February of 1983, and it had been about six months since the arrest—and Starr's hot tip was that Dub Bentley was going to get McArthur off on a technicality, because the Speedy Trial Rule would expire in February of 1983. I was familiar with the Speedy Trial Rule. It had come up in a couple of other cases that I had covered. I knew that Starr's tip was not right. The law at the time, if you were out on bail—as McArthur was—then they would have to try you in about eighteen months. If you were in jail, they had to try you within a year. I immediately told Starr that it was eighteen months. He said, "Well go check your facts. I don't think you are right." He was saying that he wanted a story about it, so I went over and interviewed a couple of judges. I made a photocopy of the state law—Speedy Trial Rule. So I went back to the office that evening to write the story up, and I really wasn't sure of what I was going to write. My information told me that the Speedy Trial Rule wasn't going to run out for another year. I told [city editor] Ray Hobbs that, and he said, "Well, Starr wants a story though, you know." So I was over at my typewriter, and I was just kind of sitting there scratching my head. Starr was standing there. I hadn't even noticed him at first. He said, "Don't worry about it. I'll handle it." He said, "But write me up some notes." I said, "Okay. I'll do that." I left him maybe a page and a half of some notes. I believe I [had] talked to Judge Langston. I talked to Judge Lowber Hendrix. I had talked to the prosecuting attorney [and] a couple of other lawyers. I believe this was a Friday afternoon. I just left it in Starr's mail slot, and went home for the weekend. That Sunday I see the paper, [and] on the front page there is this story by Starr that the Speedy Trial Rule was about to run out [and] that Prosecuting Attorney Bentley was pulling shenanigans to try and get McArthur off. I didn't like how he was using some of the quotes that I had given him in the notes. They were used in a way to make Dub Bentley look like he was pulling something over on people. I knew the story was wrong. I knew that there would be repercussions. I was sort of concerned that maybe some of the fallout was going to hit me. But the very next day, Monday, before I had even gone into work that day there was this front-page correction that Starr wrote. I believe he even addressed it in his column. He said, "Well, my brain slipped a notch," or something. But as I recall the correction just said "his source." I never knew who his source was. I suspect it was Tommy Robinson, but I don't know that. He just said that his source had called him and said, "Well no, actually, the Speedy Trial Rule won't run out for another year." Fortunately, that was all there was to it. I went on my way covering the courthouse. Starr went on his way.

Two of the more dramatic confrontations with Starr involved Leslie Newell Peacock. She was a copy editor whom I had hired about 1976. She quit around 1978 or 1979, mostly because of bad hours, she said, but reapplied and was rehired after Starr took over. Leslie had never been really fond of the Democrat *as a paper but liked the people she worked with, she said. She was never shy about speaking her mind, and that included to me and also to Starr. As it turned out, she detested Starr.*

Leslie Newell Peacock: John Robert Starr was in charge and he was so critical—hypercritical of everybody. He would put a note on the wall called "Random Thoughts." And in "Random Thoughts" he just trashed everything he had read in the paper—who did what wrong. That's just the kind of personality he had. He was just not a friendly editor. All he would tell you is how bad you got it. He called the copy desk in for some meeting at some point, and I don't why. He went on and on about how the paper had put Steve Clark [former attorney general of Arkansas] in office, and he was proud of that. And the paper would continue to do things like put people in office because of what we knew and how we reported. So he was not my favorite person. So I worked there, I had a great time there, and I really liked the people that I worked with, but I never was proud. When I worked at the *Gazette* I was so proud to work there because I had always wanted to work there. I was really proud to be associated with it—even with Gannett—just because I thought it was a real paper.

Leslie had worked briefly for Bill Clinton between her stays at the Democrat, *and her brother Frank Newell, an attorney, had been appointed by Clinton to the Public Service Commission. The rules apparently specified that the appointee had to be supported for confirmation by the senator for his home district. That was Joe Ford, who then worked for Allied Telephone Co., which merged with an Ohio company and became Alltel, with Ford as the CEO. Leslie said the utilities did not support Clinton's picks and that Ford had no intention of supporting Newell. She said the* Gazette *reported in detail about that situation, but the* Democrat, *whose reporter did not understand it, barely mentioned it. She was attending one of the* Democrat *staff's "drunken parties" one night, and the subject of the newspapers war came up and she said, "I hope the* Gazette *wins." That was promptly reported to Starr, and he fired her the next day. That was not a surprise, even to Peacock, but she marched into Starr's office and asked him for his reason.*

Peacock: I said, "What for? What are you firing me for?" And he said, "You're a traitor, and you're a spy." I said, "What are you talking about?" And he said, "Well, I don't have to explain myself to you." He said, "I will not have anyone working here who is not loyal to this paper and believes in this paper and supports this paper and thinks it's better than the other one." And I said, "Well, you might be losing some employees!"

That might have been the end of it, except for Jan Cottingham and

Omar Greene. Jan had been hired as a copy editor, and she had been trained by Leslie, and they were close friends. Jan had also married Omar Greene, a reporter on the Democrat *staff.*

Omar Greene: We got married in John Robert Starr's office, and it was on television. Starr would do anything to get publicity for the newspaper, so he called people at the TV stations—and he got John Purtle [a Supreme Court judge] to do it. We got married in John Robert Starr's office, and he gave us one day off to go on our honeymoon. So we went to Eureka Springs. And he thought he was really doing us a favor.

She [Leslie] was real sassy to him [Starr]. We'd have these staff meetings—and people were pretty intimidated, generally intimidated by John Robert Starr, but she wasn't intimidated by him. He said something about wetbacks one time, and she called him on that in front of everybody: "You might have hurt Miss Trujillo's feelings using that word. That's kind of a derogatory word, to call somebody a wetback and everything." He was real embarrassed. And she did some other things like that to him. She eventually ended up getting fired. My wife, Jan, liked her a lot and was going to have a party for Leslie. Starr called Jan into his office and chewed her out and made her cry and told her it was a shitty thing that she was going to have this going-away party for Leslie. Jan came out of there, and she was crying. I got all mad, and I was going to go in there and whip Starr's ass—I was really furious.

Peacock: She was really angry [when I was fired] and threw a huge party, a going-away party for me. Everybody came. It was another drunken brawl, and we had arm wrestling and dancing on the tables. You may recall how we acted back then when we were young and could drink a lot.

Greene: I had enough of him bullying everybody, and I was just going to go in there and kick his ass. I was in really good shape then. [Greene had been a Golden Gloves champ while attending Subiaco Academy.] Jan was a pretty tough newswoman, you know. She was not easily intimidated, but he'd made her cry, and he'd fired Leslie, who I liked. So something just rang in my head. And Bob Sallee and Damon Thompson, who were a lot bigger than me, they actually had to hold me down on a desk until I calmed down and told me, "You'll go to jail if you do this. You'll lose your job. You might kill him. You might seriously injure him." So they calmed me down, and then I didn't do that.

Peacock: She [Jan] got in big trouble for having that party. But she was too good for Starr to get rid of, but he never gave her another pay raise. And he put a sign up, you know, "Random [Thoughts]," the next day saying that he was ashamed of the people who had gone to the party, and he wanted to know who had gone to the party and wanted people to name names.

Leslie Peacock eventually went to work for the Gazette *and worked there until it folded and then went to work for the* Arkansas Times, *along with several other former* Gazette *employees. Jan Cottingham eventually resigned from the* Democrat *and went to the* Gazette, *its last city editor. She then went to work for the* Dallas Morning-News *but, professing homesickness, joined the* Arkansas Times. Greene *left the* Democrat *about the same time as his wife, and eventually went back to law school and became a lawyer. He and Jan divorced. Jan talked about the run-in with Starr in an interview for the* Gazette *oral history project: "I was very upset because the talent pool at the* Democrat *was not deep, and she [Leslie] was very gifted. He [Starr] called me into his office, and he said, "I hear that you are upset that I fired Leslie." I said, "Yes I am. She is good. We have a lot of idiots and it is unfair." He said, "Disloyalty is like a cancer. You have to cut it out." I said, "Okay, fine. That is your position. You are the boss. I understand you can do what you want, but you may as well know I am going to have a going-away party for Leslie. She is my friend." He said, "I think that is a shitty thing to do." We went ahead and had the party, and all the good people who had any character came from the* Democrat, *and all the butt-kissers didn't come. It was one of the best parties we have ever had, and I didn't get a raise for a year.*

"Later, when I was a general assignment reporter, we are talking probably 1982, Starr told me that I didn't get a raise because I had supported Leslie but that he admired me for moving from the copy desk and showing some gumption and becoming a reporter and also for being loyal to my friend. And after that I started getting raises like, you know, ten dollars once a year. [Starr] was a very shrewd man, like Walter Hussman, very shrewd. He [Starr] was a demagogue. He played to the base instincts of the populace. He was very astute, very manipulative. I don't think that he honestly believed some of the things he wrote, but he thought readers would like them. He pandered, but he was insightful. He had a sense for what readers wanted. He was dishonest. He was a coward. He had a chip on his shoulder. He played to a kind of class

consciousness in Arkansas, where he portrayed the Gazette *as the paper of the elite and the* Democrat *as the scrappy paper of the working class. That was very clever and effective."*

Starr had support from some members of the news staff.

Nelson: When I came back [to the *Democrat*], Wally [Hall] said, "Look, now. You worked for me only for about a year, and then you left me to be editor at Arkadelphia. If you come back, I need you to stay a few years." And I said, "Fine." I was *loving* being assistant sports editor. Wally was letting me write some, so it wasn't all administrative. I had covered the Super Bowl that year. I was really having a good time, and I saw that the Washington [DC] correspondent's job had come open, but I really had no interest. I still remember I was asleep late on a Monday morning because, of course, weekends were your big time in sports. I remember the phone ringing. I answered it, and he said, "Bob Starr." Boy, *that* would wake you up if you worked at the *Democrat* in those days. I thought, "Oh, man, what did we screw up if he's calling me at home?" I said, "Yes, sir." And he said, "Why haven't you applied for that Washington job?" And I said, "Because I'm not *interested.*" He said, "Why not?" And I said, "Well, I'm enjoying what I'm doing. I told Wally I would stay for a few years." And he says, "Well, Wally works for *me.* Wally's going to do whatever I *tell* him to do, and I've already decided you're the one I want going to Washington. That's an important beat, and I like the work you do. Now, we have to kind of play the game because we've got some other people interested, so I need you to apply. We've got a few people in the newsroom that'll interview you, but I've already decided you're the one going." Basically, [he] gave me no choice. It ended up being the greatest thing that ever happened because I met my wife when I was living there and made a world of contacts and have kind of been in the political realm ever since. Now I'm a presidential appointee, and I go to Washington a lot. But I ended up living there and covering Washington for the *Democrat* from the summer of 1986 until basically the end of 1989.

McConnell: What was John Robert Starr like to work for?

Nelson: He scared people to death, but he had a soft side. He was very good to me; I'll put it that way. I've told people before, "If you want to hear bad things about Bob Starr, you've come to the wrong person," because he plucked me out of the sports department and sent me to Washington.

Wally Hall and Starr had an interesting relationship, pretty smooth in the early years and then a little rocky toward the end.

Wally Hall: In 1975, I took a job for the United Press International [UPI] in New York City. I moved up there—first month was great, like a paid vacation. The next six months were hell. I just didn't blend in too well. At that point, I returned to the *Arkansas Democrat* and started school again. I worked here about two years, and I got fired. They said I missed an assignment, which I didn't, but it was a wakeup call for me. I spent two years working for the Arkansas School for the Deaf, and John Robert Starr hired me back as investigative reporter—not sports. About five months later, the sports columnist, Jim Lassiter, left, and his job came open, as did the Capitol Bureau. Starr called me in, and he said, "You can have either job you want, sports columnist or the Capitol Bureau chief, and I'd rather you went to the capitol. I will give you a raise if you go there. If you take the sports job, I won't." I took the sports job. I had broken a story on a chain-letter thing and had [received] some threats. I was newly married at the time, and it made her [my wife] a little nervous when people camped out in front of our house. I took the sports job in 1979, and in 1980, I believe, Todd Gurley, the sports editor, went to work for Southwestern Bell [Telephone Company], and Starr called me in and said, "You know, this would be a great way to be your own boss. You can do both jobs"—I was writing five columns a week and thought that was pretty taxing—"plus I'll give you a raise," and he did. And I assumed the sports editor's role, too. He gave me a five-dollar-a-week raise.

Frank Fellone: [When] Walter Hussman bought the newspaper and eventually brought John Robert Starr in here . . . things began to get tumultuous. How tumultuous, and in what ways—how was it working for Starr?

Hall: It was the best of times, and it was the worst of times. The best was his spirit of adventure, his fearlessness, his love for the written word. You know, the man was the managing editor and wrote seven columns a week, which I always thought took away from his administrative part. But he became very competitive with me. That was later, that was when things began to change, but I'll never forget we had a consultant come in the early 1980s. Starr came into my office—or my cubicle—and he said, "What are some of the things you've always wanted to do?" I said, "What do you mean?" And he said, "You know,

I've always wanted to climb the Matterhorn," he said, "but I'm old now and I'm not going to. What have you always wanted to do?" I said, "I've always wanted to run with the bulls in Pamplona, Spain." He said, "See how much it costs!" I said, "What?" He said, "Our consultant thinks you have a smidgen of talent, and [we] need to start taking advantage of it and doing things the other newspapers are not doing."

Fellone: Tell me about some of the mistakes you made during the newspaper war.

Hall: I made tons of mistakes. You know, I don't know if this was a mistake or not, but it was the beginning of the end of the relationship between John Robert Starr and myself. Arkansas had just lost to Texas Tech. Jack Crowe was the coach, and just he and I were standing there. ... All the other reporters had left. And he said, "We've got one game left, and I'm not sure what to do." They had a quarterback, a good kid, but he just couldn't pass very well—his name was Peanut Adams. I think he's a state trooper now. Good kid, but couldn't pass. And I said, "Why don't you run the option? You've got one game left, you could put the option in [for] one game." And he said, "Will you keep that off the record?" I said, "Sure." You know, no big deal. Word leaked out, and [Texas] A&M was completely prepared for it. The Razorbacks lost, and in my Sunday column I wrote, "We sat on this all week, and it still leaked." Starr was livid that we sat on what he considered was a huge news story. I told him it was off the record, and my word is my bond. He wrote a column that said he was considering firing me.

Fellone: Which he did not.

Starr used to write some critical things about people working at the Gazette. This is not the norm in the newspaper business. Most papers seem to take a hands-off approach when it comes to commenting about people or mistakes at other newspapers. I can remember when I was writing sports at the Gazette, *and on a rare occasion someone in Democrat sports would write something that I knew was incorrect, and I asked Orville Henry if I could write something to correct the misinformation. He told me no, to let the* Democrat *correct its own mistakes. Starr didn't pay any attention to such niceties, even if they had been suggested by Hussman. Sometimes he lambasted Bob McCord, who had recommended him for the job. More frequently, his target was Orville Henry.*

Randy Moss: I used to be entertained by a lot of the things he wrote. But the day that he wrote in the paper that Orville Henry became sports editor of the *Gazette* when all the good men were away at war—that's when he lost me. I felt that was not only inaccurate but an incredibly vicious thing to say.

Well, that was accurate up to a point, but Starr seemed to have ignored a salient piece of information, as outlined by Jim Bailey.

Jim Bailey: Well, you know, Orville fell into the job as a teenager in the middle of World War II when he was draft exempt because of his small size. At that time, he was about five feet tall and weighed about 100 pounds. He eventually grew up to be about six-two and 120.

It is also not the norm in the newspaper business for an editor to respond to a letter to the editor. The editor has a built-in advantage. He or she may write as often as they want. Many papers allow letter writers to be printed no more than once a month. Starr disregarded that precept. He decreed that no one was entitled to a "free shot" at him or the newspaper without him writing a rebuttal.

Many people speculated on Starr's perceived animosity for the Gazette. Most of that touched on his unhappiness with the way the Gazette used his byline when he was working for the Associated Press or the way the Gazette used AP bylines in general. He commented on that in a column he wrote in 1998: "It is the policy of most newspapers to call people what they want to be called, but the Gazette, which didn't like me even when I was a humble staff writer for the Associated Press, made an unappreciated exception for me. Usually, the Gazette, not wanting to recognize that anyone but its own editors and reporters practiced good journalism in Arkansas, only used AP bylines on stories that might blow up in their face. It was always ready to share the blame. When I complained about the byline change, the Gazette's policy became locked in stone. From then on the Gazette spited me by calling me John Robert Starr, even in news stories. The policy continued when I became managing editor of the Democrat, although the name on the Democrat masthead and the byline on my column was John R. Starr." It isn't clear from this when the Gazette made the change or whether it involved using his byline on AP stories when it didn't use that of other AP writers. I suspect it went back to when he was covering Governor Orval Faubus for the AP. There was a general feeling at the Gazette that he treated Faubus tenderly. I can remember Gazette staffers saying they felt Starr slanted his stories to favor the governor or to be less harsh than he could have been. I suspect some of that talk got back to Starr. Carrick Patterson later admitted that the Gazette had "tattled about it" to the AP head office. Starr admitted in his book Yellow Dogs and Dark Horses that he became the favorite reporter for Faubus after George Douthit of the Democrat fell out of favor. "I didn't realize for awhile that I had been anointed," wrote Starr. "What happened was that with Douthit sulking in the press room, Faubus began to corner me in corridors away from other reporters and tell me things off the record. From then until Faubus left office, I got a number of stories "not for attribution" that I attributed to "a source close to the governor. I had forgiven Faubus by then for his sins of 1957–58 because I felt that, with the exception of his irrational actions to the prospect of integration, he had been a good governor."

Starr was also known to hold a grudge, sometimes for a long time. I recently found a letter he wrote to George Fisher, the Gazette editorial cartoonist. I found the letter in the Margaret Ross collection at the University of Arkansas in Fayetteville. The letter was dated November 4, 1982, and here is how it reads, verbatim: "Mr. Fisher: Word was circulating around the AEA convention Tuesday that you were threatening to pull out as the banquet speaker because I got an award for standing up for the first amendment rights of teachers. If this is true, I hope you realize what a cheap little shit it makes you look like. I can remember a time when you would have cheered anyone who stood up for First Amendment rights. That was, of course, before you whored for Rockefeller, a dereliction for which I had long since forgiven you. I guess you are living, breathing proof of th [sic] old adage, 'If you run long enough with turdheads, you risk becoming a turdhead.' [Signed,] John R. Starr." He put down Fisher years later in one of his columns.

Starr thought about retiring immediately after the Democrat won the war but decided to stay on during the transition. That ended after about eight months when Hussman picked Griffin Smith, his travel editor, to head the news staff. Smith, a Little Rock native who has a law degree, had helped found Texas Monthly magazine and worked as a speechwriter for President Jimmy Carter and then as a travel writer for National Geographic.

Griffin Smith: As I understand it, Starr had told Walter when the newspaper war was over, "If you decide you need to replace me, you won't get any back-talk from me." The war ended on October 18, 1991. What Starr may have said to Walter and when—I was not privy to that. But in November of 1991 my wife remarked, "Well, you know, Starr's not gonna be there forever. Why don't you tell Walter you're interested? Put your hat in the ring." Of course, by this time, Walter had seen my work and knew my friends, and I had a track record. I paid a visit to him around Thanksgiving of 1991 and said, "If Starr ever leaves, I'd be interested." And we continued to talk through the early part of next year—of 1992. I became editor on June 23, 1992. Walter said, "My plan is, I'm gonna call Starr in the morning and tell him that we're making the change. And then you can be in the WEHCO conference room next door waiting when I'm through with Bob and have thanked him for all he's done and told him this is his last day." And Walter probably was thinking he wanted Starr to stay on as a columnist. When Walter and I talked, certain things clearly clicked. One was that I said, "I don't want to write a column." Walter clearly wanted separation of news and opinion. After Starr and I met on June 23—I guess I learned this from Walter because he met with Starr—they were the only two in the room—that Bob had expressed some doubt that the newsroom would accept me. Not a vociferous objection. It probably came up as, you know, "What problems would you see for Griffin?" "Well, one is, you know, he's not [Bob] Lutgen, and the newsroom might not accept him." Otherwise, I didn't know what their conversation was. But Bob Starr came over into the conference room, and we sat down. He wished me well. He clearly did not seem like a man stunned or anything. I'm still puzzled that if that's the first he'd heard of it, that's pretty quick. But, again, he was staying on at the paper and had worked out his arrangements with Walter for his column. I'm sure I told him, "I'll need your help and advice," and I'm sure he said, "You've got it." And for most of the rest of his life, he was a joy and a pleasure in that he freely gave me advice when I asked and didn't offer any when I didn't.

McConnell: Did your relationship with him remain good throughout the rest of his life?

Smith: You sure you want to get into that?

McConnell: Yeah, if you do. That's your option. [Starr had made it clear in some of his late columns that he was unhappy with his successor.]

Smith: Okay. Well, I'll try to walk carefully here. He died on April Fool's Day of 2000. That's one reason we had a hell of a time covering his death because by then relations between him and me were so deteriorated that everybody thought, "Maybe he's capable of pulling this prank just to embarrass the editor." We really had to run our traps to be sure he was actually dead. No disrespect to Bob or his family. But things were that bad by then. They had not been that bad as late as Christmas before. It was basketball season when it started, and Bob loved to tell [University of Arkansas head basketball coach] Nolan Richardson how to run his business. It was a Saturday, and Nolan Richardson had done something that displeased Bob. And as you may or may not know, the "Perspective" section is an advance section on Sundays, so it had already gone to press. So all of a sudden on a Saturday afternoon Bob has thoughts about Nolan, and there's no place to put them. He's determined to get them out. At the same time, Wally Hall was having a very difficult time with Richardson, I forget just why. [Starr complained in a column that by this time Hall had become a sycophant of Richardson.] But Bob announced that he was gonna run his column in the sports section the next day. For reasons having to do with the good management of the paper and the principle that columnists run where people expect to see them, I told Bob no. And I told the people in the sports department that if he tried that this was my direct order not to do it. That's the only time I've ever called something "a direct order." I guess Bob tried, and somebody in sports told him what I'd said, because from that point on, it became open warfare. During that period I thought Bob wanted to kill me if he could. He started sending me weird stuff in the mail every few days—derogatory notes, pictures of lions, rubber ducks. He seemed to have lost his mind. It was getting to be a very bad situation. You could see it in his published columns during that period. He had a heart attack going over Wolf Creek Pass [in Colorado]. He and his family had been in Arizona, and he loved to come back to Colorado. And he chose a pass that's twelve thousand feet high, and I'm guessing his heart couldn't take it. Because he was dead when they came down the other side. It was that sudden. And he still had bizarre stuff in the US Mail pipeline that arrived to me after his death.

Starr maintained in his columns that what he had was news about *what was going on in the Razorback athletic department, and he was giving the Democrat-Gazette sports department notice that the information was available, and if they hadn't reported it in two weeks, then he would reveal it himself in his regular column slot. He said that in a column that ran on March 30, and he died on April 1. A little over a week earlier, in a March 19 column, he had taken shots at Wally Hall, by name, and Griffin Smith, unnamed but the obvious target. He was unhappy, really unhappy, with Wally for a column praising Nolan Richardson. "I created Wally as a bold sportswriter, dedicated to 'telling it like it is' every day in every way," Starr wrote. "He transmogrified into a homer right before my eyes. . . . I called Wally to congratulate him on the column." He said he thought it was fair and objective. "Walls, you kissed his a** 33 times," I protested. "You have set a state record. Maybe a national record. . . . Do not take what I have said here as anything but constructive criticism of Wally. . . . I believe in my heart we could not have won the newspaper war without him. My gratitude to Wally comes from the heart and is everlasting and unshakeable. Unfortunately in some hearts, gratitude is on a short tether. It happens to everybody who stays around awhile, including me. People whose journalistic talent cannot balance with that in your little finger get into places from which they can give you orders." That obviously was a shot at Griffin Smith.*

Starr apparently started suffering heart problems while working for the Democrat.

Rusty Starr: I think there were times that he got so focused on [his job] that he wasn't paying attention to his own personal health. My dad had a heart attack in Colorado on April the 1st, 1981, and a full lunar cycle later—nineteen years on April 1, 2000, he had a heart attack in Colorado and died. I happened to be on that trip in 1981 with him. When he went skiing and then came back in and basically, you know, spent a couple of days talking about how bad his indigestion was . . . and then we got on a plane and flew back to Arkansas. And he went to get some kind of award that someone was giving him. I forget exactly what it was. And he went to pick up that award, which, you know, those kind of things never seemed very important to him, but that one was for some reason. And he picked up that award, and as soon as he got through accepting the award or whatever, he went to somebody and said, "Take me to the hospital." So he basically suffered through a heart attack to go get that award. He went to a doctor who told him he needed to have bypass surgery.... And he then went and found another doctor who would treat it with medication. And so they treated it with medication and patched him up and kept him going for a while. [His] first bypass surgery was in 1983. I think the first time he did a quadruple, and then he had to have another one—another set of bypasses done twelve years later. And it was kinda interesting that the doctor said he was one of the people who basically had a heart that bypassed itself that formed capillaries and stuff around the blockages, which apparently is not unheard of, but not that common, either, which really made things complicated for him after he had the second surgery. They basically told him that they could never do it again.

McConnell: Did you ever notice—after either one of those bypass surgeries, did his temperament change any? I've heard some people say that even if they were successful your temperament [can] change with all that [trauma].

Starr: How would anybody have been able to tell? One of my personal frustrations was that he died too soon after he had completed the transition from hectic newspaper editor to doting grandfather. When he made that transition, the things that he was doing for my kids—taking my oldest son, who has Downs syndrome, out to dinner with his girlfriend and sitting in the car while they ate so that they could have a real date, you know? Taking my youngest son out when he was no bigger than a matchstick and driving around a golf course 'cause the kid liked to play golf. And my dad would just drive him around out there and let him play, and he—you know, they spent basically a summer, you know, with my dad driving him around playing golf. And when he first started doing that kinda thing, he wasn't terribly comfortable with it. But in the last year or so he did get very comfortable with it, and not only that, was just enjoying it immensely.

CHAPTER 10

No Net for Gannett

FOR WALTER HUSSMAN and his staff at the Arkansas Democrat, *the euphoria that followed the victory in the antitrust suit did not last long. Hussman welcomed the respite as a chance to cut out some of his money-losing competitive practices and to finally start making money again. Before Hussman could even begin to dig out of the hole in which seven years of head-on competition with the* Gazette *had left him, the Pattersons sold that proud old paper to Gannett Co. Inc., the biggest newspaper chain in the country. When Gannett officials arrived at the* Gazette *talking about "deep pockets" and winning the war, it didn't take Hussman long to figure out they had no intentions of coexisting with the* Democrat.

Walter Hussman: A very interesting thing happened in 1986, right after the lawsuit was over. We said, "We are so close." We had made money in 1984. We didn't make money in 1985 because it cost us $1.3 million to defend against the lawsuit. Plus [it was] a tremendous drain on my time, on management's time here. But we were so close that when the lawsuit was over, we said, "What are we going to do now? Now is the time to move into the black. Now we can make money." So the best thing to do to get into the black is to eliminate your circulation discounts. And circulation discounts produce far more red ink than advertising discounts. And the economics of that is that newspapers [base] their retail price on seven-day home delivery at enough to cover the newsprint and the carriers' profit and the ink and just the out-of-pocket expenses. So you really don't make any money on circulation. Somebody will say, "Oh, you did that to sell more circulation." Well, if you sell a thousand extra copies in a day, it doesn't help your bottom line at all. If you do it every day for 365 days, well, maybe you can add a bit more to your advertising rates, and that does help. Anyway, when you start cutting your circulation rates, you're cutting right into the bone, and you're bleeding. So we said, "If we'll just do away with the circulation discounts, that alone will put us into the black." We even had a big meeting over in our new production facility, which was the Terminal Warehouse building on Markham. We told everybody, "We're eliminating discounts. This is going to put us into the black, and the *Democrat* has a bright future because we're going to be profitable. We've gained a lot of market share, and hopefully we can gain some more market share. You employees—you've got a bright future here."

Anyway, at the same time, the people at the *Gazette* were sitting over there looking at a very different situation. They were saying, "We've lost the lawsuit. We're going to sell the newspaper. What makes the most sense to sell this newspaper? What makes the most sense is to try to gain as much circulation [as possible], because the new owner is going to come in and look at the competitive situation and look at the circulation of the two newspapers as opposed to looking at the income statement, because they're going to come in and they're going to say, 'We're going to operate with our own people and our own policies. We can do our own income statement.' Gannett knows about a newspaper this size—how to man it, how to staff it, what their operating costs are." And I think the *Gazette* probably was a little bit scared because we'd almost caught them in Sunday circulation. I think the first quarter of 1986 we were 155,000 on Sunday and they were 157,000 on Sunday, so that's as close as we ever got. They probably didn't have those numbers on March 26th, which was the day the trial was over, but they had them maybe a month or two later. And I think they said, "Let's start discounting circulation with a vengeance. And let's do it to get our circulation numbers up."

So here are these two newspapers that made diametrically opposite decisions on marketing. We cut out our discounts to get into the black; they had never done a lot of discounting, but they really started doing a lot then in order to help sell the newspaper. Well, good grief! You report your circulation twice a year. So on October 31, we got the *Gazette*'s numbers. We were within two thousand of them in the first quarter of 1986. Now in the third quarter of 1996, we were about fifteen thousand or twenty thousand behind. How discouraging! Well, the same day, October 31, they announce they're selling to Gannett. I mean, it was a double-whammy. And we thought, "We really made a mistake cutting out all those discounts. Here we were about to pass them, and now Gannett is buying them, and they paid $51 million. They assumed $9 million in debt. Gannett is not investing $60 million in order to have two newspapers in the Little Rock market. I still thought two newspapers could survive. I thought that if we could make money— we had about 36 percent of the revenues when we started making money in 1984—well, if we could make money with 36 percent of the revenues, maybe the *Gazette* couldn't make money with 55 percent of the revenues, but they could change their operation, and they could be more efficient and not pay for all these costly work rules with the labor unions. We could both have 50 percent of the market and both make money. But when Gannett bought the paper, that changed the dynamics, because obviously they were not buying the newspaper to have one of two newspapers in Little Rock. They were buying the newspaper to have the whole Little Rock market. So at that point we said, "Oh, this is not going to work, trying to sit here and make money. These guys are going to try to kill us, and we've got to respond." We're now in something that we really never had when we were competing with the *Gazette*. We never had a circulation war. We really were mostly competing for advertising. We were mostly competing journalistically. We were competing for readership, but it wasn't a circulation war, and circulation wars are documented in the history of newspaper publishing where one newspaper says, "Get circulation at all costs, no matter what it costs. Get circulation—drive your circulation higher than the other guy." And the *Gazette* had never done that, and we had never done that. We talked to Steve Starr—he was a brilliant guy, and he taught at the Harvard Business School. He later taught at MIT [Massachusetts Institute of Technology] Business School. He'd come down about once a year, and we'd visit with him about "What do you think we're doing right? What do you think we're doing wrong?" And we called Steve Starr after they sold to Gannett and said, "What do we do now? Do you have any thoughts?" He said, "It's going to be a circulation war. They're going to do everything they can to drive their circulation so far higher than yours that the advertisers will give up on you and they'll have to go to them. So you've got to respond. You've got to gain circulation as fast as you can, any way you can. If people don't have the money to buy a subscription, take a can of corn, take a can of pork and beans, do anything to sell your paper." And we thought about that, and we said, "Of course, if you do that, it's a bloodbath. It's just red ink everywhere because now you're cutting back into that circulation price, and there's no profit margin as there is in advertising. You can cut your advertising rates 25 percent and you can still make money. But you can't do that in circulation." Anyway, we said, "Okay. We've come all this way. We've made all this progress. Now they're selling to Gannett. Gannett is going to force the issue so there's only one newspaper in the market. What are we going to do?"

So we had to come up with a new strategy. One was to gain circulation as fast as we could. And we said, "You know, this is going to be terrible financially. We've got to forget about the financial part. We've got to dive back into huge losses again." Gannett had a unique advantage here in Little Rock they'd never had anywhere else. They were able to buy a newspaper, and they were able to get all our financial information from the trial. And I'm sure when they looked at that, they said, "Look at this guy. He bought the newspaper in 1974. He cut his losses for several years as an afternoon paper. Then he incurred larger losses when he went to the morning edition. Then he started cutting those losses. He got into the black and was pretty close to breaking even. Now we're coming in and he's going to have to plunge back into a sea of red ink. That's going to be really demoralizing." They were right. It was really demoralizing. I remember May of 1987—boy, I think we lost maybe a million dollars in one month. We had never lost that much money. It made me sick. I was driving, and I just started beating on the steering wheel. I thought, "This is terrible. I can't believe that this has happened. We've gained all this market share, and now we're losing all this money. I don't know if we can afford to lose the kind of money we're losing. Maybe we're going to lose all we have gained just because maybe they can outspend us." We weren't so worried about being outspent, but maybe they can do things in circulation that would force us to lose so much money that we can't stay in the competition. But, you know, it was really interesting. We sat over there in the conference room, and we said, "What can we do to compete against these guys?

We can say we're Arkansas's largest newspaper. That's what we've been saying since 1978, since we published two more pages or four more pages than the *Gazette*. They can take that advantage away from us tomorrow. They can publish ten more pages than we publish on any day." So we changed. We dropped "largest," and we were "Arkansas's newspaper" by deleting the "largest." The only thing they can't take away from us is that we're locally owned." We said, "Well, that's a great comfort. We're locally owned. Most people could care less who owns the newspaper. They just care about the paper." And we said, "Well, maybe so, but it's an advantage, and we've got to use it for whatever it's worth." So we said, "Well, we'll take this piece by piece. What are they going to do?"

It didn't take them long to find out or to respond. Paul Smith, the general manager who had been the advertising manager, knew where the Democrat *had come from and the challenges they faced.*

Paul Smith: At the time when we switched to a morning newspaper, we had 18 percent of the newspaper revenue. The *Gazette* had 82 percent of it. By the time the *Gazette* sued us, we were up to 38 percent. And when the lawsuit was resolved, we were up to 42 percent. And so we were encouraged that we had increased our market share to the point that we thought we could survive in this market with the *Gazette*. When the *Gazette* was sold to Gannett, that changed everything, because we knew they didn't buy the *Gazette* to publish in this market with another newspaper. I heard from some employees at the *Gazette* that when the CEO of Gannett came to Little Rock he told the *Gazette*'s employees that they had deep pockets and they would win the battle here. I understand that he suggested that management at the *Gazette* be preparing a wish list of [the] things that [they] would like to have when there was only one newspaper in the market.

After Gannett had owned the *Gazette* for less than a month, we heard from a telephone employee who was working in our building that there was some big hush-hush project at the *Gazette*. He said they were installing a lot of phones in a big room and that it was a big secret. When Lynn Hamilton [then the *Democrat's* vice president for operations] relayed the information to me, I assumed they were getting ready to introduce free want ads, which they did. That was the first thing they did, and that concerned us, because that had been an advantage of ours for a long time. We knew that we had to do something to make our free-want-ad program better than theirs.

They copied ours program exactly. We did a couple of things initially. The first probably didn't have much effect, but we did it to try to send a message in the marketplace. I told Walter what my assumptions were, that I thought they were getting ready to start a free want ad program, and I told him that I thought we should announce the program for them. We checked with the TV stations and asked if anyone had reserved a large TV buy. We learned that Cranford and Johnson had, and we assumed it was for the *Gazette*. The ad agency had not announced who their client was, but it tied in perfectly with the assumption that they were getting ready to start free want ads. So I wrote a couple of TV commercials and proposed to Walter that we produce the commercials at some location away from Arkansas, so that no one would know what we were planning. The TV buy scheduled by the Cranford and Johnson Agency was to start on a Saturday, and I proposed that we break a TV commercial in the market on Friday night that would announce the *Gazette*'s free want ad program one day before their ad was scheduled to start. We brought two actors from Kansas City to Dallas, where we shot the commercials. In the first commercial we had two businessmen types walk onto a set that was designed to resemble the old Bard's Restaurant here in Little Rock, with the checkered tablecloths. They sat down at a table, and one of them had a *Democrat*, and the one with the *Democrat* said, "What do you think about the latest rumor about the *Gazette*?" The other fellow said, "What rumor?" And the first man said, "I hear they're getting ready to start free want ads." The other man said, "Oh, I can't believe that." He said, "They sued the *Democrat* over free want ads. They said they were illegal. Surely they wouldn't do something that they thought was illegal." And the other fellow said, "Well, I don't know, they've copied just about everything else the *Democrat* has done."

That was the first commercial. And they did announce their free want ads with a massive TV campaign starting the day after our commercial was first aired. Two days after they first aired their commercial, we came out with the second commercial with the same two guys who went into the same restaurant set, and one of them said, "Well, you were right. They did start free want ads," and the other one made a couple of comments. And then the first one said, "I wonder what's next, Orville Henry T-shirts?"

The second thing that we did to try to compete against their free want ads was the thing that really helped us the most. We talked to our people about the fact that when we were offering the only free ads in Arkansas, people would wait on the phone for several minutes to get an operator on the line. We had eight people taking free ads. And so we concluded that free want ads had suddenly become a commodity. They could get them at either newspaper. We decided that we had to give better service when giving away free ads. So we expanded our phone room from eight ad-takers to sixteen. I had my secretary call the free want ad numbers every day at both newspapers. She did that every hour each day from eight a.m. until five p.m. She recorded how many seconds it took to get an operator on the phone to take her ad. And we paid a bonus every day to our supervisor in that department and to those sixteen operators if our response time was quicker than the *Gazette*'s. It usually took no more than three or four rings before we would have an operator on the phone. Sometimes the delay at the *Gazette* would run three or four minutes. I suppose they thought at the *Gazette* that if they were giving away ads it was not important how long people had to wait. But we felt that if they could get on the phone in a few seconds at the *Democrat*, they probably wouldn't wait several minutes on hold to get their ad in the *Gazette*.

Jerry McConnell: Did they ever match you in amount of free want ads that ran in the paper?

Smith: No, they never got close to the volume we had. I think partly because people wouldn't wait a long time to try to get their ad in the *Gazette*. Plus, they were accustomed to running them with us. And they knew they produced good results in the *Democrat*.

Gannett took control of the *Gazette* in early December of 1986. And each year in March, we typically had a moderate rate increase. The next March, about three months after they took over the operation of the *Gazette*, we had a 6 percent increase in classified advertising rates. Classified had been our strength for some time. That was on March 1, 1987. On March 2, 1987, the *Gazette* announced a 50 percent advertising rate decrease for large classified advertisers. That was a big one. Their strategy was obvious. Classified was our strength. They thought their rate reduction would take most of our advertising if we didn't match their rates. I believe they assumed that if we did match their rates we would bleed to death. They probably thought they would win either way.

We had really good relationships with most advertisers. That had been one of our strategies when the *Gazette* had a lot more circulation and we realized that we had to have some advantages, and that was one of the things that we concentrated on. We went to great extremes to try to help our advertisers and develop good relationships. That was an advantage. When the *Gazette* reduced their classified rates, we showed our advertisers rate cards from Gannett's other newspapers, such as Shreveport and Jackson, Mississippi; and Springfield, Missouri; and others. And we calculated the advertising cost-per-thousand at those newspapers and compared them to the advertising cost-per-thousand at the *Gazette*, and we just reasoned with them. We asked why they thought the advertising cost-per-thousand was so much less in Little Rock than it was at their other papers and tried to help them to understand that this was a strategy to try to eliminate competition. We were frank with them and said, "If we match these rates we'll bleed to death, and if that happens you will likely have rates in Little Rock that are similar to those in Gannett's other markets." Most advertisers understood and continued advertising with us.

We lost some, but not a significant amount. In fact our advertising revenue increased significantly during the five years Gannett owned the *Gazette*. The *Gazette*'s ad revenue was less when they closed than when they bought the *Gazette* five years earlier. The *Gazette*'s advertising revenue decreased 16.7 percent from their first full year of Gannett ownership to their last full year. During this period, the *Democrat*'s advertising revenue increased 26 percent. We were gaining market share in circulation and advertising, even though Gannett was a lot bigger company with more resources. In fact, they outspent us by $50 million during the five years they operated the *Gazette*.

McConnell: Then what happened after that? What other moves did they make?

Smith: At about the same time that they implemented their rate decrease, they started a horse-racing contest. The racing season [at Oaklawn Park] started in February, and just before they announced the classified rate decrease—they announced a contest where they offered readers $350,000 in prize money during the length of the Oaklawn racing season. They gave away that much money to their readers who played their racing game. We talked about trying to react to that, but we couldn't spend that amount of money on a contest, especially considering our other increased costs. Walter and I discussed that and came up with a contest that we called "the $2 million Arkansas Sweepstakes." When I talked to Walter about my idea he said, "Well, we can't give away $2 million," and I said, "I don't think we'll have to give away $2 million." And the way that we designed it, every day we'd run a reproduction of about a dozen dollar bills in the *Democrat,* and readers could win money or merchandise if they had a dollar bill with the serial number shown on one of the bills in the paper. And every day for fourteen weeks we had a full-page ad from some auto advertiser in the newspaper. Each of these auto ads contained a reproduction of a dollar bill, and anyone who had the dollar bill shown in the ad would win a new car. We sold the program to seven car dealerships, with each car dealer buying one full-page ad each week. The duration of the contest was fourteen weeks. So each of the seven car dealerships ran fourteen full-page ads, and they paid for all those ads. And we gave away two or three cars during that period and gave away considerable cash and other prizes. But the money that we gave away didn't exceed the amount of advertising revenue that we took in from those full-page ads. All dollar bills were spent in Arkansas the day before their facsimiles appeared in the *Democrat-Gazette.* We traveled all over Arkansas to circulate these dollars. We ran an ad each day in the *Democrat* revealing the cities and towns where dollar bills had been spent. We got a call from Kroger, asking us to stop the contest. They said, "We can hardly get our bank deposits done each day. People in our office are checking every dollar bill to see if they have a winning number." It worked really well for us, and the *Gazette* never had another contest. I think the readers really thought that we one-upped the *Gazette.* But, you know, the only way we would have given that [amount] away would've been if every one of those dollar bills had been brought in by readers, and that obviously wouldn't happen. But every one of those dollar bills was put in circulation, so you know, readers had a chance to win on any one of them, but that ended the contests.

The next thing they did is funny now, but it wasn't as funny then. We heard about a radio disc jockey contest, which they conducted at the *Denver Post*. So John Mobbs, [the *Democrat* advertising director], *and* Larry Graham [the circulation director], and I went to Denver and spent a day at the newspapers there. John and I went to the *Denver Post*, and Larry went to the *Rocky Mountain News* to see what ideas he could get from them. During that trip we got the details of a radio disc jockey contest. The way it worked was the *Denver Post* announced the contest, and they encouraged all radio disc jockeys to participate and ask their listeners to vote for them as the best disc jockey in the market. The winning disc jockey chose a charity, and that charitable organization got ten thousand dollars, given by the newspaper. The strategy was to get the disc jockeys competing with one another over the air, encouraging people to vote for them. And the way they voted was to clip a coupon out of the newspaper and mail it to the newspaper's office. So we came back and quickly started making plans to do the contest in Little Rock. We had a full-page ad prepared to run the following Sunday, and on Thursday, the *Gazette* came out with a double-truck [two-page] ad announcing a radio disc jockey contest. We assumed they had heard about this from somebody here or from one of the disc jockeys, even though we had tried to limit the number of people who knew about our plan. We were convinced they had stolen our idea. I remember the morning their ad broke. Walter asked to meet with Estel Jeffrey, our director of promotions, and with me. I've worked with Walter for close to forty years, and only two or three times have I seen Walter really, really angry, and this was one of those times. The *Gazette*—in their contest, had added a couple of features that wasn't in the Denver contest. They announced that the disc jockey that got the most votes would get a Pontiac Fiero and from the coupons that were returned by readers, they would draw one of them and the reader that sent that coupon in would win a Pontiac Fiero. And they planned to draw three more coupons, and the three readers who sent those coupons in would win a trip to Disney World. Walter was furious, and he took the *Gazette*'s ad, wadded it up, and threw it against the wall and said, "They might think because they've got more money than we have, that we're going to roll over and play dead, but they're wrong." He said, "We're going ahead with our contest, but we're not giving the winning disc jockey a Pontiac Fiero. We're giving a Porsche. And we're not giving a Pontiac Fiero to the winning reader, we're giving him a Mercedes. And the three readers who win a vacation aren't going to Disney World, they're going to Hawaii." It was interesting how this played out. Back at that time, the single-copy price of both papers was twenty-five cents, and I heard of disc jockeys saying on-air things such as, "Vote in both contests, but if you've only got one quarter, buy the *Democrat*. I would much rather have a Porsche than a Pontiac Fiero." And we had a really successful contest, probably better than we would have had without the *Gazette's* entry, which caused us to raise the ante.

Meanwhile, Hussman was also thinking about other ways to compete with Gannett that didn't break the bank. Some of Walter's department heads had been thinking about that, too. And Larry Graham came up with some ideas of his own.

Larry Graham: In October or December of 1986, we found out the *Gazette* had [been] sold to the Gannett Company. Gannett had announced that they were sending in Bill Malone to be their publisher. Bill Malone was their corporate circulation director prior to this job. I think that sent us a signal of what Gannett was going to come in here to do. That they were sending in a circulation expert to grow their circulation. A lot of things changed at that time. We were afraid they were going to come and get our subscribers. Over the next month or two, we visited a whole bunch of different newspapers in the country. We visited Fort Lauderdale, Orange County [California], Houston, [and] Chattanooga, to look for ideas on what we should do. Probably the best idea we picked up was from the Chattanooga paper. Over in Chattanooga the afternoon paper had won the circulation war. We spent hours talking to Roy McDonald about how they grew their circulation. What he pointed out as one of his biggest keys was this program called "Ten-Twenty-Forty." He sold subscriptions for $10 for three months, $20 for six months, and $40 for a year. He offered people a discount if they would pay in advance for their paper. Prior to this time, I didn't think in a competitive market that you could get people to pay in advance. It's a mindset that I had that—since people could make a decision to read the *Gazette* or the *Democrat*, I didn't think they would pay me in advance. After visiting with Roy

McDonald, we came up with this plan that I presented to Walter that was called "Twenty-Forty-Eighty." The way that worked was that if someone would pay in advance for a year, they could get it for $80. Prior to that, our price was $109. So for a $29 discount, you could pay us $80 in advance. The reason we thought this was important [was that] we were afraid Gannett was going to come and take our subscribers away. We were sort of desperate to keep our subscribers. We thought if we could get them to pay us in advance, it would make it hard for them to take them away from us. We introduced this, I think, in about February of 1987.

We paid all our carriers and our employees to go out and try to get all of our subscribers to pay this advance. We were afraid that Gannett knew tricks that we didn't know. At that same time—I sort of got lucky—in January of 1987 I had this fellow by the name of Louis DeNicola walk into my office. He was a contractor. At that time, we had our own employee telemarketing operation selling two hundred or three hundred orders a week. We were trying to collect them in advance. He walked into my office and said, "I can sell you a thousand paid-in-advance orders a week." I said, "Show me." I contracted with Lou to start selling paid-in-advance orders for us. Before I could implement this Twenty-Forty-Eighty, I had to get Walter Hussman's approval. I went into a meeting early [in] 1987. I wanted to start offering these discounts for people who paid us in advance. I presented the whole program to Walter. I remember explaining to him that it was going to cost us about $900,000 a year or something like that. The meeting lasted about ten minutes. He made this million-dollar decision in about ten minutes. As part of the plan, I thought I could increase circulation by about twenty thousand for the next year or two. I sort of stuck my neck out. He let me spend almost a million dollars to try to implement this plan.

In this meeting was myself and David Enoch, our city [advertising] manager at the time, and Paul Smith. I had this big chart made up. I remember walking out and looking at David and going, "Holy cow! We just got a million more dollars to spend a year." Remember, we never spent very much money. We were desperate. Over the next year, we started to get subscribers to pay through the office. I think about a year later we had about fifty thousand subscribers who paid through the office, so we went basically from zero to fifty thousand in a year. This telemarketing contractor came in and started selling one thousand orders paid-in-advance a week for us. I remember him walking in and saying, "Why don't we sell them for a year?" I said, "What do you mean, sell them for a year?" That's what he said. "Right now we're selling for three months. Why don't we just collect the whole year in advance?" I thought, "You can sell the whole year at one time?" He said, "Yes." I said, "Okay." Over the next twelve months, I don't know how many of them he sold—about thirty-something thousand of them. A year and a half later, we had our circulation increase on Sunday by about thirty thousand. We exceeded our expectations. We built our circulation base by getting people to pay us in advance. We learned how to compete, is what we did. We were lucky that our competitor allowed us to exist all these years while we learned how to compete, so that by the late 1980s we had our service lined up. We had about forty or fifty district managers by this point. We were really doing a much better job on the service side. I guess at the height of the circulation war in 1988 or 1989 we were selling thirty-five hundred—even four thousand—paid-in-advance orders every week. Our goal was to sell more orders than our competitor every week of the year but collect them all in advance. Of course, they sort of laughed at this. "Laughed at it," meaning not openly to our face, but they were trying to sell the traditional way. They were calling people up and starting their subscriptions on promise-to-pay. A lot of those people don't wind up paying. We were collecting all of our sales door to door and everything in advance, so we had a nice circulation gain. It was beyond what we thought would happen.

In 1988, things began looking up. That's when Gannett began changing the Gazette.

Hussman: By now both papers had the ability to print quality color reproduction. So that was one of the reasons they went to color. But it wasn't just color. What happened is *USA Today* was their flagship, and it's still their flagship, I guess. But *USA Today* is different now than it was back in 1986. And the idea then was shortened stories, more feature stories. Put more feature-oriented stories on the front page. And we would do focus groups, and we would get four different groups of people in and let them be interviewed. And we would sit behind a one-way mirror and listen to this. And the four groups would be the *Gazette*-only readers, the *Democrat*-only readers, the people who read both, and the fourth group would be the people who read neither. And we asked them different questions. And the whole idea was, "What do we need to do at the *Democrat* to get more readership? What would it take to get you to read the *Democrat*?" For the *Gazette*-only readers, the answer was: "Nothing could get me to read the *Democrat*. I'm not going to read the *Democrat*." You talk to the *Democrat*-only readers. "What would it take to get you to read the *Gazette*?" The answer was: "I'm not going to read the *Gazette*. I like the *Democrat*. I only have time to read one newspaper. I don't need to read the *Gazette*. I don't like the *Gazette*. It's liberal." Or the *Gazette*-only readers would say: "I don't like the *Democrat*. It's conservative." Well, one of the things we learned in all this research is that the *Gazette*-only readers—there was virtually nothing we could do to get them. And we'd say, "Well, surely there's something the *Democrat* could do to get you to take the *Democrat*." And they'd say, "Well, if the *Gazette* threw the newspaper on the roof for a month and I couldn't get it, maybe I'd take the *Democrat*. Or if they totally change the *Gazette*, its format, its content, maybe we would take the *Democrat*." You know, the *Gazette* totally changed under Gannett. It didn't even look like the *Gazette* anymore. It seemed like a totally different newspaper. Well, as a result, maybe readers would now consider taking the *Democrat*. Gannett did for us what we couldn't do for ourselves by changing the *Gazette* so fundamentally that it put those readers in play where they would consider reading our newspaper. If Gannett hadn't changed the *Gazette*, I don't know if we would have ever caught them in circulation.

Cary Bradburn and David Davies, two reporters who had previously worked at the Democrat *and left for the* Gazette *while the Pattersons still owned the paper, could tell about Gannett's changes from the inside.*

Cary Bradburn: I started at the *Gazette* in December of 1985. In my first year there, it was owned by the Pattersons. They sold it in late 1986 as I recall. Then for the next year, 1987, Carrick Patterson continued on as the chief editor, and things went along like they had. There really weren't too many internal changes. I mean, some of the Gannett people would show up in the newsroom from time to time. But they hired Walter Lundy to be the editor at the start of 1988 [replacing

Carrick], as I remember, and that's when things started really fundamentally changing in the news coverage. They wanted shorter articles. They wanted offbeat little feature stories. I think one I had to write was about a pig that was suckling a little cat [or] a pig suckling a dog? But, it was just something that would have been laughed at—you know—even a year earlier. I always felt like when I worked during the Patterson period that the editors would send you out somewhere to cover something, but when you came back, they'd want to know, "Well, so what's the story?" You know, they left the judgment with the reporter who was out there. Once Gannett firmly got a hold, it was more of a top-down [management style]. It was, "This is the story. You go out, and write us this." And they didn't seem to want to know what we thought.

David Davies: At first, particularly, it was an absolute revolutionary change in worldview. The *Gazette*—at least in the early years—did its own thing and went its own way no matter what the *Democrat* did. And by that I mean the *Gazette* was pretty confident at that point that it was the leader, and the editors trusted the reporters and what they said the news on their beats was. I'll never forget Max Brantley was asking me something about some story, and I asked him something to the effect of, "What should I do on this story?" And he said, "Well, you tell me. I trust your judgment." And I found that very empowering, and it was typical of the *Gazette* early on. Because they trusted the reporters. It was kind of a reporter's paper.

Now that changed a bit after Gannett [bought the *Gazette*].

Meanwhile some of the people at the Gazette *were trying to tell the Gannett editors that neither they nor some of the readers liked the changes that were happening. Deborah Mathis, who had become a popular columnist at the* Gazette, *was one of them.*

Deborah Mathis: I certainly didn't like these changes that were being brought to the paper that, in my view, didn't need the change. The people weren't asking for it. You know, the times weren't really asking for it. So I didn't understand why. I thought it was arbitrary, and once I went to work there, I found just how arbitrary it was. [They were] so patronizing to us when we tried to tell them, and when citizens and well-regarded, high-powered people tried to say, you know, "Leave it alone," they would kind of just pat you on the head and tell you, "Okay, cute—now go away."

With nothing else working, Gannett made one more bold and costly gesture.

Hussman: What happened is we continued to compete . . . and in 1988, Gannett got frustrated. And they thought, "This was not supposed to last [this long]." They had bought it in 1986, had it all of 1987, and we were about in the middle of 1988—so over a year and a half that they've operated the paper, and they were frustrated. They said, "This battle was supposed to end by now, and we're losing money. We're losing lots of money. And our market share is not going up. These guys are actually gaining more circulation than we're gaining." And I looked at that every quarter. That's what gave me the encouragement to continue, despite losing all this money. This is my assumption: Gannett said, "We've got to put this thing in fast-forward. We've got to bring this thing to an end, because we've got to get this thing down to a one-newspaper town." So they said, "What we're going to do is we're going to cut the subscription price from $2.00 a week to 85¢ a week." That move alone cost them an extra $7 million a year in operating losses—that one move. So we sat down, and we said, "Wow. We charge $1.80 a week. We said, "All right, if we match that price, that's going to cost us maybe an extra $5 million a year. We can't lose another $5 million a year." Our people worried that just because of the lower price, subscribers were going to gravitate over. We finally came up with a solution. How much more can we lose? We can sustain another $1 million or $2 million in losses, and that was about it. They said, "Okay, instead of putting in the discounts, let's add another $2 million a year into marketing—hire more door-to-door salespeople. Hire more telemarketing people." We were already delivering the newspaper on the porch. We were already giving better service. That was already showing up in gains. People who took both papers would read ours first because ours was on the porch and theirs was in the yard. So we put that money in marketing, and, to me, that was a classical, fortunate decision in marketing, of how to use limited resources. It was far more important to spend your money on direct marketing than it was on discounts. That ended up hurting the *Gazette*, not helping them. Their circulation did get a bump initially. I think maybe that one year we lost some market share for a few quarters, and they were gaining more circulation than we were. But then we started gaining more. And it hurt them. I remember sitting on an airplane. I was thinking, "How do we respond to this from a public perception, advertising-wise." At that point we were having such large circulation gains, we were the fastest-growing newspaper in the country percentage-wise in the ABC Audit Reports. So we had a sign that we created, a rack card. And the *Gazette* had a rack card that said, "Now only 85¢ a week." And our rack card said, "America's fastest-growing newspaper." So we ran newspaper ads that said, "A tale of two papers," and they showed the two racks standing side by side, and under ours it said, "America's fastest-growing newspaper," and on theirs it said, "America's cheapest." So what ended up happening, in people's perceptions, when they cut their price, it's like people started saying, "Well, you know, the *Gazette* just isn't as good as it used to be." So I see why they cut their price. It was interesting.

Lynn Hamilton: The one thing that I can think about that doesn't get a lot of attention, the quality of our circulation department, made a tremendous difference in the competition with Gannett. The one thing, I think, that made more difference in selling circulation and increasing our number of readers than any other thing we did was the effort that was put into door-to-door sales crews. I can't give you the exact numbers, but we had up to thirty, forty, maybe as many as fifty people at a time knocking on doors offering people the opportunity to buy the *Democrat,* and we had extremely lucrative commission plans for those folks. This was in [the] late 1980s. We had some salespeople making fifty thousand dollars a year selling subscriptions door-to-door. They were motivated to work, and I don't think the Gannett people copied that at all.

Hamilton had another accolade to pass out.

Hamilton: Paul Smith gets so much credit for our marketing strategy. You know, he has recently been made president of the newspaper division and president of the *Democrat-Gazette.* Paul, for years, has been the marketing guru. "Genius" is a word that gets tossed around, but Paul is an incredible marketer. I think that this operation—like an award-winning movie you have a producer and director. Well, Walter is the producer, and Paul is the director. Paul is the artistic guy. In a movie, the director is the artistic person who is creating a work of art. Well, if the *Democrat-Gazette* is a work of art, Paul is the director.

Not all of the things that the Democrat *did that helped were strictly business issues. One innovation that almost everyone seems to think made a difference was the creation of a new Sunday newspaper section, "High Profile." This was sort of a takeoff on a newsy society section that combined parties, personalities, weddings, and homes. The front page was devoted almost exclusively to a big picture and profile of an interesting or important person in the community. The time came when people were almost salivating to be picked for the "High Profile."*

The section was a smash hit almost from the start, and one reason was that the Democrat *picked the ideal person to run it, Phyllis Brandon. Phyllis seemed to know everyone in Little Rock. She was born in Little Rock and graduated from Little Rock High School and the University of Arkansas, where she studied journalism and worked for the school papers, the* Tiger *and the* Traveler. *She also had worked for the* Democrat *and the* Gazette, *then quit for sixteen years to raise two sons, Phillip and Alex. She then went to work for Systematics, which she thought was nice but boring. Her son, Alex, graduated from the University of Missouri and went to work as a photographer at the* Democrat *and lived in his mother's garage.*

Phyllis Brandon: He came home one day and said, "Mother, I understand they need someone to cover parties at the *Democrat*. I told them my mom could do that. I want you to go down there and talk to them about that." I didn't do it, and he came back around again. He said, "I want you to go talk to them about that." I said, "Okay." So, I went down and talked to Jane Dennis, who was a style editor at that time, and, I guess, John Robert Starr. I had known John Robert Starr when he was with the AP [Associated Press] when I was at the *Democrat*. I liked John Robert Starr. We were friends. I started covering parties as a second job. I'd go to the party at night and write them up on the weekend. I did that for a while, and then next thing I know, John Robert Starr was calling, and he wanted to talk to me. I said, "Okay." He called me in and said, "Phyllis, would you like a full-time job?" I said I already had a full-time job. He said he didn't know that. But they were interested in starting a new section for the paper called "High Profile" and wondered if I wanted to work on it. I said, "Well, it's just a matter of money. We've got to survive." So, they called a meeting one evening. It was a pretty amazing meeting. It was in Walter's conference room. Walter was there and John Robert Starr was there and Lynn Hamilton and Paul Smith—all the honchos. And we planned that section—what was going to be on the cover, what it was going to be about—that we were going to have the top six houses, that we were going to have volunteers, that we were going to have those two pages of color weddings, and it has pretty much remained the same, except for the design, since then.

McConnell: How soon did it start catching on with the public?

Brandon: It caught on really fast because at first it was only distributed in western Little Rock. The whole goal of the section was to make the *Democrat* socially acceptable, so it was distributed in west Little Rock. Well, everybody started yelling. Park Hill, North Little Rock—they said, "We want it!" And then downtown said, "We're being discriminated against." [We] gradually added more places that it was distributed. Of course, the war was so interesting. They [the *Gazette*] were copying everything I was doing. They started a similar section. They made some *very* bad mistakes. Thank goodness this has never happened to me, but they had brides' pictures with the wrong write-ups, and that sort of thing. And they would just copy everything I would do, which, you know, I didn't care for.

It would have been difficult for the Gazette *to find someone with Phyllis's credentials.*

Brandon: When I was home for sixteen years, I was president of the Cathedral Church Women at [Trinity] Cathedral. I was president of the Little Rock PTA Council. I was a member of the Pulaski County Election Commission, representing the Democratic Party for five years. I was a member of the Garden Club. I think everything you do builds on everything else, so that I have never gone to a party where I didn't know at least one person.

McConnell: When did it become obvious that the *Democrat* was being accepted?

Brandon: [You could tell] because people were calling and inviting me to the social events. And it has become a coveted honor to be on the cover. I mean, people just died to be on the cover.

McConnell: Who makes that decision?

Brandon: I do. In the first years, I would supply Walter with a list, and he would pick who he thought would be good. But he finally just got too busy, so now I make the decision and pick the weddings that we're going to feature. The weddings part just goes to Pulaski County. We feel that the small-town papers do a big deal about their weddings. This is our Little Rock weddings—Pulaski County and all.

I think one of my things that I've been very lucky with is I have a nose for news. We don't write the stories in the old-fashioned, gushy way. We write the party stories as real news stories. There is always something new and different at every party, and that's how we write them. And it's work. Also, I've pointed out that we don't really have society anymore. It's more just that people like to have their pictures in the paper. It's not a society thing. We don't worry about that.

See, I had the full backing of Walter Hussman. Therefore, I had the full support of John Robert Starr. I have been very lucky I've gotten to do pretty much what I wanted to do. I've been to many places abroad. I went to Paris to a wedding.

McConnell: Did the *Democrat* pay your way?

Brandon: Yes. I've been to London. I was in London when Princess Diana died, by coincidence. I had a front-page story from London for four or five days there. I stayed over for her funeral. I went to Mons, Belgium, and interviewed [General] Wesley Clark when he was head of NATO. I've been to New York many times to interview Arkansans who are working up there. They let me go where I think the story is. I never would have thought that we'd have a president of the United States from Arkansas, so I was very lucky that I went to the White House several times to cover events. I've covered several state dinners and other things. I have covered four [presidential] inaugurals, and I've covered two Democratic National Conventions and all the parties around all these things and the inaugurals and the inaugural balls and all that. I have met Margaret Thatcher. I told Margaret Thatcher to smile. She didn't.

There were a number of observers, inside and outside the Democrat, *who thought "High Profile" had a significant impact in the war. One was Ron Robinson, who worked at the* Gazette *as a teenager and became the president of a major advertising agency that represented the* Gazette: *Cranford, Johnson, Robinson and Woods.*

Ron Robinson: In my mind—and I've always told her this— Phyllis Brandon was one of the reasons why the *Democrat* won the newspaper war. When she started publishing "High Profile" in 1986. It really was a very highly professionally done publication. It took society news off just the weddings and the country club and made it more of a community activity—more of an arts in the community, charities in the community, personalities in the community kind of thing. And obviously those people and things that they covered certainly were not selected because they also could be or were very high-volume advertisers in this community, but just because of [who] they were. So to be on the cover of "High Profile" was a big deal. And Phyllis certainly deserves a lot of credit for personalizing that and providing a counterbalance to the kind of wide-eyed editorship of John Robert Starr. [It] provided some class and legitimacy, and it all wasn't dog-eat-dog journalism.

Another development that had a major impact on the outcome of the war was William Dillard Sr.'s decision in May 1989 to pull the ads for Dillard's out of the Gazette *and then keep them out. Dillard's was by far the largest advertiser in Little Rock and in the* Gazette. *In fact, the second-largest advertiser spent no more than a third of what Dillard's spent, Paul Smith said. Some people estimated that Dillard's spent between $1 million and $2 million a year at the* Gazette.

"That's a hell of a blow to the Gazette," *said the late Bob Douglass, a former* Gazette *managing editor who was a journalism professor at the University of Arkansas at this time. "There is a loss of prestige and a loss of readership because so many people shop at Dillard's. The paper with the leading advertiser has a distinct advantage."*

People at the Gazette *were convinced that Dillard pulled out his advertising in anger over a story that ran on the front page of the* Gazette *on May 2. That was likely the case. However, it also seems likely that he kept it out because Hussman showed him that the* Gazette *had been giving cheaper rates to companies that advertised far less than Dillard's did.*

The story ran on May 2. Dillard's ran its last full-page ad in the Gazette *on May 7. Gannett officials had a nonproductive meeting with Dillard executives on May 15.*

Kenneth Eaton, who has retired and now lives in Rogers, said he handled advertising for Dillard's in twelve states, including Arkansas, when Dillard decided to pull all of his ads out of the Gazette. *Eaton told me that he did not want to do a taped interview, because Dillard had asked him not to talk about it, and he had agreed. Eaton told me there was a front-page article in the* Gazette *that upset Dillard and maintained the article wasn't correct and shouldn't have been on the front page. He confirmed that Hussman did come to talk to Dillard (presumably about ad rates) and that Dillard then called him. Regarding the different opinions about why Dillard pulled out of the* Gazette, *Eaton says that the recollections of John Mobbs, advertising director at the* Democrat, *and Hussman "would probably be accurate."*

Hussman: How that happened is this. Gannett got frustrated that we were hanging in there with them, and so they started getting very aggressive on discounting their advertising rates. They would target those advertisers that still ran most of their advertising in the *Democrat.* And they would target them by saying, "If you will run with us, we will charge you a really low, discounted rate," thinking if they could get the business out of us, that would hurt us. I remember they did that with Kroger. Kroger was one of our bigger advertisers, and I think they cut the rate in half. And we said, "What are we going to do?" And I said, "We have to cut the rate to Kroger to match the *Gazette.*" But Gannett kept doing this with more and more advertisers, and literally they were going to bleed us to death if it continued. So we told advertisers, "Here's how we're going to respond to this. If the *Gazette* makes you an offer that is a lower rate than what we're charging, and if you will document it, then we will either match the rate or we'll say, 'We're sorry, we can't match the rate. And if you [switch] to the *Gazette,* there's not much we can do about it.'" And so they said, "Well, how are we going to document it?" I said, "You have to have an invoice. We need to see an invoice." We started getting tons of invoices over here that advertisers gave us. By the time this thing came along with Dillard's, it was months after we started getting all these invoices. And so I had told Bill Dillard that we were really having a tough time, because the *Gazette* was undercutting us on prices to advertisers. He asked, "How are they doing that?" Well, I told him kind of how they were doing it. He said, "Nobody's paying a lower rate than we are." And I said, "Well, actually, they are." I was telling him the truth. And so he just kind of filed that away in the back of his mind. And so after he pulled out of the *Gazette,* he called me one day, and he said, "You told me that the *Gazette* was selling advertising for rates lower than what Dillard's was paying. Can you prove that?" And I said, "Yes, sir." And he said, "Well, come down here. I want you to prove it to me." And so I pulled out some of these invoices, and I got the tear sheets which referred to the ad. And so I took the tear sheets and the invoices, and I sat down with him in his conference room, and I said, "Here's Rex TV. They're a much smaller advertiser than you are. Look here. The first ad every month, they pay the full rate, and every ad after that they pay half price, which is less than what you're paying, you know? Okay, here's Jimmy Karam." A tiny advertiser was paying less than Dillard's. And so he looked at several of those things. I said, "I got more." He said, "I don't need to see any more. I've seen enough. You've got me convinced." And so I left, and as he told me later, the people from Gannett came down here, and he asked them point blank. He said, "You're selling advertising to my competitors at less than I was paying, and I was your biggest advertiser." He said, "Isn't that true?" They said, "We never did that." Now, either the person from Gannett didn't know they were doing it, or they just weren't being honest. But I think that cemented his decision that he couldn't trust those people.

McConnell: How much of an impact would that have been on the paper at that time, to lose all the Dillard's advertising?

Hussman: It was a pretty major impact. It not only had an impact on them financially; it had a major impact on them from a circulation standpoint because Dillard's was the biggest store in the whole market. And a lot of people shop there, and a lot of people wanted to see the advertising information in the newspaper. And then suddenly, you know, they couldn't get it in the *Gazette* anymore. So that hurt them.

Smith: Dillard's would probably have eventually resumed advertising in the *Gazette* if Mr. Dillard had not learned that some other advertisers had lower ad rates than his company. I think that gave Mr. Dillard the resolve to continue holding out. If being out of the *Gazette* had hurt Dillard's significantly, I think they probably would have gone back. I think what happened, Jerry, was that when people realized that Dillard's ads were not in the *Gazette,* they knew they could find them in the *Democrat.* Dillard's at that time had the same ad schedule in both newspapers. The *Democrat's* schedule didn't change, but we benefited from having them exclusively.

Roy Reed: You say that your losses were greater than ever. How big did the losses get during that competition with Gannett?

Hussman: You know, we've never disclosed our losses, but I will tell you that the *Gazette* lost $108 million. That number has been out there. Under Gannett, the *Gazette* lost $108 million. The *Gazette* had never lost money until 1986. You know, they had the cost of the lawsuit. They had the cost of the discounting in 1986. So they did lose money, and they sold the paper in December of 1986. That was their first unprofitable year. I think they made money all through the Depression.

I can tell you that our losses were significantly less, but they were in the tens of million of dollars. They were huge. They were horrendous. And, really, they were bigger for us than they were for Gannett because Gannett was such a bigger company.

Reed: Even the Gannett people now acknowledge that they handled things poorly here. When did they start seriously thinking, "We're going to sell the paper"?

Hussman: I think what happened was that we passed the *Gazette* in circulation on Sunday, in the first quarter of 1990; it was the first time in thirty years that the *Democrat* had more circulation than the *Gazette*. And I felt that if we could ever pass the *Gazette* in circulation, it was over because I felt like Gannett's only hope was to come in here and drive their circulation so it far exceeds ours, and if they couldn't do that, it was hopeless for them to have the only newspaper in town. So that's why the circulation was so important. So when we passed them in circulation . . . on Sunday, they were still ahead of us daily. Sunday is the biggest advertising day of the week. So we had a party. We said, "We've got to celebrate." So we had a party for over one thousand people. We invited all of our advertisers. We had it down at the State House Convention Center and had a big band and a big outdoor dinner. We wanted our advertisers to celebrate that they helped us get where we were. But I think that also sent a message. We really wanted everybody to know we passed them in circulation. So we kind of drove the point home with the party. I think that's when they must have started thinking about it.

It was in the spring of 1991 that they called. I remember Doug McCorkindale called me and started talking. We had bought a vacation home in Vail, Colorado, in early 1991. And I paid more for that house than I paid for my house in Little Rock, which seemed crazy at the time. Anyway, we did. We had young kids, and we went skiing every year. Anyway, Doug called, and he said, "How have you been?" I said, "Fine." He said, "You been doing much skiing lately?" I said, "Yes, I've been skiing." He said, "Yes, I think I'd heard you were out in Vail. You been playing golf lately?" [Hussman had recently played in a golf tournament in San Francisco.] I thought, "These guys are keeping tabs on me." And it started dawning on me, you know, "I bet they know about that house in Vail."

Doug McCorkindale was the CFO [chief financial officer] for Gannett.

And I thought, "You know, it's a matter of public record. I bet they know what I paid for that house out there. And I bet they're thinking, 'We have to squeeze this guy financially, and here he is having these lavish parties, and he's buying houses in Vail, Colorado. This guy doesn't look like somebody who's being squeezed to me.'" This is my interpretation. I've never asked Doug if that's what he thought. Anyway, I think they said, "Maybe we need to do something." So that's when we first started talking. So we had a number of conversations. One time we looked at doing a three-way trade with a Little Rock TV station, and that kind of all fell apart. I flew over to Savannah, Georgia. The first time I met with the people at Gannett was in Savannah, in an airplane hangar, in someone's office there. And we talked about it. That probably would have been in May of 1991.

The first contact was probably in April. So then we kept talking, and in July we went up to Washington, and we ended up signing the agreement then. And I remember after we signed the agreement, Doug McCorkindale stood up and put his hand out, and he said, "Congratulations. I have a lot of respect for what you did there." I thought, "Gee, I've been thinking of these guys as the enemy and the evil guys all along." I was really impressed with that gesture.

And, of course, it was the oddest situation because we couldn't acquire the *Gazette* if anyone else would acquire it. This doesn't have anything to do with the failing newspaper act that was passed in 1970, the Newspaper Preservation Act. This has to do with a Supreme Court decision that was handed down in a shoe case where one shoe company wanted to buy another shoe company. It went all the way to the US Supreme Court, and the law was determined and set by the Supreme Court. They ruled that one shoe company couldn't buy the other shoe company because they're competitors. And if this shoe company says they're going to go out of business—the only way they can sell to their competitor is not just to say, "We're going to go out of business," because who knows if they're really telling the truth? But if they try to sell their shoe company to other people, and if literally nobody will buy it because they've obviously been losing lots of money, maybe losing market share, if they can prove that, then the other shoe company can buy them because there's going to be an elimination of competition anyway. And I guess that's maybe what Hugh Patterson was thinking when we talked to him back in 1977. I didn't understand that part of the antitrust law at that time. Anyway, the only way we could buy the *Gazette* was if no one else was willing to buy the *Gazette*. Any other buyer is more suitable than the other competitor. I think it's a valid antitrust concept, and I think it's a good law. So when they talked to us about buying the *Gazette*, of course, we couldn't buy it unless it was going to be approved by the Justice Department under this antitrust law. So what that meant is if we were going to buy the *Gazette*, we couldn't see any of their financial statements for the last five years. We couldn't get a list of assets. It's sort of like you're buying a pig in a poke. Well, it wasn't that bad because we knew what their assets were. Their second-biggest asset was that printing plant. They had two brand-new printing presses, very state-of-the-art, modern equipment. That was important. Very important. The biggest asset they had was the name, the *Arkansas Gazette*.

The Justice Department forced them to try to sell it. They made them hire two different brokers. Not just one broker, but two brokers. They tried to sell it nationally and they tried to sell it in Arkansas. And, of course, by the time they were trying to sell it, they were losing $29 million a year. We had to borrow $68 million to buy the *Gazette* assets. We had never borrowed anything like that in the history of our company. And this was sort of a make-or-break deal for our company. And I remember the banker sitting down and saying, "Let's see, the *Gazette* lost $29 million last year. You lost millions. You're going to buy their assets, and you're going to become profitable. How are you going to do that? Because we're getting ready to loan you $68 million, we want to get our $68 million repaid. So tell us how you're going to do that." So we had to come up with a plan, and this plan had to work or I was going to lose the *Gazette* and the *Democrat* and everything we had worked for all those years. One of the things we couldn't do was accept the liability of buying the *Gazette* and operating it for a while. You either buy assets, or you buy the stock in a company. You can buy the stock and you take on all the liabilities. But we didn't know what their liabilities were because we weren't privy to them because the Justice Department wouldn't let us see any of their financial statements and contracts. Anyway, the people got mad at us—people like [those now at] the *Arkansas Times*—because the *Gazette* didn't publish a final edition. The *Gazette* could have published a final edition. Gannett could have operated the paper one more day and let them do that. But I was not willing to buy the *Gazette* and operate it for a day because if I had bought the *Gazette* and operated it for one day, I would have been buying the stock in the *Gazette*, assuming all their liabilities, and not knowing what those liabilities were. I was only willing to buy their assets. Anyway, that's kind of a minor footnote. So it was a Herculean effort. And I had grown up admiring the *Arkansas Gazette*. I thought it had been a great newspaper, and I wanted to perpetuate their name. And that's why we changed the name of the newspaper to the *Arkansas Democrat-Gazette.*

We never published a single edition of the *Arkansas Gazette.* We published the final edition of the *Arkansas Democrat,* and the next day we published an edition called the *Arkansas Democrat-Gazette.*

Reed: And this was part of your satisfying the bankers that you knew what you were doing?

Hussman: Right, and satisfying the bankers that we weren't picking up any of their liabilities. And it also happened at the most inopportune time. We asked the Justice Department, "Would you please call us, call Gannett if you decide to approve this? Would you call us and give us some advance notice?" Because I was starting to think about, "How do we publish that first paper?" And I was thinking that it would be easier to do on a Tuesday or a Wednesday, [than] if we had to publish on a Sunday. So they decided, and they didn't call either one of us. They issued a press release that they had approved this. And it was on a Friday afternoon. And now we're confronted with getting the Saturday paper out, which was okay. But on Saturday you've got to be producing a Sunday paper.

At noon on Friday, October 18, 1991, the computers at the Arkansas Gazette *went dead, and the deal that would close the* Gazette *was soon announced to the staffs of both papers and naturally produced widely different reactions. The staff at the* Democrat *enthusiastically cheered the announcement by Walter Hussman Jr. The staffers at the* Gazette *cried, cursed, and moaned when they learned the 172-year-old* Gazette *had already produced its last newspaper. They would not have a chance to write their own obituary. Their dismay grew as they learned they would have until five p.m. to box up their belongings and take them out of the building, walking past security guards who eyed their loads.*

Philip Anderson: We closed on that Friday because of the concern about damage to property and the like if the *Gazette* continued in operation over the weekend. There were serious concerns about property damage, so we closed the purchase that day. There were concerns that there could be damage to the presses or to other property at the newspaper. The situation in the *Gazette* newsroom was bad that day. There was drinking going on there, and a general undercurrent of rowdiness. There had been some comment made about changing the locks on the *Gazette* building. But, given the animosity of the *Gazette* staff towards the *Democrat* at that time [and] given the unruly behavior that was going on in the *Gazette* newsroom, I would say that we all came to the collective notion that it would be better to just to go ahead and secure the physical assets as best we could.

Bob McCord said the decision to close the Gazette *was announced to the staff at one thirty by Maurice (Moe) Hickey, the publisher who had only been on the job a few months and who many believed (he denied it) had been sent in by Gannett to close the paper down.*

Bob McCord: Hickey talked for twenty-seven seconds. He said, "The paper has been sold, and the *Arkansas Democrat* will take it over today." He turned [the meeting] over to the personnel director. He walked out of the room and went downstairs, where he had a limousine waiting for him. He got in the car, went to the airport, and never came back to Little Rock, Arkansas.

Hussman said the Democrat *intended to hire about two hundred of the* Gazette's *seven hundred employees, most of them in production, and several others in advertising and circulation. Employees not hired would be offered a sixty-day severance package, and employees with* more than ten years at the Gazette *would receive an extra four weeks of pay, up to an extra twelve weeks for those with more than thirty years of service, Hussman said. The package was estimated to cost $3.6 million, and Hussman was paying about $3.2 million of that, the* Democrat *said.*

When the Democrat *sent department heads over to the* Gazette *that afternoon to look for employees, they were not exactly met with open arms.*

Leroy Donald*:* And then Paul Smith [general manager of the *Democrat*] came in, and somebody was hollering obscenities at him, and I thought that was pretty stupid.

Smith spoke to Gazette *employees for about five minutes and offered them a chance for a temporary job at the* Democrat *and was booed, according to a* Democrat *article. "You would expect some of that. There were some people who were visibly upset and there were some boos," Smith said.*

Larry Graham, the Democrat *circulation manager, sampled some of the same attitude.*

Graham: A whole team of us went into the *Gazette.* My job was [to] try to meet with circulation staff and decide what employees I wanted to hire. We sort of had a good idea. We had met with the management staff of the *Gazette.* Their circulation director had recommended—"Hey, you probably want to talk to these people." They were very professional about it, but think about this. I was flying high. I was excited. "Hey, I'm coming in. Hey, we got a new deal for you." Debbie Pennington, who still works for me, had worked for the *Gazette* since, like, 1980. She loved working there. She loved working for the Pattersons. Loved the *Gazette* company. She loves our company today. She's a great employee, but when I came and offered her a job she was devastated. She just did not want to come and work for us. I'm glad she decided to.

In a signed editorial that ran on the front page of the Arkansas Democrat-Gazette *on October 19, 1991, Hussman noted that on that day there were only sixteen cities in America that had two separately owned competing newspapers. Two years earlier there were twenty-four, he said. And the year before he purchased the* Arkansas Democrat *in 1974 there were thirty-seven. This was down sharply from ninety-one cities in 1953, when television started serving cities throughout America.*

Hussman said later he truly believed in 1986, just before Gannett bought the Gazette, *that two newspapers could survive in Little Rock. He no longer believed that, he said.*

Hussman explained in an email in 2014 why he was willing to pay $68 million for the Gazette, *which was more than Gannett had paid for the paper in 1986.*

Hussman: I did not know how much Gannett was losing with the *Gazette,* but I knew they were losing market share in both advertising and circulation. I didn't know how much longer the competition would continue, and I knew that newspaper battles like this were risky and subject to unknown developments. For example, what if I had been killed in a car accident? Or if Paul Smith had? Or if Gannett decided to continue to battle, even a losing battle, for another ten years or more? We never lost as much money as Gannett, but we were losing money, and this offered a possibility of ending our losses. And if we did not offer to purchase their assets, and they suddenly closed the paper, and they moved their two press lines to another market, we would have had a serious problem trying to serve the entire market with just one press. And if they did we would have a harder time reselling all the former *Gazette* subscribers than if we bought their subscription list and immediately continued their subscriptions. I realized we would have a much larger circulation if we bought their assets, especially their presses and subscription lists, and with a much larger circulation we would have a much more valuable newspaper.

CHAPTER 11

Uncharted Territory

A LOT OF things had changed in the newspaper business in Arkansas and the country during the thirteen years the Democrat *and* Gazette *fought their own private but spectacular war. A lot more were in the offing, some of them so surprising they could hardly have been imagined in 1991. Besides, there were more immediate concerns. Finding a job, or even an occupation, had to be on the minds of the seven hundred or so people at the* Gazette *who suddenly were without a paper. Figuring out how to merge two papers into one and whom to deliver it to was on the minds of the key people at the* Democrat-Gazette.

Paul Smith: We realized that if the Justice Department decided to not object to the sale, we wouldn't have any idea when they would tell us that they weren't going to object. So we had to be prepared. We met with our department heads and worked out a plan as to how we would roll these two papers together. And we planned for several months how to do that. Walter received a call from an attorney who said the Justice Department had notified him that they would not object to the sale, and Gannett shut the *Gazette* down that day, which was a Friday. We asked Gannett to wait until the following Monday to close the newspaper. We didn't want to combine the two newspapers for the weekend editions. They [Gannett] wouldn't agree to delay because they would lose too much money publishing the Sunday edition. They said they had published their last newspaper.

Jerry McConnell: I know that some people at the *Gazette* were very unhappy because they never got a chance to publish another paper, and they felt they should've had a chance to publish that paper.

Smith: We wanted them to publish another paper. We would have preferred a Monday issue to be the first combined issue. Combining the Saturday and Sunday newspaper was much more difficult because they were larger, with a lot of advertising that was in varying stages of being created. After the announcement, their composing and advertising employees just walked out, and we had no idea what advertising had been scheduled. If it had been scheduled, we didn't know where the ads were in the process of being typeset and composed. A Monday or Tuesday paper that didn't have much advertising would have been much easier.

We knew we couldn't depend on [the Justice Department] to work on our timetable. We had to merge our subscriber lists and our advertising lists with the *Gazette*'s. We had done preparation work in case the sale was approved, but no one at the *Gazette* could see our competitive information, and we couldn't see theirs. So we turned our circulation and advertising databases over to a third-party contractor, and they merged them and had everything ready in case the transaction was approved. We had done some work like that, and we had requested rate cards from other newspapers in similar-sized markets to try to come up with a reasonable rate for the merged newspaper that would survive the competition. We got advertising rates from about fifty different newspapers and did cost-per-thousand comparisons on each paper and came up with an average. That helped us set our advertising rates. We did other similar things prior to the merger.

The man who really caught the brunt of the circulation problem was Larry Graham, the circulation director.

Larry Graham: It was July or August when Walter Hussman called me over for a meeting. It was Walter, Paul, and myself. We sat down on the sofa in Walter's office. He said, "It's over." And I think that's all he said. I said, "Well, what's over?" He said, "The war is over." And I said, "What are you talking about?" He told me about the deal with the *Gazette*, that we were buying their assets. I never dreamt that they might sell their assets and close. When he told me—he said I couldn't tell anybody—when he told me, goosebumps went from my head to my toes. The only other time I had that feeling was when we won the Grantland Rice Bowl Game. It was just this great elation. It was the ultimate high, I guess. [Graham had played football for East Tennessee State, and in 1969 his team had beaten Louisiana Tech, quarterbacked by Terry Bradshaw, in a bowl game in Baton Rouge.] Of course, over the next couple of months all the details got worked out. The day it finally happened, a whole team of us had to go over to the *Gazette* to hire some of their people. And we must have looked like mafia walking in. We all had our suits on. We all had these brick phones. The few things that we knew were going to happen—we knew that we were going to shut down the phone system of central Arkansas. Think about this. When we started merging our subscription list [and] merging our routes, we had letters set to go out to one hundred thousand subscribers telling them what was going to happen to their subscription. One thing the *Gazette* had done the last year, [they] had gone out and sold a lot of one-year ten-dollar-a-weekend subscriptions. So for ten dollars a year you could get Friday, Saturday, and Sunday. And that was going to cost us a fortune. This whole thing was expensive anyhow, so we made this business decision not to honor the *Gazette*'s expiration date. Maybe that wasn't a great marketing decision, but it was a financial decision. We needed cell phones to call each other. I mean, thousands and thousands of people were trying to call. They got upset with us. We took all of the *Gazette*'s money and applied it at the *Democrat*'s subscription rate. Let's say that you had paid ten or twenty dollars through August of this year. I took that money and applied it to our rate, so maybe it only paid you through June.

We also stopped delivering a weekend subscription. We started delivering just a Sunday subscription. We didn't want to offer a weekend subscription. We were afraid that people would just take our paper two or three days a week, and not seven days a week. So we upset people by eliminating the weekend subscription. We upset people by not using the expiration date. Here again, it was not a good public relations decision. We knew that. It was a financial decision. It was going to cost millions of dollars to do what the *Gazette* was doing, so we made these difficult decisions to try and bring them in the other way.

McConnell: So you got so many complaints, did it shut down the phone system?

Graham: You know, I don't know—we sure shut down our phone system. I could not hire enough people to answer the phones. We really thought we would possibly cause every number in Little Rock to ring busy. I don't know if we ever did or not. We got bags and bags of letters. I had about thirty or forty extra people answer the phone for months. It was a nightmare trying to work all that out.

From day one we tried to keep the *Gazette* carriers and our carriers. We delivered the same paper to every carrier statewide and told them to "Keep delivering to your customers until we get to you." So a lot of people got two papers. Here in Pulaski County it took us less than a month to go out and eliminate all this duplication and merge their routes together. To go work on routes down in Gurdon or South Arkansas—it took a long time. It probably was six or seven months before some of these areas got fixed.

We kind of wanted to make sure that people got papers. I would just sit here and answer mail all day long and go and fix people's accounts. People got upset with us. I would, obviously, try to do it whenever I could to keep subscribers, even if it meant honoring the *Gazette's* expiration date. There were some people that I did that for. But about a year later—one day there was no mail [and] no phone calls. It just stopped. Took about a year really to fix things.

Then we had excess employees, excess carriers, and plenty of subscribers. We probably hadn't sold a new subscriber in about a year because we were just working to try and get our service straightened out. And we had to go back to selling at some point. We probably sell as hard today as we did in 1988.

McConnell: Do you?

Graham: Not quite. The job is different now. It's harder in different ways. Back in 1988 you knew who your competitor was. I could point across the street and [say] "There's my competitor. It's the *Gazette*. [We] were trying to get readers from them to take our paper." Today our competitors are all around us and everywhere. You can't find them. They're the Internet, Play Station 2, X-Box, DVDs, Direct TV, Yahoo!, Showtime, HBO. Back in the 1980s we knew who our competitor was, and now I don't know who they are. They're harder to find.

Things weren't quite so tough for some of the other department heads. In fact things quickly got better for most of them, such as Lynn Hamilton, in charge of production.

Lynn Hamilton: When we became profitable, things immediately got better. Salaries have improved, and the equipment. Not only did we get their printing presses and production equipment, but we got all of the desks. We had so many chairs that didn't have backs on them or that were ragged and torn. We threw all of those out and brought over the *Gazette's* furniture, and even that was a tremendous improvement. Now if we wear out a chair, we replace it. Back in the old days, we didn't.

Immediately what we did was print on all the presses. They had two presses, and we had two, and we were running four printing presses. The first few months we printed a new *Democrat-Gazette* on all four presses. Anyone who had been a *Democrat* subscriber and a *Gazette* subscriber got two papers because we didn't know who we had in common. I want to say that a few of those first Sundays, we printed about four hundred thousand papers and delivered them. We had their comics that we had to marry into the paper along with their features. You know, their columnists that we were including and keeping—we had to figure how to change the format of the paper and make all that happen. We were working directly with them, and they were really nice cooperative folks at that point, but it was strange having them over here and doing that.

Another person whose job got easier after the merger was Jim Shuemake, the maintenance man who for years ran himself ragged trying to maintain the Democrat's *limited and inferior computers and terminals on which, eventually, the news was written and produced.*

Jim Shuemake: We got their [the *Gazette's*] photo comp type-setters, their cold-type news—it was a lot better than ours. And their computer system was a lot better than ours. It was a dual system. It was all in one system, but everything was backed up in the system. And we got people from the *Gazette*. We got a lot of the *Gazette* people—some of them were good, and some of them weren't. Some of them stayed, and some of them didn't. But we did get some good ones. I got a good one from the computer room [Rick Stegall], who knew their computer, and we tore it down over there and moved it over to the *Democrat* and set it up. I mean, we two by ourselves did it. I learned a lot about it in tearing it down and putting it back [together].

Another question that the readers had was whether the paper would continue with free classifieds once it had won the war. The answer was yes, on a somewhat restricted basis. John Mobbs, the advertising manager, explains the current parameters.

John Mobbs: We operate it a lot like an airline reservation system, where if there's space available, you can travel. That kind of thing. We have allotted a certain number or certain amount of space that we will run each day by each classification that will run free ads. If when we take all those ads, that fills up that allotment for that day, then it pushes out the first day that you can run a free ad. So you basically have a choice. If you want to place an automobile ad to sell your car, you call in, and we might say, "Sure, we can get your ad in the day after tomorrow." Or we might say, "I don't have any free ad space left that day. My next free ad day available might be next Tuesday." Well, then you have a choice. You can say, "Gee, that's fine. I'll do that. I'll wait until next Tuesday to run my ad," or you can purchase the ad, and it will start the next available day. So that's a little bit different, but we still run an awful lot of free ads, and we'll continue to do that. That's extremely important. We average almost three full pages a day of free ads.

Another important question was whether Hussman would retain Starr as his managing editor. Starr had written a series of critical columns about politicians and other well-known figures at the same time he was in charge of the newspaper coverage of those figures. A lot of people, including Hussman, were not comfortable with that arrangement. Starr was replaced as the managing editor in about six months, although he remained on the staff as a columnist. He was replaced by Griffin Smith, a lawyer and the paper's travel editor, who made it plain he was not interested in writing a column. He said Hussman clearly did not want an overlapping of news and opinion, nor did Paul Greenberg, who had been recently hired from the Pine Bluff Commercial, where he had won a Pulitzer Prize, as the paper's head editorial writer. Hussman named Smith as the executive editor and retained Bob Lutgen, Starr's deputy, as the managing editor, under Smith. Smith held the position for about twenty years, before stepping down in 2012.

McConnell: Now I think we need to get into how the *Democrat* has developed as a newspaper since you've been the executive editor. What changes has the paper made?

Smith: My mind is spinning because there are so many different tangents on that. One of them is that when I became editor, I was struck with how young the staff was and how little institutional knowledge we had. And I have been pleased to be able to recruit people like [features editor] Jack Schnedler, who started his career in the 1960s at the *Chicago Daily News* as a rewrite man and had been at a number of major papers. People like [graphics editor] Kirk Montgomery, and

Guy Unangst, who was the managing editor of the *Fort Worth Star Telegram* and became an enterprise editor at the *Democrat-Gazette*. Both of them were Gene Roberts and Gene Foreman disciples. We've kept Leroy Donald, who does a well-read business column with great institutional and community knowledge. [Donald died in July 2009.] Part of the plan was to recruit methodically to get the best people we could, including people who had careers elsewhere and who found that this paper freed them to do what they wanted to do.

I think we did it in a way that didn't tell our own people, the ones who won the newspaper war, "That was then, this is now." We kept our loyalties to them, and we surrounded them with other good people. People who have both institutional and, in some cases, more local knowledge. We opened the doors to, I think, the best the *Gazette* had to offer. We got people like [former "Style" editor] Karen Martin. Jerry Jones when he was at his best was fine. I mentioned Leroy Donald. [They also eventually hired Jim Bailey, an exceptional sportswriter.] We had a fairly limited number of *Gazette* folks who chose to come. But we hired some, and my impression is that their friends told them, "Well, be Benedict Arnold if you want. The *Democrat* is a terrible paper." And they came and they thought, "It's not. I like it here."

I think the most important thing is what didn't happen, because the paper still believes in putting news in the paper, treating news seriously, and having a lot of it. I didn't invent that. Go look at that *Arkansas Democrat* on my wall, the one from the end of World War II. It was just bulging with news. This was the real stuff. The *Gazette* had news in it. Arkansans expect that from their paper. That was Gannett's mistake. "Let's tart up the Old Lady."

The core value that animates our budget meeting when the front page is planned at three thirty every afternoon is, "What are the five most important stories in the world today *for our readers*?" Some days they're all local. Usually it's a mix of local, national, and international. The theory is, people respect the paper because judgment is shown about what's news. The animating principle is the one that I inherited, the one Walter believes in, the one that won the newspaper war, which is: Give your readers serious news. Don't be dull if you can avoid it, but don't play games. Walter's given us enough news hole. We've got enough staff. If we're not doing our job it's our fault.

McConnell: Did the salaries improve, though, after the end of the newspaper war?

Smith: Yes, they did. Walter's benchmark goal is to be the Southern Newspaper Publishers Average [SNPA]. David Bailey [the managing editor] and I—every time we do a raise, we have a computerized table. It shows where this person fits in the SNPA scale for that job. The problem is that we've got a lot more newsroom staff than a paper our size would normally have. The economics are that we're working from an advertising base of a much smaller community, and yet we're staffing and covering and distributing the paper to all seventy-five counties. I mean people are amazed. We have two interns [from the] University of Texas—they're amazed that our paper is bigger in circulation than the *Austin American Statesman.* The city of Austin has a population somewhere over 750,000.

Griffin also had two other former Gazette writers, columnists Charles Allbright and Richard Allin. He inherited them because Gannett got antsy when Orville Henry jumped ship and switched to the Democrat. *So Gannett put Allbright and Allin under contract for a big bonus and big boost in pay. When Hussman bought the* Gazette *assets, Allbright and Allin were part of those assets. Smith set off something of a furor when he fired Allbright and Allin in October 2003, effective on December 31. Neither Allbright nor Allin was happy about that decision.*

McConnell: You would've preferred to keep writing your column.

Charles Allbright: Yes, I would. Because, actually—between you and me, it was going good. There was good readership. And for Richard, too.

McConnell: You got a lot of support from the readers that ...

Allbright: Enormous. Thousands. Wally Hall even wrote one thing in his column one time. He said, "I'll be glad when the protests about Allbright and Allin are down to one hundred a day."

Allbright was convinced that Smith would not have made that decision without consulting Hussman.

Allbright: How would he? No way. In fact, he told Richard and me, "Mr. Hussman has said this is entirely my decision." Well, that's [BS]. It is unless he [Hussman] wants something otherwise.

Allbright said their contracts with Gannett (reputedly for $75,000 a year) were for one year. At the end of that year Hussman called him in *and said he was cutting the salary to about $60,000 or $65,000, Allbright recalled. He said he protested but did nothing else. Smith insisted that it was his decision to fire them.*

Smith: I had felt that their columns had run their course. I don't think it's appropriate for me to elaborate on the record as to why, but my feeling was, "We don't have an unlimited amount of money. That's a lot of money. What am I getting for it?" Their readership had declined, but they still had readers. I certainly counted myself as one. But as a steward of the company's money, could I spend it better in another way? And I decided, yes, I could spend it better on news coverage. And down the pike came Iraq, and we sent [reporter] Amy Schlesing to Iraq. She's been there a total of sixteen months now. Where did the Allin and Allbright money go? We spent it on Iraq.

In 2004, Roy Reed asked Hussman how the victory of the Democrat had worked out.

Walter Hussman: I think it has worked out well. Of course, it's sad to go from two newspapers to one newspaper. Obviously, newspaper competition is great. It really keeps people on their toes. Competition is great. It's great in the newspaper business, and it's great in every other business. Would Little Rock be better served by competition? Probably so. Most markets would. Is newspaper competition realistic in America today or twelve years ago? No. You can look—it has been a steady decline. The world has changed, and there are lots of other ways people get news. Television has gotten much more dominant. Direct mail—we still don't have Kroger's advertising in the *Arkansas Democrat-Gazette*. They go with Advo here in this market. So the loss of competition is sad, but it has worked out well for us. It has worked out well for the community, too, I believe, because I think we publish a quality newspaper. As evidence of that—we pumped a lot of money into the news operation. Ten years later we were spending more than double what we were spending when the *Gazette* closed. We have won lots of national journalism awards. I feel like we publish a real quality product, journalistically. We still serve the entire state. We have the lowest subscription prices of any regional newspaper in Arkansas or any border state. We charge less than twelve dollars a month. Nashville is over fifteen dollars. Memphis is over seventeen dollars. Austin is over nineteen dollars. So we have low prices. So even though we're the only paper, we keep our prices low. Our advertising rates are not low, but they're very typical. They're very average for a newspaper our circulation size. The advertisers are not getting taken advantage of because [there is no] competition in the market. We don't make as much profit as Gannett makes, but we do still make—we've been profitable every year since 1992. We made some money in 1992. And we make a respectable profit.

While things were going well, Hussman expanded. He started a Northwest Arkansas edition and built a printing plant in Lowell, which he furnished with one of his old presses in Little Rock. He expanded the staff in Fayetteville from five to more than three hundred. He bought the combined newspaper in Chattanooga, Tennessee—the Chattanooga Times Free Press—in 1998 and later bought the papers in Bentonville and Fayetteville. He bought the Jefferson City News Tribune in Jefferson City, Missouri, the state capitol, and paid cash for them, according to Paul Smith.

While newspapers across the country had been struggling for some time because of competition from television, and then later the Internet, things really got tough when the economy tanked in 2009, which was when I revisited Hussman.

Hussman: So even a newspaper like the *Democrat-Gazette* [that] has not been affected much by the secular trends [the Internet and other new developments)] we are certainly being hit by the cyclical downturn [recession], and our advertising is down significantly. The *Democrat-Gazette* made a profit in 2008. It was nowhere near the profits we've made. It's down significantly from what it's been. And we could possibly lose money in 2009, and so we're having to—as I say, we're having to trim some newsprint expense here and there and trim the size of our staff some, and we've had a wage freeze and a hiring freeze since August. We're making a few [changes]. For example, we changed the format of our television magazine, and that saved us $350,000 a year. So we're having to try to still provide a great newspaper but trim expenses where we can.

McConnell: Have you trimmed your news hole some?

Hussman: A little bit, but not much—more in the feature areas. We haven't had any across-the-board or mass layoffs. But we have selectively had to have some people take early retirement. In this case, many of the people were over sixty-five. And we're probably gonna have to have a few more of those. We did something recently where we asked anyone if they would take a voluntary reduction in hours worked. For example, would they want to work four days a week instead of five days a week and make 20 percent less? And we've actually had some people come forward and agree to do that. I'm taking less salary. I've reduced my compensation 26.5 percent, because I feel like it ought to be throughout the organization. It ought to come from the top and affect the people at the top as well as the rank-and-file people throughout the company. So, you know, we're having to trim our sails a bit just to try to get our costs down to—and we'll get through this recession at some point. It may be longer than we'd like, but we want to make sure we come through with as much of our circulation as possible and as much of the newspaper intact as it was so that, you know, we can thrive another day. Spend more money, and you're gonna prosper.

McConnell: Are there any other reasons that newspaper circulation is going down?

Hussman: In a lot of cases the quality of news has gone down. And some of that's because some companies really emphasize short-term profits. And the public companies are under more pressure to deliver quarterly results as opposed to, say, private companies that can maybe think longer term and not have to produce the quarterly results. That's part of the problem. Part of the problem is it's just a changing society. One part of the problem with online news . . . in just recent years is the great increase in the [percentage] of households in America that take high-speed Internet service. So before, when you had dial-up service and it took a long time to get the news delivered onto your screen, it really may not have been such a great substitute. But now that you can get incredibly fast delivery in color and great graphics and everything, it is a better substitute for the print version. So there's a whole host and variety of reasons. You know, the advent of cable television news has resulted in a decline in circulation.

McConnell: Why are so many of the major newspapers in real financial trouble now, though?

Hussman: Well, a variety of reasons. You know, number one is all of 'em have pretty much embraced this idea of giving all their content away free, and, as a result, they have lost a lot of circulation. You know, it really, really pains me to see the *Dallas Morning News:* they've lost 300,000 Sunday circulation in ten years, from 780,000 to 480,000.

And so I think the main culprit is just giving away your content for free. Now, there are other problems, though, besides that, and one is classified advertising and the migration of that to the online world. And that's happened in different formats, because classified covers a lot of different categories. Employment, real estate, and automotive are the three big categories in classified. And so a company was started to try to just do online employment advertising, which was Monster. com. And some newspaper companies responded to that by [saying], "Let's create an alternative to Monster.com and try to out-Monster Monster." And that was called Career Builder. And some of the biggest companies in the newspaper industry created that. I think Tribune and Knight-Ridder and Gannett maybe were the three companies that started that. Anyway, and so what they did is they did out-Monster Monster, but when they out-Monstered Monster.com, they really dealt a devastating blow to their [own] newspapers. They really every Sunday would promote Career Builder in their classified pages, and they really trained their readership that, "Hey, you know, instead of looking for this in the newspaper, go look for this online." And it has really hurt especially the big-city papers. Do I have any empirical evidence for that? Well, I looked at our own newspaper. And the year 2000 was the best year ever in the history of the newspaper industry in America in classified advertising. I can't remember the number, but it reached its peak, and it's gone down since then. In 2007 newspapers in America were running less than half of the employment advertising that they ran in 2000. The *Democrat-Gazette* was running about 12 percent less. We never affiliated with Career Builder. We never affiliated with Monster. We never affiliated with Yahoo Hot Jobs. And those are the Internet online sites. Those exist, and people in Little Rock can go there, but not as many people in Little Rock think about it because we don't promote it to 270,000 print readers every Sunday, you know? We still think print is a good way for people to find jobs, and so people still do.

McConnell: I know that you for some time now have been charging for your newspaper on the Internet—do you see any signs that any of the other major newspapers are switching?

Hussman: Yeah. Let me answer that with a preface and say that there's a lot of misunderstanding about why we charge for content. We and the *Wall Street Journal* and maybe just a few other of the sixteen hundred daily newspapers in the United States do this [this was 2009], you know? And I'd like to say, first of all, we used to give all our content away free, too. And when the Internet first came along, we followed exact conventional wisdom of everybody else: "Let's embrace the Internet. Let's be the leading source of information in our community." Having the benefit of owning the newspaper and actually living in the town the newspaper's published in—people would come up and say, "We really appreciate your putting all that content—all your newspaper online for free. We used to subscribe to your newspaper, and we don't have to anymore, and you're saving us money."

And I started thinking, "This doesn't make a lot of sense," you know? So that's when we, years ago, decided to say, "Look, let's give the online version to all of our print subscribers as an extra bonus-added value. But anybody that doesn't subscribe to our paper, they need to at least subscribe online to get it. And that way it will minimize the loss of circulation. So that's why we did it. It's not really to collect the $4.95 from [each online customer]. I think we have 3,400 people that do that. That represents not even 1 percent of our revenue.

The purpose is to maximize the print circulation. So we recently went back and said, "How have we done over the last ten years with our circulation? And how do we compare with other newspapers?" And we said, "Why don't we compare ourselves with other newspapers in this region?" So we took Arkansas and the six border states, and we said, "Let's look at larger markets like Little Rock. Let's don't look at the real small markets. Say, Little Rock's 130,000 households within generally the county or what's called the city zone. Let's look at other markets in these seven states that have 100,000 households or more, and so we did. And there's probably twenty-some-odd newspapers in those markets; generally, one in each market. And I've got the figures right here.

If you look at daily circulation, in the September six-month period we had 176,275. Ten years ago we had 173,316. We are the only newspaper of these twenty-some-odd newspapers that had a circulation gain in the last ten years. You look at Shreveport. They've gone from 75,000 to 48,000. Dallas has gone from 479,000 to 338,000. I mean, several of these newspapers have lost over 30 percent of their circulation. Quite a few newspapers have lost over 20 percent. Most of 'em have had double-digit losses in their circulation. We've had a gain. You look at the same information on Sunday—we're 270,477; ten years ago, 273,505. We've lost right at 1 percent of our Sunday circulation. I mentioned to you Dallas has lost almost 300,000. The *Houston Chronicle*'s lost 168,000; Oklahoma City's lost 50,000. So, you know, that's why I think—that's why I think not giving your content away for free makes economic sense.

The cyclical thing that's happened is this recession we've been in now for a little over a year [this was in 2009], and newspapers have been losing revenue since 2006. The whole newspaper industry lost revenue in 2006, 2007, and 2008, and, of course, [is] losing revenue in 2009. So because of the secular factors, it started losing revenues early—before there was a recession. Now that we have a recession, the recession has particularly hit the automotive business very hard, and it's hit housing and residential sales very hard, and now unemployment is the highest it's been in decades. Those are the three mainstays of classified. So it's really hit newspapers hard.

Probably not as many people are going to read newspapers twenty years from now as they do today. But I think the people who are going to continue to read newspapers are going to be the best educated, the most affluent, the people who are the most concerned and committed to their communities. And if that's the kind of audience you deliver, that's going to be a great audience for advertisers to reach.

Hussman's success in those years did not go unnoticed around the country. Warren Buffett, at one point the third richest man in the world, surprised people when he started buying newspapers at a time when newspapers were in a steep decline. Buffett said that local newspapers that deliver reliable information to tightly bound communities with a sensible Internet strategy will stay viable. "The main exemplar for local newspapers is the Arkansas Democrat-Gazette, *published by Walter Hussman Jr.," Buffett wrote in early 2013 in an annual letter to his Berkshire shareholders. "Over the past decade his paper has retained its circulation far better than any other large newspaper in the country."*

As of early 2014, Hussman is still trying to deal with some of the seismic shifts in the newspaper industry. He said there has been a fun-

damental change in the business because of the decline in newspaper advertising due to a huge increase in the number of companies selling advertising, often for far less than newspapers must charge. Thus, for decades and decades newspapers were able to sell their papers cheaply because advertising paid the freight. Now, he concludes, the people who take the paper are going to have to bear more of the cost.

Thus, in June 2012 he doubled the price of the paper and spelled out his reasons in a long letter to subscribers. He noted that ad revenues nationally dropped from $49 billion in 2006 to $24 billion in 2011, a decrease of 51 percent. Some newspapers have responded by cutting their news staffs sharply and reducing space. Some major papers plan to only publish three days a week, and many have severely reduced their circulation zones.

Hussman: Our plan is to remain a statewide, seven-day-a-week daily newspaper. We also plan to maintain our news staff and provide the type of complete, in-depth reporting that Arkansans have expected from us for decades. So far the response has been favorable. In the third quarter of 2013 the daily circulation had dropped by 10.3 percent, while the Sunday circulation had dropped by 12.6 percent. However, we made a profit in 2013. We didn't make as much profit as we used to make. However, each quarter we make a profit we give a 2 percent bonus to our employees. I feel good about the *Democrat-Gazette*, but to make this work you have to put out a good newspaper; you have to have good content, good writing, and good editing.

INDEX

Donald, Leroy, 215, 223
door-to-door sales, 129, 130, 203
Doty, Gerald, 4–5, 74–75
Dougan, Michael, 5, 21–22, 23
Douglas, Bob, 49
Douglass, Bob, 207
Douthit, George, 53–54, 60, 63, 65, 182
Downie, Tom, 80
Dred Scott's Advocate: A Biography of Roswell Field (Kaufman), 42
drinking. *See* alcohol use
Dumas, Ernest, 10, 128
Dunn, Si, 59, 65

E

East Tennessee State, 218
Eaton, Kenneth, 207–8
Economist, 72
El Dorado, 97, 98, 99, 157
El Dorado News-Times, 13, 97
Engel, August (father), 25
Engel, August (grandfather), 25
Engel, K. August: biographical background, 25–26; as business manager, 23; death, 3, 5, 6, 57; editorial focus and policies, 32–34; frugality, 28–32, 44; integration views, 33; as owner/publisher, 6, 17, 19–20, 26–34; television station ownership, 8, 30, 31–32
England, 38
engravers, 104
Enoch, David, 198
Epstein, Ben, 47
Estrin, Dick, 70
Eureka Springs, 176
Evening Star, 21

F

Face in the Crowd, A (film), 52
Farley, Dan, 74
farm labor movement, 22
Faubus, Orval E., 10, 32, 34, 53, 81, 181–82
Fayetteville, 40, 128, 226
Federal Communications Commission (FCC), 31

Fellone, Frank, 5, 179–80
female journalists, 73
Ferguson, Bob, 63, 65
Field, Roswell, 42
Fields, Arlin, 5, 69
Fields, Gene, 112
Fisher, Bob, 13
Fisher, George, 182
flat-bed presses, 99
focus groups, 199–200
Ford, Joe, 175
Foreman, Gene: biographical background, 5, 6, 8, 13; cash awards, 92; departure from the *Democrat*, 69–70; and Hussman, 74; as managing editor, 57–63, 68; move to *Newsday*, 69–70; staff hiring, 65–66
Foreman, JoAnn, 58
Fort Chaffee, 84–85
Fort Lauderdale, Florida, 197
Fort Smith, 6, 53
Fort Worth Star Telegram, 223
Francis, Ken, 37
free want ads: *Arkansas Gazette*, 134–35, 146, 191–94; classified revenue, 115–16; competition with the *Gazette*, 166; effectiveness, 120–25, 134–35; post-merger advertisements, 221–22; as predatory practice, 140, 145, 155; resuscitation plans, 115–16, 117, 118; telephone operators, 193
fringe benefits, 39, 43, 46–47, 69, 102
Fulbright, J. William, 31
Funston, Lelia Maude, 54–55

G

Gamble, Marguerite, 5, 46–47, 54–55
Gamino, Denise, 81, 83–86
Gannett Corporation: advertising rates, 193–94, 208–9; circulation war, 188–91, 197–99; closure of *Arkansas Gazette*, 217; free want ads campaign, 146, 191–94; horse-racing contest, 194–95; meeting with Hussman, 210–11;

ownership of *Arkansas Gazette*,
187, 188–211; radio disc jockey
contest, 196–97
Garden Club, 205
Garrett, Chester, 5–6, 19, 27–28, 29
Gates, Bill, 74
George, Marcus: biographical
background, 6; as editor, 26, 27,
57–60, 70, 71; employee meeting,
69; newspaper career, 37, 44, 52
George Mason University, 74
Gillette, Mr., 38
"good old boy" system, 173
Graham, Larry: biographical back-
ground, 6; as circulation manager,
129–31, 196, 218–20; on competi-
tion with Gannett, 197–99; on the
competitive market, 129, 220; on
Democrat-Gazette merger, 218–20;
and *Gazette* employees, 215
grand jury probes, 79–80
Graphic, 22–23
Great Energy Department Retreat
of 1980, 167–68
Greenberg, Paul, 222
Greene, Omar, 6, 176, 177
Greenville, Mississippi, 98
Greenwood, Ramon, 6, 36–39, 54
Griffee, Carol, 172
Guaranty Building and Loan
Association, 26
Guggenheim, Harry, 69
Gulley, Tom, 80
Gunter, O. D., 48
Gurdon, 220
Gurley, Todd, 179

H

Hackler, Tim, 6, 163
Hale, David, 173
Hall, Eugene, 172
Hall, Wally: biographical background,
7; offer to Moss, 132–33; as sports
editor, 126, 127, 132, 178, 179–80;
and Starr, 179–80, 184, 185
Hamilton, Lynn: biographical
background, 7; on door-to-door

sales, 203; High Profile section,
205; on Paul Smith, 203; on
printing presses, 221; as production manager, 220–21; as
vice-president for operations, 191;
on working conditions, 220–21
Harrison, Eric, 7, 156
Hatch, Leon, 65
Haverford College, 7
Hawaii, 197
Hays, Steele, 7, 74, 166
health care benefits, 43, 102
Heidt, Horace, 40
Heiskell, J. N. (John Netherland), 4,
17–19
Hemingway, Collins, 74
Hendrix College, 3
Hendrix, Lowber, 174
Henry, Orville: and Bailey, 127–28, 181;
move to Fayetteville, 128; move to
the *Democrat*, 224; Razorbacks
coverage, 66, 67; as sports editor, 7,
11, 67, 127–28, 132–33; as sports-
writer, 47; and Starr, 180–81
Henson, Ronnie, 106
Herrington, Gene: biographical
background, 7; departure from the
Democrat, 65; on editorial policies,
33; newspaper career, 37, 42–43, 44,
57, 58; newspaper editions, 20
Hess Oil, 74
Hickey, Maurice L. (Moe), 214
High Profile section, 204–7
Highway Audit Commission, 79
Hobbs, New Mexico, 6
Hobbs, Ray, 174
Hoffmann, Garry, 74
Hoge, Alyson, 7–8, 162
Holiday Bowl, 126–27
Holmes, Leon, 151
Hope, 157
horseracing contest, 194–95
horseracing handicapping, 132–33
hot check story, 82–84
hot metal printing process, 71, 95
Hot Springs, 53, 67, 76, 97, 98, 100,
120, 157

Kirkendall, Mike, 74
Knoxville, Tennessee, 117
Koonce, Gerald, 9, 74, 76
KRAY, 137
Kroger, 208, 225
KTAL-TV, 98
Kumpe, Peter, 151

L

Laman, William F. (Casey), 15, 90–91
Lancaster, Bob, 9, 69, 76
Lane, Harlan, 92
Laney, Benjamin, 80
Langford, Dick, 115
Lang, Fred, 38
Langston, Judge, 174
Lassiter, Jim, 179
lateral moves, 61
Laventhol, David, 70
Lemke, Bud, 64, 65
Leveritt, Mara, 9, 73, 76–77
Levy, Henry, 45
Levy, Paul, 167–68
Lindenwood College, 3
linotype processes, 1, 71, 95
Lippmann, Walter, 34
Liske, Ed: and Allbright, 40; and
    compensatory time, 38; as editor,
    20, 40; and Gamble, 54; and
    Greenwood, 38–39; and McCord,
    36; and Sutton, 51
lithograph printing, 99
Little Rock: advertising rates, 194; labor
    pool, 154; news coverage, 44, 60;
    newspaper market, 17, 21, 100, 108,
    114–15, 137, 148–49, 189, 229; radio
    disc jockey contest, 196–97;
    society news, 205–6; television
    stations, 30
Little Rock Central High School crisis,
    32, 33, 34, 43
Little Rock Chamber of Commerce, 52
Little Rock Housing Authority, 52
Little Rock PTA Council, 205
Little Rock Publishing Company, 23
Little Rock School District, 170
Little Rock State Journal, 21

Little Rock Travelers baseball team, 45
Log Cabin Democrat, 43, 77
London, England, 206
Lorenzen, Rod, 9, 46, 68
Los Angeles Times, 4, 10, 13, 72, 73, 74, 147
Louisiana State University, 30
Louisiana Tech, 218
Lowell, 226
Lowery, Clyde, 30
Luckenbach, Texas, 25
Lundy, Walker, 200
Lutgen, Bob, 183, 222
lynchings, 22

M

Mack-Blackwell Amendment (1952), 79
Madden, Owney, 67
Madison County, 80
Magnolia, 97, 98
Malone, Bill, 197
Malvern, 112, 173
manning requirements, 103–4
Marianna, 74
Marion Hotel, 45
Martin, Karen, 223
Martin, Roberta, 52
Masterson, Mike, 9–10, 100, 163
Mathis, Deborah, 10, 73, 201
May, Al, 10, 74, 77
McArthur, Alice, 171–74
McArthur, Bill, 172–74
McClendon, Larry, 172
McClure, John, 21
McConnell, Jerry: biographical
    background, 10; departure from
    the *Democrat*, 112; as managing
    editor, 70, 71, 72, 83, 84, 102, 111;
    reporting scoops, 93; small-town
    newspaper offer, 111–12
McCord, Bob: biographical back-
    ground, 10; on Carroll, 54; on
    delivery service, 131; on Douthit,
    53; as editor, 4, 5, 6, 11, 36, 57–58,
    68, 103; on editorial policies, 33;
    and Engel, 35–36; and free want
    ads, 117; on Hickey, 214; local news
    coverage, 114; meeting with

lawyer, 88; newspaper career, 35–36, 44, 48, 52; and Patterson, 110–11; photography career, 47–50; and Starr, 180; and Sutton, 50

McCorkindale, Doug, 210–11

McDonald, Roy, 113–14, 116, 156, 197–98

McGehee, 42, 65, 67

McGuirk, Leroy, 45

McMath, Sidney Sanders, 49, 79–80, 81

Mears, Roger, 92

Medford, Oregon, 165, 166

Memphis Commercial Appeal, 13, 85

Memphis, Tennessee, 225

Mercedes, 197

merger preparation, 217–18

Microsoft, 74

Midland, Texas, 96

Midwest Video, 98

Miller, Nancy, 73

Mitchell, James, 21, 22–23

Mitchell, William S., 23

Mobbs, John, 196, 208, 221–22

modernization efforts, 72, 78, 95, 152, 154

molested boys, 87–90

Mons, Belgium, 206

Monster.com, 228

Montgomery, Kirk, 222

Montgomery, Monty, 86–87

Montgomery Ward, 115, 125

Moore, Maurice, 65

Morning Line, 132, 133

Morrow, Fred: biographical background, 11; as sports editor, 14, 61, 65–67, 73; as a writer, 76

Morton Salt, 39

Moss, Randy, 11, 132–34, 180–81

Mount Holly Cemetery, 54

movie advertising, 146

Mowery, A. C., Jr., 81

Murdoch, Rupert, 10

N

Nashville, Tennessee, 225

National Association for the Advancement of Colored People (NAACP), 51

National Geographic, 14, 74, 182

Naylor, George C., 18, 23

Naylor, Julia, 52

Nearly Home story, 87–90

negotiation impasse, 104–5

Nelson, Rex, 11, 126–27, 162, 178

New Braunfels, Texas, 25

Newell, Frank, 175

New Orleans Item, 23

News America, 144

Newsday, 5, 69

newspaper delivery, 130–31, 140, 155

Newspaper Guild, 71, 102

Newspaper Preservation Act (1970), 211

newspaper war, 17, 128–29, 132–38, 159–60, 166, 180–82, 205–7

newsprint expenditures, 28, 115, 116, 125, 128, 157, 187, 226

New York Daily News, 14, 73

New York Dress Institute, 54

New York Herald Tribune, 34, 49, 65

New York, New York, 206

New York Times, 5, 34, 57, 147

Nielsen, Paul, 65

Nieman Fellowship, 9

North Little Rock, 47, 90, 91, 131, 205

North Little Rock School District, 170

North Little Rock Times, 11, 36, 57, 68, 155

Northwest Arkansas newspaper edition, 226

Northwestern University, 90

Nutt, Houston, Sr., 7

O

Oaklawn Park, 132, 133, 134, 194–95

offset lithograph printing, 99, 120, 130

off-the-rate-card deals, 143

Oklahoma City, Oklahoma, 112, 230

Oklahoma City Times, 10, 112

operating expenses, 103–4, 107, 152, 154, 157

Orange Bowl, 127

Orange County, California, 197

Orsini, Mary "Lee," 171–74

Orsini, Ron, 171–74

O'Sullivan, Daniel, 21

Jerry McConnell, now retired, was a reporter and managing editor at the *Arkansas Democrat*, a sports writer at the *Arkansas Gazette*, and a sports editor at the *Daily Oklahoman*.